# Photo essay

1 Coastal cliffs
2 A carved Maori gateway
3 Grape-pickers in Hawke's Bay

4  Milford Sound

5 Whakarewarewa Pohutu geyser
6 Shepherd on Pohuenui Island, Marlborough Sounds

9 Lavender farm, Napier
10 Rotorua Museum of Art and History

11 The Shotover jet on the Shotover river, Otago
12 Cathedral Square, Christchurch

13 Thunder Creek Falls, Mt Aspiring National Park
14 Statue commemorating the arrival of the European settlers
15 Auckland

# The bank for New Zealanders.

## It's easy to open a bank account in New Zealand with Bank of New Zealand.

When you arrive in New Zealand, you'll notice there are things we do a little differently than the way you might be used to. You'll discover that our easygoing nature extends to the way we like to live our lives, and the way we like to go about our business. Maybe that's one of the reasons we've made it so easy for you to open an account at Bank of New Zealand. In fact, you can get set up before you've even left the UK.

To request an account opening pack or discuss your move, talk to our dedicated UK team today on 020 8614 9328 or email migrant.banking@eu.nabgroup.com

Better Off

# Welcome to Bank of New Zealand

Moving to the other side of the world can be a great adventure, but it's also a major life change. That's why at Bank of New Zealand you'll find a range of special services and a dedicated team to make the financial side of your move as smooth as possible. You'll get personal assistance and advice before you leave, and have access to a range of banking products and services when you arrive in New Zealand that are designed to help you, and your money, be better off.

Choose Bank of New Zealand and you're choosing a bank with a long proud history. Founded in 1861, today BNZ employs nearly 6,000 people nationwide. We offer the latest in Internet and telephone banking, with a full range of business and personal banking services including:

- Credit cards
- Transaction and Savings accounts
- Lending
- Insurance
- Investments
- Foreign exchange
- Corporate Business and Agribusiness banking solutions
- Private banking
- UK pension transfer and tax advice

Bank of New Zealand is a member of the National Australia Bank group, which includes Clydesdale Bank and Yorkshire Bank. National Australia Bank is an international financial services group that operates in New Zealand, Australia and the UK, and has more than 10 million customers around the world.

Together with National Australia Bank, we have been assisting new migrants for nearly 150 years.

# Bank of New Zealand Migrant Banking

## Helping you make a great start in New Zealand

When you move to New Zealand, you need banking advice that's right for you. Every year at Bank of New Zealand we help thousands of new customers make the move to New Zealand. So you can be confi dent that when we recommend a personal, business or investment decision, it's based on proven experience that has been perfected over time and will be suited to your needs.

## Our team in the UK

Before you arrive in New Zealand, our migrant banking team in the UK can help get you started by opening a New Zealand bank account.

They will also provide you with contact details for one of our dedicated migrant bankers in New Zealand to meet with face-to-face on your arrival.

## Once you arrive in New Zealand

Your dedicated Migrant Banking Specialist will have everything you need ready for your arrival and will continue to work with you to recommend the very best combination of Bank of New Zealand products and services.

The service you'll experience goes beyond banking, too. So if you've got questions about setting up a business, buying a house or even finding good schools or universities, all you have to do is ask.

# Opening a Bank of New Zealand Account

The more you can arrange before you leave the UK, the more time you'll have to explore and enjoy your new home. We've made it quick and easy to open a Bank of New Zealand New Resident Achiever Savings Account right here in the UK, so you can transfer funds before you move, and have easy access to your money the moment you reach New Zealand.

You can apply for your new Bank of New Zealand account online or through our UK Migrant Banking Team. Please visit: **www.nabgroup.com/migrantbanking**

Contact the UK Migrant Banking Team on **0208 614 9328** between 9:00am and 5:00 pm UK time or email migrant.banking@eu.nabgroup.com for an account opening pack, for more information or to discuss your move.

# Migrate to New Zealand
## Australia and Canada

**It's Never Too Late!**

New Zealand, Australia and Canada are in urgent need of tradesmen and professional people.

We can help you find a job and arrange visas for you and your family!

**Not qualified?**
We can also help you retrain and qualify for your new career abroad, and then stay on!

**Call NOW for a Free Assessment 0845 2 606030**

Immigration Unit is a well established company based upon the principle that migration does not have to be stressful or difficult. We have helped hundreds of people migrate to New Zealand – people just like you.

We employ experienced professionals to work **with** you to achieve **your** goals. We use every visa possible to ensure that you can go. Many people have been told by other companies that they cannot migrate – they now live happily in their new home! Let us know what you want and we will make it happen using our team of locally based people. We work closely with nationwide organisations and local government bodies throughout New Zealand to assist you with:

- Finding a job
- Settling into your new home
- Receiving the best advice throughout the entire process
- Ongoing service and support all the way to citizenship

Job placement is an essential part of migrating to New Zealand for many migrants. We have nationwide assistance ready and waiting just for you – and many jobs waiting to be filled.

We are unique in that we are with you all the way – we do not just get you your first visa and say goodbye. We remain with you until you have citizenship, completing all of your documentation every step of the way.

Our associates in New Zealand are locally owned and run businesses that are looking for so many people just like you. Many of our staff in the UK and other countries, are from New Zealand and have been working in the industry for many years. Like you they are migrants, they are from the place you want to go to, they can talk to you simply because they are just like you. They have lived where you are going, shopped where you are going and grew up where you are going. Experience like that cannot be learned.

Come and talk to them, let them help you achieve your dreams!

**Dolphin Movers** provides a professional portfolio of relocation services that are reliable, prompt, cost-effective and responsive to the requirements of each individual.

Our services include international and national removals, shipping and storage solutions throughout the UK.

**1. Overseas removals** to any destination in the world. We provide fully export-packed, door to door removal services, not only from but also into the UK. We offer frequent services to Australia, New Zealand, USA & Canada.

**2. Excess baggage & small consignments** can be moved by air, sea or road, in the least possible time or for the lowest possible cost.

**3. Storage** is available either for the short or long term prior to your move. We can store anything from a single box through to the complete contents of your home.

FOR FURTHER INFORMATION & TO BOOK YOUR FREE HOME SURVEY
PLEASE CONTACT US ON

Freephone **0800 032 9777**, email **sales@dolphinmovers.com**
or visit us on **www.dolphinmovers.com**

Georgina Palffy

# *Working and Living*
# NEW ZEALAND

**CADOGAN**guides

# Contents

## About the author

Georgina Palffy moved to New Zealand in 2002 to give birth to her first son. For several years she and her family lived 100 yards from the beach in Napier, Art Deco capital of Hawke's Bay, a flourishing wine region. Married to a New Zealander, she didn't really want to come to the southern hemisphere in the first place, but was been converted to the easygoing charms of life on a South Pacific island. Before leaving the UK, Georgina worked as a travel editor for Cadogan Guides, a political and media analyst for an intelligence organization, a foreign affairs journalist at the *Guardian* and *Daily Telegraph* newspapers, and an art reviewer for a London listings magazine. She has also lived and worked in Rome for several years. She currently lives in Richmond, Surrey – but now feels wistful for the open spaces and night skies of her adopted country.

**Cadogan Guides** is an imprint of
New Holland Publishers (UK) Ltd
London • Cape Town • Sydney • Auckland

| New Holland Publishers (UK) Ltd | 80 McKenzie Street | Unit 1, 66 Gibbes Street | 218 Lake Road |
| Garfield House, | Cape Town 8001 | Chatswood, NSW 2067 | Northcote |
| 86–88 Edgware Road | South Africa | Australia | Auckland |
| London W2 2EA | | | New Zealand |

*cadogan@nhpub.co.uk*
*www.cadoganguides.com*
**t** 44 (0)20 7724 7773

Distributed in the United States by Globe Pequot, Connecticut

Cover photographs: Front cover: Shutterstock: Andy Hewyward, Ant Clausen, Robert Cumming, Joe Gough, Rohit Seth, Fotolia: © Paulus Rusyanto. Back cover: Shutterstock: Colin & Linda McKie
Photo essay photographs © John Warburton-Lee, © Paulus Rusyanto - Fotolia.com
© Harris Shiffman - Fotolia.com © cosmity - Fotolia.com
Maps © Cadogan Guides, drawn by Maidenhead Cartographic Services Ltd
Cover design: Sarah Rianhard-Gardner
Layout and editing: Linda McQueen
Proofreading: Dominique Shead
Indexing: Isobel McLean

Produced by **Navigator Guides**
*www.navigatorguides.com*

Printed in Finland by WS Bookwell
A catalogue record for this book is available from the British Library

ISBN: 978-1-86011-405-2

The author and publishers have made every effort to ensure the accuracy of the information in this book at the time of going to press. However, they cannot accept any responsibility for any loss, injury or inconvenience resulting from the use of information contained in this guide.

Please help us to keep this guide up to date. We have done our best to ensure that the information in this guide is correct at the time of going to press. But laws and regulations are constantly changing, and standards and prices fluctuate. We would be delighted to receive any comments.

# Introduction

New Zealand has attracted waves of immigrants since it was first settled by Polynesians in the 13th century, 'discovered' by Abel Tasman in 1642, explored by British naval lieutenant James Cook in 1769, exploited by whalers and sealers, 'civilised' by missionaries, and colonised by the British with the Treaty of Waitangi in 1840. In the early 21st century it continues to attract newcomers, for a variety of reasons that are explored in this book. They range from disgust with the old world – its politics, overcrowding, high prices, long working hours, traffic and pollution – to a Utopian quest for a clean, green, safe, natural wonderland in the new world. For many people, the decision to give New Zealand a go will be more personal: time for a career break, a change of scene – or marriage to a Kiwi. Whatever their reasons, this book aims to be a friendly companion to those seeking to set up a new life abroad.

The book has two broad sections. The first (chapters 1–3) aims to give the reader, who may be only dreaming of a life overseas at this stage, an idea of what New Zealand is all about. Chapter 1 looks at the climate, landscapes and events that have shaped the national character. Chapter 2 takes the reader on a 'tiki tour' of the regions, from subtropical Northland to the chill wildernesses of Southland via Auckland, the biggest city, and Wellington, the capital. Chapter 3 whizzes through New Zealand today, from its politics and economics to the broader racial and cultural issues that continue to be thrown up by the nation's founding treaty. It also takes a look at the country's media and arts – relevant to the former colony's ongoing quest for an identity – and the contemporary role of women in what has traditionally been a masculine culture.

The second part of the book (chapters 4–7) looks at the practicalities of a move to New Zealand. Chapter 4 offers information on how to get there in the first place. Chapter 5 steers the reader through the convolutions of getting a long-term visa or permit. Chapter 6 is a starting point for daily life: how to find a home, set up your power supply, open a bank account, get your mobile phone and Internet connection up and running, register with a doctor, choose a school and all the other tedious business that makes up a good proportion of our lives. Chapter 7 suggests some ways to go about finding work or starting a business in New Zealand. Finally, a short reference section fills in some of the blanks, from longitude and latitude to useful Maori vocabulary.

# Getting to Know New Zealand

New Zealand is a group of South Pacific islands slightly larger than the United Kingdom, with a recent history of settlement. The first Polynesian settlers reached the archipelago, by canoe, around 1300. Dutch explorer Abel Tasman was the first European to record a sighting of the islands, landing at what is now Golden Bay in early 1643; after hostile Maori clubbed a few Dutch sailors to death, however, Tasman set sail again, naming the location Murderers' Bay. It was not until British naval lieutenant James Cook set sail for the South Pacific in 1769 that Europeans returned to what was by then known as New Zealand. A trickle of whalers, sealers and missionaries followed. In 1840 the British Crown drew up the Treaty of Waitangi, which effectively gave sovereignty over the islands to Britain, and an influx of Britons keen to make a better life away from the home country began. The rest is history (for which, *see* below).

Arriving in New Zealand today, British people will find the country in some ways remarkably similar to the place they have left – a neo-Europe on the far side of the globe: the climate is temperate; English is the main official language; government and the law are closely modelled on the British system. Yet the islands are much less crowded and there is a greater sense of opportunity. Although Pakeha (Europeans) dominate in numbers, Maori culture is resurgent. New Zealand in the 21st century is forging a belated identity as a bicultural and even multi-ethnic nation.

# Historical Overview

## Prehistory

A Maori creation myth narrates that nurturing mother earth **Ranginui** and distant father sky **Papatuanuku** were prised apart by their son **Tanemahuta** to create light and air for him and his brothers. **Tane** went on to shape a wife out of earth and start the human race, while his jealous brother **Tawhirimatea** unleashed wind, rain and storms on the land. In the alternative, geological version of events, **tectonic shifts** separated the islands of New Zealand from the Gondwana supercontinent 80 million years ago (the rest became Australia, Africa, South America, Antarctica and the Indian subcontinent).

The country's oldest rocks are 680 million years old, although much of its surface is as young as 100,000 years, formed by earthquakes and volcanoes along the overlapping tectonic plates that run down the islands' spine. The biggest seismic drama in recent millennia was an eruption of **Taupo** in AD 186, when witnesses as far away as China recorded a sky 'red as blood' and Romans saw the sky 'burst into flame'.

New Zealand was the last significant land mass in the world to be colonised. By 10,000 years ago all the other continents were inhabited by humans, but until Polynesians and then Europeans arrived within the last 1,000 years, the islands were covered with primordial forests, bush and ferns, flightless birds and Jurassic survivors such as the tuatara (a lizard-sized dinosaur) and wetas (primeval giant crickets). It did not take long for the settlers to devastate this ancient ecosystem: the Polynesians brought kiore (rats) and dogs, and hunted the giant moa (a bird with eggs the size of a rugby ball) to extinction; the Europeans cleared the land to create a 'neo-Europe', killed off most of the rest of the native birds and imported more pests. Ecological change was very rapid.

# The Discovery of New Zealand

The discoverer of New Zealand was a **Polynesian** voyager named **Kupe** in AD 950, according to the **Great New Zealand Myth** – an amalgamation of Maori myths peddled by Europeans – followed in AD 1350 by a 'Great Fleet' of seven canoes. Central to this mythology is the naming of the land **Aotearoa** ('land of the long white cloud') – a name that has recently become fashionable, but is most likely apocryphal. In fact, Polynesian canoes may have landed in New Zealand around AD 800, but settlement did not begin until the 13th century, apparently in several voyages of colonisation from East Polynesia (the Cook, Marquesas and Society islands), whose inhabitants were driven by an 'ethos of expansion' to find new land.

Polynesian culture was transformed into Maori culture by the available resources (seemingly inexhaustible but rapidly exhausted) and climate. Within a hundred years the 'future-eating' colonists had hunted the flightless moa, giant goose, adzebill, swans and pelicans to near-extinction, and seal colonies had been decimated. The settlers fell back on the harder-to-gather resources of fish and seafood, and the cultivation of eight plants, including the kumara and yam, that they had successfully imported (others failed in the more temperate climate). Initially mobile hunters moving from camp to camp, Maori settled at this time around gardens guarded by hilltop pas (forts), and tribal culture and organisation began to develop (see box, p.6), along with local art forms such as greenstone- and wood-carving.

# The European Discovery of New Zealand

Europeans first arrived in New Zealand in the 17th century, driven by their own 'ethos of expansion' – a God-given sense of racial and cultural superiority, scientific and philosophical curiosity, trade, immunity to diseases, and the maritime and military technology that enabled them to voyage around the world. On 13 December 1642, **Abel Tasman**, commander of a two-ship Dutch East India Company expedition with orders to find *Terra Australis Incognita* (presumed to exist as a counterbalance to the weight of Europe) and to establish trade with any 'wild savages' he met, sighted the alpine ridge of the island known to its

## Te Ao Maori: Traditional Maori Culture

The Polynesian settlers soon developed a culture specific to their new land. When European settlers arrived, the original inhabitants came to be known as 'maori' – ordinary people – while the later arrivals were called 'pakeha' – light-skinned foreigners. Until then (and afterwards), 'Maori' culture was marked by tribalism; there was no one, cohesive society, but a system of whakapapa (relationships) based on tribal descent from the founding waka (ancestral canoe). This ancestry was expressed in waiata (songs) and patere (chants). Inter-marriage brought intertribal allegiances, but only blood descent conferred full membership of the waka, iwi (tribe) or hapu (sub-tribe). Tribal structure was hierarchical: ariki (paramount aristocrats) ruled over rangatira (aristocrats) and tutua (commoners). Rank was conferred by birth, but could be gained or lost through mana (status conferred through noble actions) and tapu (sacredness). Children could show themselves to be tohunga (chosen) by demonstrating special abilities – often spiritual – which would ensure they were groomed for a particular role in the tribe.

Inter-tribal relations were affected by the mana whenua (authority over the land) of the tangata whenua (people of the land) in relation to tau iwi (people from elsewhere). Society as a whole was shaped by competition for resources, expressed in utu (exchange of favours or insults). Warfare was a learned, culturally determined response to offences against the rules of Maori society, which could heighten or diminish individual or tribal mana. The settling of scores was not always immediate; one tribe, Ngapuhi, gained revenge for many old grievances once it laid hands on muskets in the 19th century.

In the earlier periods, war was sporadic, and brutal. Tribal leaders were almost exclusively men, the kaumatua ('no fathers') or elders of the tribe – in their 40s. In between defending the kainga (villages) from the hilltop pas (forts) that overlooked them, the tribes gathered and grew food, made tools and maintained dwellings and canoes. Specialist tohunga developed moko (tattoos, often facial), wove flax and elaborated the carving of wood (door lintels and house gables), bone and stone. Pounamu (greenstone) was particularly prized, and traded along with obsidian and other gems, for carving into adzes (axes) and hei tiki pendants.

This culture was well established in a population of around 100,000 when the Europeans started to arrive at the end of the 18th century.

inhabitants as Te Wai Pounamu (the place of greenstone, or South Island). Signs of life (smoke) were spotted at Whanganui Inlet; rounding Farewell Spit to the bay known as Taitapu, the *Heemskerck* and *Zeehaen* were met by Maori canoes with a pukaea (trumpet) challenge, which the Dutch mistook for a friendly greeting. They cheerily trumpeted back – a clear call to arms for the Ngati Tumatakokiri tribe, who killed three Dutchmen, mortally wounded another and took one ashore for ritual cannibalisation, the traditional way to absorb the mana (status) of a vanquished foe. Dutch retaliation killed one before Tasman's flotilla beat a retreat, renaming the bay Murderers' Bay. Tasman did not attempt to land again in New Zealand, although he skirted the west coast of Te Waka a Aoraki (the Canoe of Aoraki, or North Island) on his way north.

The Maori people were to remain undisturbed by Europeans for the next 126 years. Then, in July 1769, Lieutenant **James Cook** of the British Royal Navy sailed south from Tahiti in the *Endeavour*, with Admiralty instructions to find the *Terra Australis Incognita* or 'Land Discover'd by Tasman'. The barque anchored on 8 October that year in Poverty Bay, where Rongowakaata Maori on land saw the three-masted ship as a floating island or giant bird. Despite getting off to a bad start – a ceremonial challenge was met by the panicked shooting of one Maori and another was killed for grabbing a sword, both incidents which Cook deeply regretted – the captain and his crew soon recognised Maori bravado for what it was and established good relations.

Cook's rediscovery of New Zealand was an encounter of a very different order from Tasman's. His expedition took six months to circumnavigate the islands, mapping the land to such a high degree of accuracy that the maps were referred to well into the 20th century. The naturalist Joseph Bank and two ship's artists documented Maori language and culture, as well as making detailed records of native landscape, flora and fauna. The voyagers met various tribes, with whom they communicated thanks to a Tahitian interpreter on board. Instructions from the Royal Society had described the native peoples Cook was likely to meet as 'human creatures' created by God, and stated that 'no European nation has the right to occupy any part of their country without their voluntary consent' – a relatively enlightened perspective for the day. Cook dealt as humanely and respectfully as he could with those he met.

In the course of three voyages and four visits to the country, between 1769 and 1774, Cook established a two-way exchange with the Maori: he identified natural resources such as timber, whales, seals, flax and minerals, for which he traded potatoes, turnips and metal (nails were especially prized), as well as introducing such undesirables as guns and VD. Cook was quick to see that further misunderstandings, such as the cannibalisation of 10 crew in Queen Charlotte Sound in 1773, were as much the fault of provocation by the English as of Maori belligerence. He continued to deal with indigenous peoples in a humane and respectful way, and was endowed with rangatira (aristocratic) status by the people he encountered, whom he in turn saw as 'of a Brave, Noble, Open and benevolent disposition'.

The French explorers who followed close behind the British did not display such diplomatic skills. While **Jean de Surville** sighted the islands and landed without incident in Doubtless Bay a couple of months after the *Endeavour*, in 1772 **Marc-Joseph Marion du Fresne** and 26 of his crew were killed in the Bay of Islands for breaching tapu (sacredness); up to 300 Maori were slaughtered in retaliation.

# The First European Settlers

Ex-convicts from the Australian penal colonies were the first to come to New Zealand in Cook's wake: sealers in the 1790s, then whalers, loggers and traders. Some settled, adopting the Maori way of life, intermarrying and coming to be known as **Maori Pakeha**. The first European settlement – a whaling station – was at Kororareka in the Bay of Islands (the 'Hell-hole of the Pacific'), where food, sex and alcohol were traded for European clothing and tools. Among the earliest settlers, Maori values predominated in a more-or-less symbiotic relationship, but the balance was tipped by a further influx of Europeans, bearing guns and God. Some tribes seized on the new weapons as a means to settle old scores. The first gun skirmish was recorded in 1807; by the 1820s an arms race was fuelling inter-tribal violence. By the time the so-called **musket wars** ended in 1839–40 at least 20,000 had been killed. The most famous warrior chieftain was **Hongi Hika** of Ngapuhi, who went to London and met King George IV, returning with a suit of armour to terrify his enemies. Another legendary fighter, **Te Rauparaha**, fought his way down the west coast from the Waikato to the South Island, becoming a key figure in organised European settlement.

The spread of Christianity may have hastened the end of the violence. Missionaries were able to build on strong Maori spirituality, translating concepts of atua (deity) to Te Atua (the one God) – although the idea of a fallen man redeemed by Christ's suffering was as bizarre to Maori as the notion of equality before God. The 'flogging parson', magistrate **Samuel Marsden**, started evangelizing for the Church of England's Church Missionary Society on Christmas Day 1814, but early conversions were stymied by the loutish behaviour of drunken, adulterous, arms-toting lay missionaries. **Henry Williams** made the first conversions, after 1823, helped by learning the Maori language. By 1842, 3,000 Maori had converted to Christianity. **William Colenso** took the mission one step further, printing the Scriptures in English and Maori.

The Anglicans were followed by Wesleyans, Catholics and later Presbyterians (in the Scottish colonies of the far south). All cohabited happily except Anglicans and Catholics: the Protestants waged a jealous campaign against the Catholics based on the antics of a few 'drunken, fornicating' Irishmen. However, handsome, eloquent French Catholic bishop **Jean-Baptiste Pompallier** was a striking and to the locals clearly aristocratic figure in his purple robes; he spited the Reformed Churches by baptising 1,000 Maori Catholics before 1841.

# The Treaty of Waitangi

The 1830s saw New Zealand begin to pull towards a permanent and constitutional relationship with Britain, ultimately formalised in the Treaty of Waitangi in 1840. While New Zealand's founding document was in part a product of the benevolent instincts of British humanitarianism, and its signatories had high hopes for benign outcomes, it was determined by colonial self-interest and remains highly contentious today. The process started with the appointment of **James Busby** as the First British Resident from New South Wales in 1832; assuming the mantle of diplomatic representative of the British monarch, he was received in the Bay of Islands with a feast and a seven-gun salute, in exchange handing out a few blankets. The reasons for his commission were to protect British trade, to protect British citizens in New Zealand, and as a result of a Maori request for British protection from the French and the lawless Britons (one had been involved in the kidnapping of a Maori chief). Busby's orders were to protect 'well-disposed' settlers and to guard against the exploitation of Maori – but he had no means of enforcement, and was soon nicknamed the 'Man o' War without Guns'.

In 1834 a meeting was held at Waitangi to pick a flag for New Zealand ships. This was the first of a series of farcical pseudo-consultations between the British and Maori tribes. Northern chiefs were assembled and, after the sketchiest of explanations of what it was all about, were asked to vote for one flag out of three; out of politeness, they voted for them all. After a choice was forced, they were served cold porridge while the Europeans banqueted. In 1835 an equally farcical 'Declaration of the Independence of New Zealand' by a 'Confederation of United Tribes' was signed. Designed specifically to thwart French adventurer Charles de Thierry, it had no constitutional status. It did, however, become a foundation for the assertion of indigenous rights – disunited as the tribes were.

The British government was eventually spurred to intervene by Busby's reports of the 'accumulating evils of permanent anarchy' and petitions from traders asking for their security to be guaranteed. The final catalyst for action was the formation of the **New Zealand Company** by **Edward Gibbon Wakefield** (an ex-convict who had abducted a teenage heiress) to implement a plan for colonisation of the country. In 1839 the Colonial Office dispatched **William Hobson** from London to establish a colony, by voluntary transfer of sovereignty from Maori to the British Crown. He arrived at Busby's residence at Waitangi (aptly meaning 'waters of lamentation') in the Bay of Islands on 29 January 1840. By the time a treaty was drafted, genuine concern for Maori welfare was was pushed aside by a rush to get in there before Wakefield, to create 'a settler New Zealand in which a place had to be kept for Maori'. The drafting of the treaty and its translation into Maori took place in just four days, with no legal or government advice.

Copies of the treaty were formally presented to northern chiefs at Waitangi in early February. Crucially to posterity, the English and Maori versions were significantly different in how they defined key concepts. In English, the treaty asserted that Queen Victoria wished to protect the 'Native Chiefs and Tribes of New Zealand' through a functionary authorised to treat with the Maori for 'the recognition of Her Majesty's Sovereign Authority' to bring about 'Civil

Government'. The first article asked the chiefs to cede 'absolutely' sovereignty over their territories. In the second article, the Queen guaranteed to the chiefs 'the full exclusive and undisturbed possession of their Lands and Estates Forests Fisheries and other properties...so long as it is their wish and desire to retain the same in their possession', at the same time as giving exclusive rights to the sale of land to the Queen. In the third article, the Queen extended her royal protection to 'the Natives of New Zealand', along with 'the Rights and Privileges of British Subjects'.

Many of these concepts were alien to Maori culture, a fact compounded by the woolly attempts to translate those concepts. To begin with, sovereignty was a new notion for Maori, translated with the made-up word 'kawanatanga', meaning something more like 'governorship' than 'sovereignty'. In subsequent discussions of the treaty, it would be argued that the chiefs thought they were maintaining 'mana' – true authority – while relinquishing governance to the vassals of the British Crown. The Maori rendition of article two stated that Maori were retaining 'te tino rangatiratanga o ratou wenua kainga me o ratou taonga katoa' – meaning 'the unqualified exercise of their chieftainship over their lands, villages and all their treasures' – rather more than the English version implied. 'Tino rangatiratanga', a more accurate rendition of sovereignty, was subsequently adopted as the catchphrase for Maori nationalism, while the phrase 'ratou taonga katoa' (all their treasures) was brought into use for Maori claims to not only land, but other material and cultural resources (such as fishing rights).

None of these issues was explored or discussed in the Waitangi meeting on 6 February 1840. Missionary and translator Henry Williams told the assembled Maori that the treaty was 'an act of love towards them on the part of Queen Victoria'. All assembled British government representatives and missionaries wanted the treaty signed as fast as possible, and with a minimum of fuss, and may even have believed that the treaty was in the best interests of Maori too. In the tradition of Maori whaikorero (debate), five hours of discussion ensued, in the course of which, arguments for and against signing were presented by several chiefs. While arguments began with dissenters, **Tamati Waka Nene** of Ngati Hao, a Wesleyan convert, stood up and said 'Governor! Do not go away from us; remain for us – a father, a judge, a peacemaker. You must not allow us to become slaves. You must preserve our customs and never permit land to be taken from us' – a clear indication that at least some of the chiefs gathered regarded the document as genuinely benevolent.

Debate continued overnight, and in the morning 45 chiefs were ready to sign, starting with **Hone Heke Pokai**. Subsequent signings with local chiefs took place at Waimate North and the Hokianga in February, and later in nearly 50 other locations in the North and South Islands. Hobson proclaimed British sovereignty over the country on 21 May 1840 – before the signings were complete. Much of the process of treaty-signing, not to mention the content, has remained in dispute for the intervening 160 years; in recent interpretations, attempts to define the 'spirit' of the treaty have been paramount in overcoming its anomalies. At the time, however, it brought New Zealand into the British Empire and ostensibly offered Maori some guarantees. Hobson set about 'governing', with instructions from the British Secretary of State for the Colonies, the assistance of two councils (Executive and Legislative), a Land Claims Commissioner to rule on land sales prior to colonisation, and a Protector of Aborigines (unfortunately tied in to the position of Land Purchase Officer – a conflict of interest). The tangata whenua (people of the land) would now be joined by the tangata tiriti (people of the treaty), keen to exploit the country's resources.

## Rapid European Settlement Brings Repercussions for the Tangata Whenua

The pace of European settlement accelerated rapidly after the Treaty of Waitangi. In 1840, an estimated 2,000 Europeans lived in New Zealand; by 1881, half a million had moved in. Half were English or Welsh, a quarter Scottish, a fifth Irish and the rest German (around Nelson), Dutch, Scandinavian (Norsewood and Dannevirke) and Chinese. Most migrants left Europe to escape poverty, overpopulation, the class system and religious intolerance, and headed to New Zealand in search of a 'neo-Europe' – culturally similar but with a healthier environment and greater prospects of prosperity and opportunities for social advancement.

Many settlers came on the ships of Wakefield's private-enterprise New Zealand Company, whose 'systematic colonisation' aimed to attract a good mix of venture capitalists and labourers. The company developed Wellington, then Wanganui, New Plymouth and Nelson, while similar schemes developed Dunedin and Christchurch. Much land was sold on lies – Wellington's steep hills were described as flat, fertile land in the brochures – but few immigrants off the boats were in a position to turn back.

Auckland grew up independently, and was for a while the capital. In Wairarapa, Hawke's Bay, Canterbury and North Otago land was sold off in huge acreages to become big sheep stations. A **gold rush** in the 1860s brought a new influx of settlers, followed by government campaigns to attract immigration. The character of the new country was more British than Britain, although there was a greater ethnic and religious mix than in the old country.

Large-scale immigration tipped the balance of Maori-Pakeha relations, which before 1840 had been good. While the tangata whenua (people of the land) had assimilated the first Europeans, they saw the new arrivals as 'saltwater contaminating freshwater'. Pakeha negotiated land sales unscrupulously, leaving Maori surprised to find 1,000 settlers on a plot of land ostensibly sold to one person. Buyers often ignored the communality of Maori land ownership, complicated by inter-tribal allegiances; deals would be struck without the consent of a whole tribe or all its allies. This sort of fraud and confusion soon led to armed clashes: Arthur Wakefield and 30 men were killed near Nelson in 1843; Te Rauparaha and his nephew Te Rangihaeata of Ngati Toa took arms in 1844 to dispute the sale of the Hutt Valley.

In the north, Hone Heke of Ngapuhi struck back at the British for various insults to his rangatiratanga (sovereignty), in 1844 cutting down the flagpole he had donated at Kororareka for flying the Union Jack and in 1845 besieging the town with his ally Kawiti of Ngati Hine. Tribes friendly to the Crown (kupapa) took arms against their rival Heke and his allies; the battles dragged on for 10 months, ending in a stalemate. 'God made this country for us. It cannot be sliced...do you return to your own country,' Heke provoked the Governor, before making friends with him. While a period of peace followed these conflicts, the Maori population was in decline and its future in question.

Once they had the upper hand, the Europeans set about appropriating and transforming the country: the country was explored and mapped, and English place names imposed; new species (plant and animal) were introduced, destroying indigenous ones; forests and native grassland were cleared for sheep grazing; coal and gold were mined. A British-style system of government was introduced, too. In 1852 Governor **George Grey** gave the country a constitution: regional and national parliaments and a premier (later prime minister), overseen by an appointed executive council. The Crown-appointed governor-general retained responsibility for 'native' affairs, while foreign policy powers still resided with the British government.

Initially, 100 out of a total 5,849 voters (all male landowners) were Maori; in 1867 the vote was extended to all Maori men, and in 1893 to all women (the first in the world to get the vote); in 1879 the property qualification was abolished. All this more or less set the pattern for the next 150 years. The first premier was **Henry Sewell**, who presided over a chaotic first sitting of the House of Representatives. In 1865 Wellington replaced Auckland as the capital.

## New Zealand Wars

While the new settlers were getting settled, Maori-Pakeha relations were deteriorating. By the late 1850s there was an underlying Pakeha assumption that the Maori people would die out, leaving the land up for grabs. Maori began to fear this too, and for the first time tribes united to protect Maori, as opposed to tribal, interests: a king was appointed and a move made to ban land sales. To the confident colonisers this represented an act of disloyalty, precipitating the **Taranaki War** (1860); the situation had escalated by the **Waikato War** (1864), in which 700 Pakeha and 1,000 Maori died. Confiscation of Maori lands – usually prime agricultural land, regardless of whether its owners had fought the Crown – left a new legacy of bitterness in what was now called the **King Country**. Pai

**Mairire**, a messianic sect which gained popularity by promising liberation from the Europeans, was crushed by imperial scorched-earth tactics around Taranaki.

Civil war broke out on the East Coast between Europeans, Pai Mairire supporters and kupapa Maori, resulting in the banishment of 400 Maori to the Chatham Islands. Out of this conflict came the four-year-long guerrilla campaign of **Te Kooti**, who escaped from the Chathams and returned with 300 followers. His withdrawal to sanctuary in the King Country in 1872 was regarded as the end of the New Zealand Wars. Meanwhile another guerrilla chieftain, **Titokowaru**, waged a campaign against unjust retribution in Taranaki until his personal support collapsed and he started a new life as a grass-seed salesman. He was later captured in 1881 during a non-violent occupation of confiscated land near Parihaka led by pacifist prophets **Te Whiti** and **Tohu**; singing children went out to meet the colonial troops, who nonetheless destroyed the village and took its leaders captive. Another peaceable occupying community, that of **Te Maiharoa** at Omarama, had been dismantled in 1877 and its occupants evicted, many dying on the road out. The Europeans saw the wars as a resounding victory for European sovereignty as defined by the treaty, whereas Maori saw the terms of the treaty as dishonoured by the way they had been crushed. Maori kept control of some inland North Island land, and kupapa Maori such as **Ngati Kahungunu** on the East Coast thrived, but overall Maori were left poorer and with diminished mana. As epidemics of European diseases to which the indigenous people had no immunity continued to spread, both Pakeha and Maori now saw Maori extinction as inevitable.

## Pakeha Thrive while Maori Subsist

Against the backdrop of violence, this period saw reputations won and lost among Europeans, and some notable success stories. One was **Thomas Russell**, a lawyer, speculator and minister of defence, whose career brought him profit, social elevation and political influence. Another was **Julius Vogel**, treasurer and later premier, who launched ambitious programmes to build up the colony's infrastructure (railways, roads and so on) and to assist immigration. Vogel was keen to redress the imbalance between men and women (66 per cent men to 34 per cent women – the foundation of New Zealand's masculine 'good bloke' culture: all-male logging camps were bound by camaraderie, honour, hard work and strict rules limiting alcohol or talk of sex).

By 1876, however, the **Long Depression** had set in, and many of the women who had come to the country sure of finding a husband and a settled domestic life instead found themselves working, alongside children, in sweatshops. The economy was turned around again by the first frozen meat ship, which sailed to Europe laden with lamb in 1882. New Zealand became the 'dairy farm of the Empire', exporting meat, butter and cheese to Britain and achieving one of the highest living standards in the world.

All these Pakeha achievements passed Maori by. The tribes lived a parallel existence to the Europeans. It was very variable from tribe to tribe, and not even unified by a common sense of Maoriness, despite the fact that all 'natives' looked the same to Pakeha. Four Maori seats in parliament were introduced in 1867 (15 would have been more demographically representative), but most Maori lived in isolated rural settlements. These kaiki (villages) were based around hapu (clan) membership, with the whanau (extended family) sharing a crowded whare mahana (sleeping house) and the whole community sharing a kauta (cookhouse), pataka (storehouse), whata (wood store) and wharepuni (meeting house). Some would also have had a school and church attached. Traditional building styles (earth, branches and thatch) gradually gave way to the use of European materials (pit-sawn timber and corrugated iron), but there was usually no sanitation, leading to the rapid spread of virulent European diseases like 'flu, measles and tuberculosis, often 'treated' with alcohol.

Some settlements were highly self-reliant, but most barely scraped a life from mixed subsistence farming – on the scraps of land that had not been appropriated by settlers, and without the help of land development subsidies offered to the newcomers – and seasonal cash work as shearers. At least the villages had their own rangatiratanga (sovereignty), and Maori mana (values) remained strong. The focal point of community life was the hui, a ritualised tribal gathering involving singing, dancing and storytelling as well as whaikorero – debate on political issues such as land grievances. Some Maori traditions coalesced with European ones, such as the tangihanga (traditional wake and funeral), which acquired Christian overtones.

A native land court was established in 1865 to check out the complexities of communal land ownership for sales; it may not have ensured justice, but it recorded a wealth of detail on ancestry and kinship that would otherwise have been lost. At the turn of the century, however, the 'Passing of the Maori' was still being predicted, but the activity of 'flax roots' politicians like James Carroll was beginning to lead to a resurgence of Maori culture and society.

## New Zealand Matures

Party politics emerged on to New Zealand's political scene in 1891, with the start of 21 years of Liberal rule, which set the tone for 20th-century government. The apparatus of modern government was established in the form of government departments. The country's future reputation as 'the social laboratory of the world' was laid in the foundations of the **welfare state**. While the country famously became the first to grant women suffrage (in 1893), it also produced the first woman mayor (also 1893), the first woman doctor (1896) and the first practising woman lawyer (1897). Labour laws were enacted to improve working conditions in an attempt to stave off inequality and the 'social evils' of poverty (1894). A pension was introduced for the 'deserving poor' (1898). Land was redistributed in smaller sections through Crown ballots, and a Land Act (1892) established the notion of the **Queen's Chain** – access for all to rivers, lakes, coasts, forests and mountains.

After a bubonic plague scare in 1900, measures were brought in to improve public health and sanitation, and especially to combat TB. In 1907 the **Plunket Society**, an organisation devoted to infant welfare, was set up by reforming mental health expert Frederic Truby King – although Maori still had limited access to healthcare. By 1911 the urban population of the country had overtaken the rural and, with 60 per cent of New Zealanders born in the country, the days of the grey-bearded pioneers began to seem remote. Perhaps most crucially of all to the nation's identity, the **All Blacks** made their first rugby tour in 1905.

## New Zealand at War

Surprisingly in retrospect, this era of relative calm left many New Zealand men – European and Maori – keen to go off and fight colonial wars. They got their first chance in the **South Africa War** (1899–1902), in which a New Zealand contingent fought more or less heroically.

The next opportunity was the **First World War**, where the **ANZACs**, as the Australian and New Zealand force came to be known, soon came to grief at Gallipoli. Despite winning a reputation as honourable, rugged, enterprising soldiers (in contrast to the rigid, class-ridden, uptight Brits), the New Zealanders found themselves making an impossible assault across the Dardanelles and up a steep cliff. Out of 8,450 who fought at Gallipoli, 2,721 died and 4,752 were wounded. **ANZAC Day**, which commemorates the landing on 25 April 1915, remains New Zealand's most solemn patriotic date. The Gallipoli fiasco did not stop the remaining men, so keen to enlist and participate in imperial conflicts, being sent on to the Western Front. All in all, 100,000 New Zealand men fought (20 per cent of the male population), of whom 17,000 were killed and 41,000 wounded.

## The Inter-war Years

At the end of the First World War the British dominion of New Zealand was surprised to be assigned an independent international role. Prime minister **William Massey** signed the Treaty of Versailles in 1919, and the country joined the League of Nations at its founding. (Massey's other great post-war effort was to bring the 1918 Great Flu back with him from Europe: the ship he travelled home on was not quarantined, in order to expedite the landing of the VIPs on board; 6,700 people, mainly Maori, died in the ensuing epidemic.) New Zealand continued, however, to look to Britain and the British Empire to guarantee its future economic and military security.

Back home in the South Pacific, the islands were dogged by labour issues in the wartime and immediate post-war years. In 1912–13, strikes by Waihi gold-miners and Wellington watersiders suspected of revolutionary ideals were crushed. In fact the workers were dissatisfied with the 1894 arbitration system for unions and the effects of inflation; few New Zealanders dreamed of smashing the capitalist system – most just hoped to get more out of it. By 1935, when the Labour party was swept to power by the effects of global depression, its stated aim was to improve capitalism, not abolish it.

In the interim, New Zealand once again showed its reluctance to cut the umbilical cord with the mother country. A 1923 Imperial conference permitted British dominions to form their own trade treaties; in 1926 the **Balfour Definition** (not to be confused with the Balfour Declaration, which set in motion the founding of Israel) stated that all dominions were 'autonomous communities within the British Empire equal in status, no way subordinate to one another in any aspect of their domestic or external policies, though united by a common allegiance to the Crown and freely associated as members of the British Commonwealth of Nations'. But when this declaration was recast as the **Statute of Westminster** in 1931, New Zealand refused to ratify it. This adherence to 'Home' has also been linked to the brain drain of New Zealand intellectuals: **Ernest Rutherford**, who first split the atom, Maori ethnologist **Peter Buck** and other academics left in search of supportive institutions; artists and writers such as **Frances Hodgkins** and **Katherine Mansfield** suffered from a dearth of creative colleagues and interested audiences – and also left.

In the same period, Maori culture and society was revitalised. The indigenous people had at last acquired immunity to diseases imported by the colonists, health and fertility had improved, and a new political consciousness was beginning to have some effect on issues affecting Maori – most notably land issues and redress for the Waitangi Treaty. Maori MP **James Carroll**, elected in a non-Maori seat, became Minister of Native Affairs (1899–1912); his aim was for Maori to compete with Pakeha on European terms, unlike the nationalist **Kotahitanga** (Maori unity) movement, which sought to uphold Maori tradition. Carroll's **Maori Councils Act** (1900) set up councils to supervise sanitation and suppress customs seen as a health risk (such as tangihanga, the wake). Another group, the **Young Maori Party**, superseded Kotahitanga, preaching social and religious reform along Christian lines and advocating survival for Maori through emulation of the dominant race and adoption of the Protestant work ethic. The party spawned legendary politician **Apirana Ngata**, who held the Eastern Maori seat for 38 years (1905–43). In yet another grouping, ex-Maori servicemen who had shown their mettle in the trenches became embittered by the continuing discrimination they found on returning home and joined the **Ratana** movement, a spiritual and later political movement which rejected tribalism and tradition in favour of more material progress for 'God's chosen people'.

Meanwhile New Zealand, while not yet racially enlightened, emerged from the Depression of the 1930s with a cradle-to-grave social security system, instigated by the first Labour government (1935). Welfare included Christmas bonuses, old age pensions, free schooling and new teacher-training colleges, a state-owned radio network, industrial arbitration, a minimum wage and 40-hour week and state housing. The 1938 **Social Security Act** introduced a free health system and universal superannuation at 65. Maori health was spectacularly improved, infant mortality rates dropped and life expectancy rose from the mid-40s to the late 50s. Maori education also improved dramatically, with many more children attending schools.

Curiously, as Maori ways of life began to be subsumed by European ideas of progress, Pakeha artists and writers became sentimental about 'authentic' Maori culture. Journalist **James Cowan** wrote of the 'savage glory' of 'the last of the old type of better Maori' – honourable, noble and handsome. Painter **Charles Frederick Goldie** depicted these same qualities in his portraits of 'noble and dignified' old chieftains. Even the more sensitive representations, such as those of **Frank Sargeson**, tended to the stereotypical. It was not until the 1970s, when Maori writers such as **Keri Hulme** and **Patricia Grace** began to be published, that Maori people were realistically portrayed. Maori, on the other hand, saw Pakeha as materialistic and self-centred. While the intrinsic worth of Maori values (which remained strong) began to be more widely recognised, Maori culture continued to be stymied by a lack of socio-economic advance.

New Zealand remained a conformist society, with most women based in the home as housewives and child-carers, and homosexuality unacknowledged, but from the 1930s on a new generation of writers including Sargeson and **Allen Curnow**, known as the 'cultural nationalists', began to question the consensus. Among the general populace, however, rugby and horse-racing were probably more influential, while the Church still held its own, at least as an institution in which to be born, get married and die.

# At War Again

The Labour government inherited a tradition of ideological opposition to war, but laid down the banner of pacifism at the outbreak of the **Second World War** in Europe to stand by Britain. This time around, New Zealand troops fought mainly in North Africa, in the disastrous Greek and Cretan campaigns of 1941, and with the British 8th Army contingent fighting its way up the Italian peninsula (1943–5). Many men died in **Crete** and at **Monte Cassino**, between Naples and Rome. The war in Europe was *the* war in the minds of most New Zealanders: British civilisation – and its meat and dairy markets – had to be secured. However, the war in the Pacific had threatened New Zealand's own security and brought a significant defence realignment with the United States. In all, 204,000 New Zealanders took up arms, mostly in 'Hitler's war', of whom 11,500 lost their lives. At the war's end, prime minister **Peter Fraser** established a long-standing precedent for the country by the value he placed on the UN as an international arbiter and protector of small nations.

# Post-war Conformity, the Baby Boom and Social Revolution

New Zealand emerged from the anticlimax of victory (continued hardship and rationing) a highly conformist society. As in the United States and Britain, the 1950s were typified by suburban domesticity, a baby boom, political conservatism, materialism, consumerism and the Cold War mentality. Britain was still Home and few thought it odd that British governor-generals sat at the top of the political hierarchy (until 1967). The big events of the decade were Queen Elizabeth II's **Coronation visit** (1953) and Sir Edmund Hillary's **ascent of Everest** (the same year). But things were beginning to change: New Zealand formally realigned itself with US defence (in the 1951 ANZUS pact), while Britain aligned itself economically with the EEC, jolting its South Pacific dairy farm into reality.

Cultural and social changes were afoot too. Maori began to abandon the traditional rural way of life for urban living. Television and jet travel brought cultural influences from abroad to New Zealand, along with a wartime diaspora which introduced not only specific talents but also European wine, food and manners, theatre and chamber music. These new influences were counterbalanced by a continued brain drain of scientists and academics (among notable expats was Robert Burchfield, editor of the Oxford English Dictionaries). Creative writers and artists were now, however, more likely to stay – some after a period of 'overseas experience': Janet Frame, Colin McCahon, Toss Woollaston and Ralph Hotere, among others, forged a distinctly New Zealand aesthetic.

In the main, though, conformity of dress, hair, food and recreation (beer and rugby, gardening, reading and the radio, NZ *Woman's Weekly* and the soaps) was only disturbed by a Special Committee on Moral Delinquency in Children and Adolescents, which published a report in 1954 describing the horrors of 'oversexed or morally degraded' young women in the Hutt Valley, and generated a furore over teenage sex – statistically no more or less common in this era than those before or after.

Back on the political front, the **Statute of Westminster**, granting New Zealand semi-independent status (*see* p.16), was finally ratified in 1947. Labour remained committed to social reform until it lost power in 1949, at which point the conservative National Party government committed the country to 'private ownership of production, distribution and exchange'. In the same year the Legislative Council (the appointed upper chamber) was abolished, leaving the country with a **unicameral parliament**. The 1950s also saw New Zealand caught up in the **Cold War**, along with its 'reds under the beds' fever. New Zealand troops were sent to Korea (1950), Malaya (1956) and Vietnam (1965) to combat the Communist threat, while Moscow *chargé d'affaires* **Desmond Patrick Costello** (a contemporary of Philby et al. at Cambridge) and others at home were forced out of public service under suspicion of spying, or at the very least leftist leanings.

# Social Change: the 1960s to the Present

An era of political conservatism under the National Party of Keith Holyoake (1960–72) was paralleled by the social revolution of the 1960s: sexual liberation, musical innovation, dope-smoking, long hair, colourful clothes and – crucial for New Zealand – the abolition of the 'six o'clock swill' – licensing laws which had closed pubs at 6pm. Television brought new TV stars, politicians (notably Robert Muldoon) and national events such as the 1968 *Waihine* disaster (in which 51 people drowned when an inter-island ferry struck a reef in Wellington Harbour) into people's homes. It also heralded the 1970s 'contagion of protest': against the Vietnam War, visits by US officials, the Soviet invasion of Czechoslovakia, the drowning of Lake Manapouri, the rugby apartheid of the Springboks; and for Maori, women's and gay rights.

New Zealand **literature and art** began at last to flourish under the auspices of writers such as Ian Wedde, Lauris Edmond, Sam Hunt, Maurice Gee, C.K. Stead and painters like Don Binney, Gretchen Albrecht and Robin White. Home-grown arts even gained respectability on university courses. The counter-culture against suburban mores melded with Maori spirituality in social experiments such as James K. Baxter's communes. In a radical move, the Labour government set up an 'ohu scheme' in 1973, establishing rural communes on the land (they failed, for the usual reasons).

As elsewhere in the world, all this peace and love and consciousness-raising was thrown into reverse by the 1970s oil crisis. The Lange Labour government responded by ending farm subsidies, deregulating the financial markets, cutting taxes and other 'monetarist' measures, which inspired the likes of Margaret Thatcher. The bitter pill was dispensed by finance minister **Roger Douglas** and came to be known as 'Rogernomics'. Although economically successful, these policies led to political in-fighting and a merry-go-round of governments, which in turn led to the introduction of **MMP** (a mixed-member proportional system) in 1996 – a system of proportional representation which, by 2008, seemed to have won public approval.

While Pakeha society had been revolutionised, Maori were undergoing their own cultural revolution. Pre-war Maori politicians had fought for Maori to stay on the land and preserve traditional values, but post-war many Maori chose to move into towns instead, looking for opportunities. Urbanisation brought greater interaction, and also more conflict, with Pakeha – who had long believed they had the best race relations in the world, disrupted only by the wilful naughtiness of Maori. By 1996, 81 per cent of Maori lived in cities, where jobs, education and healthcare were more readily available, but at the cost of emotional and cultural dislocation – and in many cases continuing poverty. Tribalism gave way to 'Maoriness', given cohesion by leaders like **Whina Cooper**, and tikanga (custom) was forgotten. While integration and assimilation were the continuing basis of Pakeha policy towards Maori, a revival of language

## Environmental Issues to the Fore

European immigrants from the earliest days of settlement had pursued a mission to combat nature and turn New Zealand into an agricultural landscape, in function and appearance the 'Britain of the South'. What could not be farmed would yield timber, minerals and other resources, it was hoped. So mature native forests – in their midst ancient kauri trees – were seen as a source of timber and fuel, or an obstacle to clearance for grass; if replaced at all, it was with *Pinus radiata*. Rivers and lakes were seen as energy waiting to be hydroelectrically tapped. The land was there to be turned into grass, to produce meat, butter, cheese and wool for export.

By the mid-20th century, however, this exploitation of the land was beginning to be questioned. Landslides and erosion indicated the environmental degradation caused by 'scientific' farming. While New Zealand had long been 'too desperately poor to deny the present for the benefit of the future', sustainability now became a big issue. Bush clearance, the replacement of native with exotic grasses and the intensive use of herbicides and fertilisers had turned 51 per cent of the land into grassland. But the paucity of fertile soils, combined with geological instability and high rainfall, meant that the 'virgin fertility' of cleared land was soon lost. From the 1920s on, phosphate was liberally scattered on the land (in 1985, the peak year, three million tons were applied). Since the 1970s a partial reversal has been brought about, with less use of toxic agrichemicals and a slow move to plant more suitable crops like forests and vines.

The national debate on the environment really took off with the campaign to save Lake Manapouri in the 1970s and 1980s. Plans to raise the lake by several metres as part of a hydroelectricity-generation scheme were opposed by environmentalists, who foresaw the devastating ecological impact on native flora and fauna around the lake. Eventually the government intervened to save the lake. In the wake of the lake, the last kauri trees were saved, along with some beech and giant podocarp forests. Campaigns for marine conservation and a nuclear ban were, ironically, boosted by the French secret service's sinking of the Greenpeace flagship *Rainbow Warrior* (on its way to protest French nuclear testing at Mururoa Atoll in the South Pacific) in Auckland Harbour in 1985.

Devastation wreaked on the unstable hill farms by Cyclone Bola in 1988, and more recent flooding and landslides (Manawatu and Bay of Plenty, 2004), have continued to highlight the need for action. In the 1980s the state development agencies were separated into commercial and ecological wings, to avoid conflicts of interest. Land clearance subsidies were abolished and a Department of Conservation (DOC) formed, with responsibility for preserving designated national parks. The 1991 Resource Management Act became a foundation for the 'use, development and protection' of air, land and water through the sustainable management of resources. It has not been universally welcomed: while the Green Party has broad support, there are many in the electorate who would rather their own profit interests were not obstructed by ecological issues.

(te reo), culture and history has taken place. Most dramatically, a **Waitangi Tribunal** was set up in 1975 to rule on alleged breaches of the treaty. In 1985 it was made retrospective, and the drawn-out process of dealing with claims still continues (*see* 'The Treaty of Waitangi Revisited', pp.82–6). New Zealand in the 21st century can start to call itself truly bicultural – just as it faces the challenges of greater multiculturalism brought by new waves of immigrants.

# Climate and Geography

## Vital Statistics

Situated in the South Pacific Ocean, New Zealand's nearest significant neighbour is Australia, 2,226km (1,383 miles) to the west. The island chain is made up of two main islands (North and South) and several smaller ones, with a total land mass of 268,680 sq km (103,738 sq miles) – slightly larger than the United Kingdom. The country stretches nearly 1,300km (800 miles) from north to south, from 34°S to 47°S in latitude (a bit closer to the Equator than the UK). New Zealand's coastline is 15,134km (9,403 miles) long, but at its widest the country is only 420km (260 miles) wide, and no part of it is more than 130km (81 miles) from the sea. North and South Islands are separated by the Cook Strait, 20km (12 miles) wide at its narrowest point, while Stewart Island, New Zealand's third largest island, lies south of the Foveaux Strait. Two-thirds of the country's population of 4.25 million live in the North Island (more than a million in Auckland), though the South Island – once known as the Mainland – is larger.

## Main Geological Features

Most of New Zealand is mountainous; an alpine fault line, formed by overlapping tectonic plates, runs down the middle of the two main islands. The snow-capped Southern Alps dominate the **South Island** – Mount Cook is the highest at 3,746m (12,290ft), with another 222 named peaks higher than 2,300m (7,550ft). To the east of the ranges, the warm, dry Canterbury Plains have been transformed in the last 150 years by large-scale farming from a forested area to grasslands dotted with sheep and cattle. To the west of the ranges is rainforest, overlooked by the Fox and Franz Josef glaciers. The island's ragged southwest edge was carved into fiords and inland lakes by successive Ice Ages – the last one 10,000 years ago. The coastline of the fiords stretches 1,000km (620 miles); the deepest is Doubtful Sound, at 420m (1,380ft), and the longest is Dusky Sound, which stretches 40km (25 miles) inland.

A chain of semi-active volcanoes runs through the central **North Island**. Mount Ruapehu, 2,792m (9,176ft), and Mount Nguarohoe, 2,287m (7,503ft), on the central plateau, and White Island, off the east coast, are frequently active

## Will New Zealand Survive Global Warming?

We don't know if anyone will survive global warming, but we can predict that if anyone does there will be a mad scramble for the best new places to live. Will New Zealand be among them? If sea levels rise as predicted, many coastal regions will be swamped. Even if mean sea levels don't rise by the anticipated 18–79 cm (by some estimates) or five metres (according to NASA's head climate scientist) over the next 100 years, there will be more frequent storm surges. Think again about that waterfront property you've got your eye on. The remainder of the country will be slightly warmer and wetter than now, making it more inhabitable than many other regions of the world (Australians will stop moaning about the cold and relish the rain). But there will be greater risk of tropical disease, and the country may be flooded by new immigrants.

In the meantime, fears that food miles are hastening climate change may destroy New Zealand's export markets and its lucrative tourism industry. And while the warmer climate might not sound like a bad thing for New Zealand farmers, it's unlikely to be even: heatwaves, fire risk, floods, landslides and the aforementioned storm surges are to become more frequent and more intense – not ideal for crop production. For now, New Zealand is struggling with its unusual methane emission problem: so much land has been converted to dairy farming that belching and farting cows are the biggest source of greenhouse gases; 35 per cent of the country's greenhouse gas emissions are methane, making New Zealand one of the worst emitters in the world. All those people flying to 'clean, green' New Zealand are leaving a big energy footprint too.

While some New Zealand economists urge a fundamental shift towards a weightless economy – concentrated on IT and entertainment, for example – it is hard to plan for contingencies such as inundation by migrants from Asia and Europe. Biodiversity will diminish and, in the midst of 'extreme weather events', unwelcome bugs such as campylobacter, salmonella and cryptosporidium will thrive at the new temperatures, and mosquitoes will carry diseases such as dengue fever. Forest fires will rage, cliffs and headlands fall into the sea, cyclones destroy bridges and buildings, seaside properties disappear under water; sheep farms will be turned into rice paddies and vineyards into banana groves; and pirate flotillas from the Indian Ocean may descend on the country...

cone volcanoes, while Lakes Taupo and Tarawera are mostly inactive caldera volcanoes (where the ground has collapsed on eruption). Lake Taupo itself was formed by a massive volcanic eruption in AD 186, when pumice flew 50km (31 miles) into the air. The geothermal areas around Lake Rotorua – known as the Taupo Volcanic Zone – are a constantly bubbling furnace of geysers, cauldrons, mineral pools, mud pools, silica terraces, lakes and waterfalls. All in all the landscape is notable for the diversity of its mountains, lakes, rivers, beaches, hills, plains, volcanoes, rainforests and fiords. In the north, the Bay of Islands has no fewer than 144 offshore islands, all within 50km (31 miles) of the coast.

# The Weather

New Zealanders are if anything more fanatical about their weather forecasts than the British – and for many of the same reasons. New Zealand's temperate climate is oceanic (as opposed to continental), without extreme ranges of hot and cold – but warm sun can turn to cool rain at any moment. The long, narrow shape of the archipelago and its mountainous core dictate the climate range: it ranges from almost sub-tropical in the north to icy winters in the south. Even more noticeable, however, is the range from west to east – from very wet to relatively dry.

With a bit of practice you can learn to recognise the most common weather pattern. An irregular succession of anticyclones (areas of descending air and settled weather with little or no rain, which may bring clear skies or low cloud and fog) migrates eastwards across the North Island every six to seven days. Between the anticyclones are troughs of low pressure, which bring cold fronts with them: as the front approaches from the west, northwesterly winds become stronger and cloud increases, followed by several hours of rain as the front passes over, and then a change to cold, showery southwesterly winds.

## Wind

The prevailing wind blows southwesterly across the Tasman Sea, hitting the west coast of the islands heavy with rain: Fiordland and Westland in the South Island are well known for their wet weather (but also for their luscious rainforests). By the time the wind has passed over the central mountain ranges to reach the plains of the east coast – Otago, Canterbury and Marlborough in the south; Hawke's Bay and Gisborne in the north – it is warm and dry. The North Island tends to be less windy in summer and autumn, but in parts of the South Island midwinter is the least windy period. Wellington is notoriously windy, with an average of 173 days a year on which wind gusts are greater than 60kph (37mph) (compared with around 30 days elsewhere) – and that wind comes with a chill from the south.

## Rainfall

Rainfall is dictated by the mountains too: the wettest areas are where the westerly winds hit the ranges. Despite regional differences, the country as a whole is wet. While mean annual rainfall ranges from as little as 300mm (12 inches) in a small area of Central Otago to more than 8,000mm (315 inches) in the Southern Alps, average annual rainfall is high – between 600 and 1,500mm (24 and 60 inches). The driest areas are in the eastern South Island – Central and North Otago and South Canterbury – and the Hawke's Bay region of the eastern North Island.

In much of the country rain falls evenly all year. The greatest contrast is in the north, where it rains twice as much in winter as in summer, whereas in the southern South Island winter is the least rainy season. In the west it rains every other day, in most of the rest of the North Island every third day (less in the east), in the drier parts of the South Island every fourth day and in Fiordland two days out of three.

## Temperature

The warmest parts of the country are in the north, the coldest in the south, mean temperatures decreasing from about 15°C (59°F) in the far north to about 10°C (50°F) in the south of the South Island. Temperatures also drop with altitude. January and February are the warmest months of the year, and July is the coldest, although temperatures do not vary dramatically between summer and winter – around 10°C (50°F) on the coasts, or as much as 15°C (59°F) in the 'continental' microclimate of inland Central Otago. The highest temperatures are east of the mountain ranges, where they can exceed 30°C (86°F) in summer.

The sunniest places in New Zealand are near Blenheim, the Nelson-Motueka area and Whakatane, which get more than 2,350 hours a year of bright sunshine; the rest of the Bay of Plenty and Napier are only slightly less sunny. However much of the country gets at least 2,000 hours of sun annually, and even rainy Westland gets 1,800 hours. Southland and coastal Otago are the least sunny regions. There can be many sunny days in winter.

Although most of the coast rarely has snow or even frost, it can get chilly inland in winter. The coldest winters are in Central Otago and on the central plateau of the North Island, where winter sports are popular. There is a small permanent snowfield above 2,500m (8,202ft) on the central plateau, while snow occasionally comes down as low as 600m (1,968ft) in winter. Elsewhere in the North Island winters are relatively mild. The snow line on the Southern Alps is 2,000m (6,562ft) in summer (lower on the glaciers), but in inland Canterbury and Otago heavy snowfall can cause serious sheep losses above 300m (984ft) in bad winters.

# Food and Drink

Any New Zealander aged over 40 will happily reminisce about the 'bad old days' of plain food: plain meat and boiled vegetables, meat pies and for a treat fish and chips and hokey-pokey ice cream – all swilled down, if you were lucky, with a jug of beer. But over the last 30 years New Zealand cuisine has gone through a revolution, brought about by cosmopolitan influences: New Zealanders returning from overseas have come back enthused by Middle Eastern or Mediterranean cooking, while new waves of Asian immigrants have introduced previously unknown herbs, spices and flavour mixes. Out of all this New Zealand has developed its very own cuisine – sometimes bundled in with fusion or Pacific Rim cuisine – making the most of plentiful fresh, local produce. Fish, now a rarity in other parts of the world, is truly appreciated; more unusual varieties of vegetable are being grown; and even lamb is no longer dressed as mutton. Add to all this the planting of vineyards over the last 20 years, which are now producing some excellent wines, and you have some very fine meals, not only in the high-class restaurants that have sprung up in cities and wine-growing areas, but also in New Zealand homes.

# Classic New Zealand Staples

## Barbecues

While the joys of innovation get most sophisticated young New Zealanders going, many (old and young) are still nostalgic for the staple dishes of their youth. A classic of New Zealand life is the barbecue. Not only is it a great way to enjoy the outdoors – beach or backyard – it also puts the apron on the New Zealand male, otherwise highly resistant to 'feminine' tasks. In summer, men up and down the country can be found clustered around the (usually gas-fuelled) barbecue, wielding tongs and charring hunks of meat, while the women fuss with salads and sauces. (If you are invited to a barbecue, you will probably be asked to take some meat and a salad.)

## Sweets

Around Christmas (midsummer), the barbie may be followed by pavlova (meringue with cream and fruit) or trifle (sponge cake with cream and fruit). Don't be surprised, however, even in the depths of summer, to be offered a slice of heavy fruit cake with a Santa Claus on top. New Zealand women are big bakers, and you will soon learn to feel inadequate when invited to morning or afternoon tea if you don't turn up with home-baked melting moments (buttery biscuits sandwiched together with buttery icing), ANZAC biscuits (flapjack-like biscuits), neenish tarts (tartlets with a rich lemon filling iced with chocolate and almonds), Afghans (chocolate cornflake biscuits), scones or muffins. If you have a sweet tooth, there are plenty of other options on the market too: hokey-pokey ice cream (vanilla with chunks of caramel), peanut slabs (chocolate with peanuts) and pineapple lumps (pineapple-flavoured goo in a chocolate casing) are three staples of childhood nostalgia.

## Savouries

If your tastes tend more to the savoury, look out for the ever-dwindling stands of hot pies in traditional dairies (corner shops) and sandwich shops; the most common varieties are steak and onion or steak and cheese, encased in pastry. They are likely to be on sale alongside a range of plain sandwiches: white bread and ham or cheese, although new-style bakeries have been selling focaccia like hot cakes in the last decade. Most New Zealanders, however refined their tastes, will tuck into fish and chips from time to time; the fish is so fresh and good that a spot of batter and deep frying just enhances it. A speciality rarely found elsewhere is battered oysters; the Bluff oysters are best, when in season. To find out what ordinary New Zealanders eat at home (and to learn how to cook it yourself), invest in a copy of the Edmonds cook book, in print for nearly 100 years; in winter, however, you are as likely as anything to be offered roast lamb or beef with roast root vegetables in a New Zealand home.

# Local and Seasonal Specialities

## Vegetables and Fruit

Given its distance from the rest of the world, New Zealand is largely self-reliant for its raw ingredients, which are only available in season – not necessarily a bad thing. You are likely to find yourself gorging on seasonal delicacies for the brief period they are around. Starting in spring, the first annual treat is asparagus, served with butter, lemon or Hollandaise sauce. This is soon joined by strawberries, then raspberries, boysenberries (between a blackberry and a raspberry) and tayberries (another variant). In some parts of the country you will get blueberries too. Cherries are a delicacy that appear around Christmas. More widely available are countless varieties of apricots, plums and peaches (in autumn black boys and golden queens are worth looking out for). Last in the year comes a glut of pears, apples (braeburns are among the best), kiwi fruit (look out for the golden variety), tamarillos and citrus fruits.

Oamaru new potatoes are the best of a surprisingly ordinary bunch, often served with fresh sweetcorn in January and February. Then comes autumn and a massive crop of pumpkins and squash (buttercup, butternut and crown are three common varieties), along with red and gold kumara (the 'native' sweet potato, brought by the first Polynesian settlers) and yams (another Polynesian import, a small root vegetable with a flavour not unlike a cross between an apple and a Jerusalem artichoke).

Other European vegetables, from beans to turnips, are widely grown too. Some growers have recently started to diversify into more unusual vegetables too, from countless types of aubergine (the long, white Asian ones as well as the purple ones) to cavolo nero and white beetroot.

## Seafood and Fish

New Zealand is not just a vegetarian paradise, however. Anyone arriving from the overfished and polluted seas of Europe will relish the variety and freshness of fish and seafood. Mussels and pipi (local clams) are widely fished, farmed and sold, along with the rarer (and more expensive) oysters, crayfish, prawns, shrimps and paua (a shellfish most notable for its pearly blue shell, used to make jewellery). Fish caught in New Zealand waters include snapper, John Dory, hoki, terakihi, sole, blue and red cod, hapuka, hake, ling, trevally, gurnard, moki, flounder, gemfish, orange roughy and the much-despised but delicious kawahai (a rather oily fish caught by surfcasters off beaches).

You should be able to get a selection of freshly caught fish anywhere coastal – or you can join the mass of New Zealand men huddled along beaches with their rods, or setting out to sea in boats at weekends. Whitebait (tiny whole fish) are served as fritters for a brief annual period.

## Meat and Dairy

Meat and dairy products have long been the staples of the New Zealand export economy – and of home-cooking. You may, however, find good meat surprisingly hard to come by. Old-fashioned butchers have disappeared almost as fast as they have in Britain, with much beef and lamb sold pre-packed in supermarkets. Most rural New Zealanders have a cow or a couple of sheep grazing on their property, or a contact in the field who will procure them a whole carcass, butchered, for the freezer. Venison is widely farmed too. While all cattle, sheep and pigs are 'free-range', most commercially sold chickens and eggs are not, and few of either are organic. At Christmas, baked ham is practically obligatory. Milk, cream and butter are plentiful, as is yoghurt in every variety from plain acidophilus to Greek-style or fruit-flavoured (plus sugar and additives). Much cheese is of the bland, plastic-wrapped blocks-of-cheddar variety, but the country is increasingly taking pride in its gourmet cheeses.

## Imported Foods

In the main cities and many of the larger provincial ones, you will be able to lay your hands on a range of imported foods from British and Mediterranean to Asian. Specialist shops can sell you olive oil, pasta, risotto rice, olives, capers, anchovies, parmesan, mozzarella, prosciutto, pancetta and salami (with meat products depending on the latest European foot and mouth scare), artichoke hearts and grilled peppers in jars, balsamic vinegar and so on. Christchurch, the most British of the cities, boasts its own British food shop, selling the likes of Fortnum and Mason's Gentleman's Relish. Auckland, Wellington and some of the other more multicultural provincial cities benefit from Asian emporia selling everything from noodles to jasmine, basmati and sushi rice, shiitake mushrooms, kombu (kelp), wakame (another seaweed), wasabi, spices and so on. Here the main difficulty is identifying what's in the packet, but several New Zealand and Australian published books can tell you how to use them fusion-style.

# Café Culture

One European import that New Zealand has made distinctly its own is café culture. You will find more cafés on city streets than in most Italian, French or Spanish towns, serving a full range of coffees: cappuccino, espresso, macchiato, latte, long black, flat white, mochaccino, decaf – and chai latte and hot chocolate. Cups tend to be larger and the drinks milkier than in their European countries of origin (cappuccino is often served in a soup-sized bowl), and speed rarely seems to be of the essence in getting you your caffeine fix – but the quality of coffee and service depends on the café, and with an annual national 'barista' competition coffee-making is taken pretty seriously here. Fruit juices, smoothies and spirulina (a bright green juice smoothie made with vitamin- and mineral-rich algae) are usually on offer too.

If you feel peckish while sipping your coffee, most cafés bake a variety of sweet and savoury muffins – ranging from raspberry and white chocolate to feta cheese and spinach – and make panini (always in the plural – one panini, two panini, three panini, four). Another New Zealand café favourite is a range of big breakfasts: muesli with yoghurt and fruit; pancakes or French toast with bacon, bananas and maple syrup; eggs Benedict (with bacon or smoked salmon and Hollandaise sauce) or Florentine (spinach and sauce); a full-on fry-up (sausages, bacon, eggs, tomatoes, mushrooms and so on) or plain eggs (boiled, poached or scrambled).

# New Zealand Wines

Until recently, New Zealand was beer country. If you fancied a drink, you would head down to the local hotel bar (a pretty rough and tough sort of place) and order a jug of beer on tap – most likely produced by one of the 60 or so breweries in the country, whose brands include Tui, Steinlager and DK. These days, beer-drinkers are as likely to buy imported bottled beers – or to drink wine. To many, New Zealand's burgeoning wine industry is the most radical element of the country's gastronomic revolution.

Grapes have been grown and wine made in New Zealand since the earliest days of European settlement, but it is only in the last 30 years that wine-making has taken off. James Busby, the First British Resident of New Zealand, was making wine in the Bay of Islands even before the Treaty of Waitangi (1840); his white wine was praised by French explorer Dumont D'Urville in that year, and French settlers planted vines on Canterbury's Banks Peninsula around the same time. Marist monks were producing wine for sacramental purposes in 1851 at what is now Mission Estate Winery, and New Zealand's oldest commercial winery, Te Mata Estate Winery (both in Hawke's Bay), planted its first vineyards in 1892.

It was not until the 1980s, however, when wine-makers began to focus on white varieties like sauvignon blanc and chardonnay, that the country's reputation as a wine producer began to grow. Since then the number of wineries has expanded to almost 400, which in 20 years have started to produce some world-class vintages. The wine revolution has gone hand-in-glove with the country's culinary revival. Most wineries offer 'cellar-door' sales (in fact some sell only this way) and many have also established restaurants in attractive vineyard settings or – increasingly the trend – in swanky new buildings (some of architectural merit, others more flash-cash than dash). Some of New Zealand's top chefs can be found cooking among the grapes. Sadly, to New Zealand patriots, most of the wineries are now foreign-owned.

Surprisingly to anyone familiar with French or Italian wines, New Zealand wines are rarely single vineyard wines, but made from grapes grown in vineyards dotted around the region – or even different parts of the country; the role of winemaker is consummate here. Vintages vary, winemakers move and new wineries open, so for proper guidance on wineries, grape varietals and years invest in a wine guide such as Michael Cooper's annually updated *Buyer's Guide to New Zealand Wines*.

## The Wine Regions

**Northland**, the northernmost tip of New Zealand, produces full-bodied red wines, especially merlot, while the **Auckland** region specialises in cabernet sauvignon. The wine industry here has been largely driven by Croatians who have settled in the Henderson Valley. Family-owned Babich Wines, which has a *pétanque* and picnic area among its vineyards, produces top-of-the-range wines such as Babich Irongate chardonnay, but also good cheaper wines. Some of the country's biggest wineries are here too: Montana Wines, which produces more than 150 varieties (half the country's total output) including an award-winning sparkling white wine (Deutz Marlborough Cuvée) and the highly reputed Morton Estate Black Label; and Corbans Wine, established in 1902 by Lebanese immigrants (the country's second largest winery), which makes the top-notch Corbans Cottage Block Gisborne and Corbans Private Bin Gisborne Chardonnays from grapes grown on the East Cape, and Corbans Private Bin Amberley from its Canterbury vineyards. Kumeu River is noted for its chardonnays.

**Waikato**, **Bay of Plenty** and **Gisborne** have made their name in chardonnays (*see* Corbans Wine, above), while the high sunshine hours and soil types of **Hawke's Bay** have brought 30 wineries to the region – the country's second largest wine area. All the main grape varieties are grown here, producing some excellent wines – most notably chardonnays and cabernet blends. Te Mata Estate Winery (*see* above) produces the prestigious Coleraine cabernet merlot and Elston chardonnay. The swanky Sileni Estates, Craggy Range and Black Barn vineyards are some of the proliferating flash winery-cum-eateries in the area,

## Case Study: Making Wine While the Sun Shines

Paul and Clara Guard are in the wine business. They had both been working for a wine-exporting business in Milan (where they met) when they decided to set sail for the New World. Now Paul is the general manager of one of Hawke's Bay's most highly reputed wineries. The couple made the move soon after the birth of their son, Matthew (7 months). 'New Zealand seemed a better place to bring up a child than Milan,' says Clara, who loved the pace of Italy's fashion capital as long as she was young, free and single. For Paul it was a career move: there was only so far he could go in the Italian wine industry as a non-Italian, but with the expertise he had gained in one of the world's oldest wine-growing regions he felt confident he had something to offer one of the newest – and that he could provide his new family with a better life on the proceeds.

'There's so much space,' says Clara, looking over rows of vines to distant mountain ranges at an open-air winery lunch. As the rather housebound mother of a small baby she hasn't had a chance to make many friends yet. 'We seem to have spent most of our time so far just getting set up,' she says. 'Now we've found a house we'll get out and about more too.' Paul is out at the winery every day and travels frequently to wine industry functions around the country, so has more opportunity to meet people. He is enthusiastic about his job, too. The winery is already well established, with some award-winning wines and a high profile for its restaurant, so his task is to maintain and improve a successful formula. 'I'd like to attract a less conservative crowd out here,' he says. One idea is to have live music playing on Sundays – 'either for brunch, or late afternoon into evening'. Clara would like to go back to work too in due course. One of her ideas is to set up a pizzeria, using knowledge she gained in Italy. It's still early days, but just about anything seems possible, and optimism rules the day.

but some of the smaller wineries have more charm – and may produce better wines: Clearview has made a name with its Clearview Estate Reserve Chardonnay – and for the understated charm of its seaside restaurant – and Esk Valley produces a top-of-the-taste-buds Reserve Merlot blend as well as an excellent Reserve Chardonnay. Coopers Creek, Church Road, Brookfields, Trinity Hill, Te Awa, Sacred Hill and Vidal also make some above-average wines in Hawke's Bay.

New Zealand's newest winemaking region, **Wairarapa** started off with four wineries in 1980. It now has 25, and hosts the annual Martinborough Wine and Food Festival. Pinot noir is the most widely planted variety of the region, and Palliser Estate has gained a high reputation for its pinot noir, as well as its chardonnay and sauvignon blanc. Dry River makes some of the best whites in the country (especially gewürztraminer, pinot gris and riesling) and an excellent Pinot Noir. The Ata Rangi vineyard also produces the top-quality Craighall chardonnay and pinot noir. Martinborough Vineyard is another reputed pinot noir producer in this area.

**Marlborough** is New Zealand's largest wine-growing region. Here the wide, flat Wairau Valley and a dry, sunny climate combine to produce the country's finest sauvignon blancs, as well as some chardonnays and sparkling wines. Grape planting was begun here in the 1970s by Montana Wines; now there are nearly 50 wineries in the area and the Wine Marlborough Festival is held here every February. The Cloudy Bay winery has established an international reputation (partly through good marketing), especially for its whites: its sauvignon blanc is one of the best, and its chardonnay not far behind. Award-winning Hunter's Wines produces a full range of reds, whites and sparkling wines, including its classic sauvignon blancs. One of the 'big four' wineries, Villa Maria, produces much of its wine here, including the excellent Clifford Bay and Wairau Valley sauvignon blancs (it makes some top wines in other parts of the country too, as does Nobilo, the country's other big wine producer). Grove Mill, Isabel, Lawson's Dry Hills, Seresin and Wither Hills are some of the other top Marlborough sauvignon blancs, while Pegasus Bay makes a good chardonnay and riesling.

The small vineyards of **Nelson** and **Canterbury** produce chardonnay, pinot noir and riesling. Waipara, north of Christchurch, is one of the region's most important wine-growing areas. **Central Otago**, the world's most southerly wine area, produces gewürztraminer, riesling and burgundy varieties. Gibbston Valley Wines here has an underground cave cellar, where it stores its pinot noir.

# New Zealand *Haute Cuisine*

The best of New Zealand cuisine is found either in slick city restaurants or in and around the wineries in some of the more affluent regions. As with wines, it is best to consult a current food guide for specific eating out recommendations, but here is a rough guide to the sort of dishes you might find on the menu. In general, New Zealand chefs are busy combining ingredients and flavours from around the world; the Asian influence is particularly notable, but European antecedents are also clear.

Choices might range from brains with a garlic custard and Madeira sauce to lamb loin baked in potato and sesame, on a bed of Breton-style flageolet beans with a rosemary and cabernet sauce; terrine of South Island crayfish and crab served with brown meat salad bouquet and champagne, pine nut and truffle vinaigrette; eggplant (aubergine) stack with marinated courgettes, oven-roasted tomatoes and peppers warmed and smothered in a balsamic dressing; black risotto; white chocolate mousse; *saucisson de mer*; pork fillet in green ginger wine with figs and *risone*; smoked salmon with gruyère sablé biscuits served with a dill and mustard cream dressing; giant cerignola olives stuffed and crumbed with parmesan, lightly fried and served with sundried tomatoes, artichoke hearts, red pepper oil and *crostini*; grilled salmon and mussels on a bed of spiced kidney beans with bok choy and ginger; pineapple, coconut and palm sugar tart; steamed layers of Akaroa sea-run salmon and crayfish with oyster ravioli and caviar *beurre blanc*; steamed orange roughy and sautéed king prawn with parsnip timbale and prawn and leek sauce; Marlborough Sound salmon with confit of pear, blini and kikorangi blue *mousseline*; or poached persimmons with blueberry mousse and *gaufres*. After all that, you might be ready to head home for a plain steak and kidney pie.

# Profiles of the Regions

New Zealand may be world-famous as a natural wonderland, but you are unlikely to pitch up in a remote picture-postcard setting unless you marry a sheep farmer, opt for an alternative lifestyle or set up a beachfront B&B. Eighty per cent of New Zealanders actually live in towns. That said, New Zealand's towns are not the sprawling brick and concrete conurbations of the old world. Even Auckland, the megalopolis of this southern nation, boasts less than half a million residents within its city boundary. Most of the metropolitan remainder are much smaller, even when you include the rambling suburbs and semi-rural districts that many inhabitants inhabit.

From the Kerikeri in the 'winterless north' to Dunedin, the 'Edinburgh of the south', every regional centre has its own attractions. While most expatriates seek what they can't get at home – sunny climes and open space – practicality constrains them, like previous generations of migrants, to move to areas with established communities, work, schools, shops and hospitals. Perhaps it's no surprise that the regions most popular with 'blow-ins' are Nelson and Napier, both attractive small towns by the sea, with high sunshine hours and all that boring but essential stuff, topped off by an easy 'lifestyle', a nod at an arts scene and good food and wine; more rugged locations are never far away.

The coastal Bay of Plenty and Marlborough are not far behind in settler popularity, while richer foreigners are keen to snap up prime real estate in out-of-the-way Northland and the Bay of Islands. Other, lesser-known regions may attract pioneering types: the isolation of the West Coast has a frontier appeal if you don't mind the remoteness, while the backwoods of Waikato, Taranaki and Wanganui are surprisingly untapped rural regions.

For most people moving from overcrowded Europe, the high-stress lifestyle of Auckland, the sombre artiness of Wellington or the English-style snobbery of Christchurch may not obviously attract – but in the cold light of day they may have more to offer than the boondocks. If, however, it's the spirit of outdoors adventure that draws you to New Zealand, head for the bungee-jumping action capital, Queenstown, or the white-water rafting volcanic region of the Central North Island plateau.

# North Island

## Auckland

Auckland is New Zealand's largest, fastest-growing and most multi-ethnic city, with a population of approximately 415,300 within the city boundary and 1.25 million in the greater Auckland area – almost one-third of the whole population of the country. Auckland has the largest number of Pacific

## Case Study: Goldilocks, or Mechanics in Demand

Bill Bedford had seen pictures of New Zealand and wanted to go fishing. 'I took stock of my life and jumped on a plane,' he says. 'I was 30, and my teenage years had extended long enough.' That was 30 years ago, in the days when 'a British passport got you anywhere' and there was no visa hassle. 'I just had to cut my goldilocks off to get through Singapore.' When he touched down at Auckland airport, he had a tremendous cultural shock: 'It was the bungalow-type houses, which reminded me of the outback of Spain.' But after 12 months he met a Kiwi girl, and has never looked back. In all that time he's only been back, to Birmingham, three times: once three years after he came out, when he 'couldn't get back quick enough'; last year for his godson's wedding, and the year before that – which was a big shock: 'Birmingham's been all done up, and there are just too many people,' he says. He still regards himself as British, has kept his British passport and sees no benefits in becoming a New Zealand citizen; he talks about 'home' in a flawless Brum accent and phones his 93-year-old mother every week, although he adds that he'd still rather be here. And what about the fishing? 'I don't go fishing much any more, but I used to. And lots of boating.'

Bill is a motor mechanic by trade, and still plies his trade part-time although he is now old enough to draw a pension. He has never been out of work, having turned his hand to floorlaying and carpentry, among other things, in times of recession. 'There's plenty of work for those who want to earn a dollar,' he says. In his opinion, New Zealand has been 'going backwards' in the time he's been here, in its values and 'how we respect one another'. 'You used to be able to give your word, or a handshake,' he says. 'Not any more.' On the other hand, the country is 'no longer off the map', it's just a question of whether joining the rest of the world has been a good or a bad thing for it. Sceptical about what he sees as the Waitangi Tribunal 'gravy train' for lawyers, with hindsight he wonders if more conservative Australia might not have been a better place to be. 'The Maori culture and history are wonderful,' he says, 'and should be retained, but not to the detriment of others.' He adds: 'these soft politicians will never fix it.' All the same, he has his house, family, safety – and the beach, all of which make it a pretty good life.

Islanders anywhere (including the islands themselves) and large Asian communities cheek-by-jowl with the Maori mana whenua (indigenous people), Ngati Whatua o Orakei, and white tribes – a multicultural combination that spices up the ethnic flavour of the city.

The city and its suburbs sprawl over an area of 60 square kilometres; while much of the action is in Auckland City, the six suburban 'sister cities' have their own characters – and are where many Aucklanders live. Auckland is commonly critiqued for its lack of heart: downtown Auckland is soulless, and any hunt for the spirit of the 'taone' involves traffic jams – it's the only place in New Zealand with serious congestion – while the view from the provinces is that Aucklanders are as heartless as their city. On a random sampling, this last proposition is probably untrue: most Aucklanders started off in the provinces themselves, and if they are a little harder-nosed than their fellow countrymen and women it is probably down to the effort they put into climbing the property ladder – and getting around. Many of the million-plus suburbanites commute daily into the city, a few by bus, ferry and rail but most by car, thousands over the one bridge that connects the city with its North Shore suburbs. Plans to improve the public transport network and to build a second bridge and inner-city motorway bypass are frequently mooted, but may take years to realise even if consensus on the best way forward is ever reached.

New Zealand's capital until 1865, Auckland still considers itself the country's most important city (a claim hotly contested by other cities, to which Auckland is largely indifferent). It is where most big businesses, national and international, have their head offices. The proliferation of bars, clubs and restaurants, shops and art galleries is a testament to the money being made in the 'business capital' – as are some of the glossier suburbs and smartly restored old districts. In some circles, tedious talk of yachts, cars and millionaire buddies lends some credibility to the assertion that Aucklanders are infatuated with lucre; in other, Dante-esque sub-circles, constant chatter about schools (Auckland Grammar and King's) is just as symptomatic of status-driven ambition. Property, finance, insurance, education, manufacturing and distribution are key industries supporting Auckland and the rest of New Zealand. Not entirely coincidentally, Auckland is called the 'gateway' to New Zealand, with the country's largest airport, serving 45 airlines and most overseas flights.

Auckland is built on a narrow isthmus between the Waitemata and Manukau harbours, and is surrounded by extinct volcanoes and the picturesque islands of the Hauraki Gulf. It has been known as the 'City of Sails' since its Viaduct Basin hosted the Americas Cup sailing tournament in 1999 and again in 2003.

Auckland is warm – in summer temperatures average 24°C (75°F), in winter 16°C (61°F) – but notoriously rainy. The wet does not deter Aucklanders from enjoying the city's open spaces: Greater Auckland is strung along a string of beaches; the volcanic craters of the inner city like the Auckland Domain give it green lungs as well as great concert venues (the Big Day Out is an annual event to rival Glastonbury); to the west there are remote surf beaches (Piha and Karekare), native forest (Waitakere) and vineyards (Henderson) within reach, and to the east are the islands of the gulf. Cultural attractions within the city include the Auckland Museum Te Papa Whakahiku, which houses one of the best Maori and Polynesian collections in the world; the Maritime Museum on the waterfront; Auckland Art Gallery Toi o Tamaki and its New Gallery, which exhibit a prized collection of New Zealand art including Charles Goldie's Maori portraits (*see* pp.17 and 93) and contemporary exhibitions (it's also a good place to pick up information about Auckland's art gallery scene). The city's two universities and technical institute are among the country's top-ranking institutions, and are soon to be joined by a commercially backed business school.

**Queen Street** is the city's dreary downtown hub, leading to the sterile waterfront development, but for funk and spunk head for **Karangahape**, or **K, Road** and **Ponsonby**, where you will find the city's trendiest bars, restaurants, dance and music venues; it is the city's new bohemia, where artists and media types congregate – Wellington may like to refer to itself as the 'cultural capital', but it is in Auckland that commercial artists, advertising and TV people and magazine publishers rendezvous. **Parnell Road**, flanked by wooden villas, and Newmarket are more upmarket centres of eating, drinking, shopping, fashion and art. **Mount Eden**, **Takapuna** and **Mission Bay** are among the more lively suburbs. For a feel of the city's ethnic diversity, the Otara markets in **Manukau City** (South Auckland, the location of *Once Were Warriors*) are the place to go. Of the outlying areas, **Devonport** on the North Shore is the most historically interesting, a well-preserved Victorian township now crammed with quaint craft and coffee shops. **Tamaki Drive** to the east is the most exclusive beachfront suburb. **Great Barrier Island** and **Waiheke Island** are two of best in the Hauraki Gulf, the former proudly hanging on to its primitive state, the latter a fashionable bohemian-cum-luxury paradise.

# Northland

Northland's motto is 'live, work and play', though it's best known as the playground of holidaying Aucklanders, wealthy foreigners and backpackers on bus tours. It is the North Island's most spectacular, remote and historic region, popular as a tourist destination but with sadly limited opportunities to live and work. With a subtropical climate and 1,700km (1,050 miles) of coastline, from the golden sand and rocky shores of the east coast's small coves and islands to the long surf beaches (Ninety Mile Beach) and dunes of the west coast, the region has everything to offer the seaside holidaymaker, from diving and snorkelling to big-game fishing, sailing and windsurfing – but when the tourists have gone home the underbelly is more evident. While millionaire golf-players helicopter in to clifftop luxury lodges, much of Northland's underskilled native population (146,600) lives in substandard housing, with not enough jobs to go around; at 6.7 per cent, official unemployment levels here are lower than in much of Europe, but still the highest in New Zealand.

A long, narrow peninsula north of Auckland – the tail of Maui's fish – Northland juts north as far as **Cape Reinga**, the northernmost tip of New Zealand, where the Tasman Sea and the Pacific Ocean meet and the souls of the Maori dead make their final leap into the beyond. Most visitors drive up the east coast to the cape and back down the west (or vice versa) along the twin highways. Heading up the east, they might stop at **Whangaparaoa Peninsula** en route to **Whangarei**, the region's major city (population 45,800), and where most work is to be found. Pausing for a swim on the **Tutukaka Coast** and a quick dive off the **Poor Knights Islands**, they would probably head on to explore the **Bay of Islands**, famed for its turquoise sea, tiny coves and unspoilt islands.

**Paihia** is now the bustling tourist hub of the bay – hard to recognise as the place where Henry Williams established the first missionary settlement in 1823. A few kilometres away is **Waitangi**, where the nation's founding treaty was signed in 1840. Just across the bay is Russell, nicknamed the 'hell-hole of the South Pacific' for its drunken, whoring whalers in the 1830s, when it went by the name of Kororareka. It was the site of a famous Pakeha rout in 1845, when the Nga Puhi besieged the town and chieftain Honi Heke felled the flagstaff. It's now a charming town of old wooden houses, popular with more sophisticated tourists. At the north of the bay is **Kerikeri**, another pretty small town with a history – including Kerikeri Mission House, New Zealand's oldest surviving wooden house, and Stone Store, the oldest stone building – surrounded by citrus and kiwi fruit orchards.

Carrying on to the Far North, travellers pass Matauri Bay, Whangaroa Harbour, Doubtless Bay ('doubtless a bay', Captain Cook laconically noted) and the Karikari Peninsula before heading up the Aupouri Peninsula to Spirit's Bay and **Cape Reinga** – signposted John o'Groats-style to the far-flung rest of the world – then back down **Ninety Mile Beach**, one long, straight sandy beach, which doubles up as a highway, to **Kaitaia**, the major northernmost town.

Heading back down the west coast, you pass **Hokianga Harbour**, another site of early colonial settlement, and the last of Northland's kauri trees at Waipoua and Trounson forests. The huge trees, which take a couple of thousand years to grow to their full dimensions, were mercilessly logged by Pakeha colonists for ships' masts and building timber. Tane Mahuta is the tallest survivor, at 51m (170ft) tall, while Te Matua Ngahere's trunk is over 5m (16½ft) in diameter. Last stop on the 'Kauri Coast' is **Dargaville**, the kumara-growing capital.

Northland's main industries are agriculture (dairy, beef), horticulture (kiwi fruit, kumara, oranges), forestry and fishing (including aquaculture), food processing and the transport of food products out and people in. Tourism is another big employer: shops, hotels, cafés and restaurants provide jobs for quite a few people. The region has a higher than average proportion of both young people and old people, which means education and healthcare workers are in demand too, and real estate and the construction trade are growing, due to an influx of overseas migrants. The regional economy is strong, with a shortage of skilled workers, but relies on the global economy for both food export and tourism (so is easily affected by fluctuations in the exchange rate). Much work is seasonal (fruit harvesting and tourism), and most of the rest is in Whangarei and around. Many of the remoter areas in the west and north are quite poor – many people here do not even have a phone or email. A high proportion of Northland's population is Maori (one-third across the region, and

41 per cent in the Far North). Government-promoted work-generation schemes include the retro-fitting and relocation of houses, the construction of a prison at Ngawha, and house building for the Te Rarawa iwi. While Northland may seem the ideal setting for a dream home, it's worth assessing if there is a real-istic economic basis for moving here: just how many fashion boutiques and flash restaurants can such a far-flung region support?

## The Bay of Plenty

The Bay of Plenty is a land of socio-economic contrasts, where wealthy resorts border towns that have had the economic heart sucked out of them. From the coastal boomtown of Tauranga in the west of the bay to the down-at-heel port of Opotiki at its eastern end; from the moneyed lakeside playground of Taupo to the cast-off worker towns of Mangakino, Turangi and Kawerau; from the glossy-brochure façade of Rotorua's thermal wonderland and Maori tourist villages to its seamier ganglands – rich and poor lie cheek by jowl in this region, named by Captain Cook for the abundance of its land and sea and the hospi-tality of its Maori people.

In the western Bay of Plenty, the commercial port town of Tauranga and its surfy sister Mount Maunganui are real-estate hotspots, popular with New Zealand holidaymakers and retired people who move here in droves for the sunshine, sandy beaches and shopping malls. Close to Auckland (three hours' drive) and proudly claiming that it is within 200 kilometres (118 miles) of 44 per cent of New Zealand's population, **Tauranga** markets itself as a lifestyle loca-tion on the beach with 'big city' shops, restaurants and cafés. It's growing fast: its population is estimated to grow by 53 people a week and 88 new dwellings per month, and the town boasts of its high levels of (mortgage-free) home ownership. It's also very white (89 per cent of its inhabitants are Pakeha, compared to a national average of 83 per cent) and has a high proportion of people aged 65 and over (17 per cent compared with 12 per cent nationally). If you're looking for unspoilt, this is not the place to head for; if you're keen on your suburban comforts and golf course, go for it.

As well as the white sand of its beaches and its pleasant climate, this end of the bay is sustained by the shipping of logs and fruit from Tauranga's port. Further up the coast is **Katikati**, an Ulster settlement of the 1870s, which now lives off its reputation as an open-air art gallery (murals adorn many of its walls), while down the coast **Te Puke**, another Ulster settlement, is the kiwi fruit and avocado capital of the country. The first Maori who settled here harvested sea food. The early European colonists planted maize and potatoes and logged the native forests. Pastoral farming took off in the 1930s when cobalt was added to the soil, but has now given way to horticulture and 'exotic' forestry (*Pinus radiata*). In the eastern Bay of Plenty, **Whakatane** shares the same long, sandy beaches and is one of the sunniest places in the country, with more than

2,500 sunshine hours a year, but is far less developed than Tauranga. Its main attraction is offshore: **White Island**, New Zealand's most active volcano, which can be visited from here.

**Opotiki**, the easternmost coastal settlement in the bay, is at the other end of the socio-economic spectrum too – a prelude to the East Cape: beautiful but poor. A farming service centre and small coastal port, it suffered badly from the decline of pastoral farming that followed free-market reforms in the 1980s. Its local economy is still weak, with unemployment high since its dairy factory and bacon works, clothing manufacturer and footwear factory closed in the 1990s, and local forestry was 'restructured'. Despite an unspoilt coastline, it is not really on the tourist itineraries, and its port is not big enough for commercial fishing. Its future may lie in the kiwi fruit, avocado, passion fruit and tamarillo orchards that are just being planted.

Contrary to Tauranga, which has the sixth-highest population density in New Zealand, the Opotiki area is sparsely populated; 54 per cent of its inhabitants are Maori, with most of the tangata whenua (78 per cent) living on the coast, and a significant number of the four main iwi – Whakatohea, Ngaitai, Te Whanau A Apanui and Te Ehutu – in their own rohe (tribal area). Opotiki's population is young, with households often overcrowded as extended families on low incomes crowd in together and unemployed young people stay at home. Nearly half (46 per cent) of Opotiki residents have no formal qualifications, and only two per cent have a university degree, while rates of crime including drugs-related and violent crime are higher than the national average – a classic picture of deprivation.

The Bay of Plenty region stretches inland too, encompassing most of the North Island's central plateau. **Rotorua**, with its bubbling mud, spouting geysers and hot spa pools, is one of the country's most popular tourist destinations. Enterprising Maori have cashed in with replica Maori villages, where coachloads of Japanese visitors rub noses with costumed tribespeople. Rotorua is also one of the crime capitals of the country, where the conspicuous consumption of foreign travellers meets the poverty and violence of the town's native population. South of Rotorua is **Taupo**, on the shores of Lake Taupo, a prime location for holiday homes, boating and dare-devilry. At its southern end, **Turangi** borders the spectacular **Tongariro National Park** and the volcanic region of Tongariro, Ruapehu and Ngauruhoe, traversed by the 'desert road'. Turangi was developed in the mid-1960s during construction of the Tongariro Power Scheme, and now serves mainly as a launch pad for the park and white-water rafters.

Historically, the Bay of Plenty was one of the earliest areas of Maori settlement, and still has a high proportion of Maori inhabitants. Three canoes landed in the eastern bay after making the journey from Hawaiki in the 14th century, most tribes settling along the coast to make the most of the mild climate and abundant seafood, while the Arawa people moved inland and settled around

Rotorua, founding the villages of Whakarewarewa and Ohinemutu, among others. The western area of the district (Tauranga Moana) was peopled by the iwi of Ngati Ranginui, Ngaiterangi, Ngati Pukenga, from the waka Takitumu and Mataatua, while Arawa descendants from the waka Te Arawa inhabited the eastern area of the district and south to Rotorua. The tribes fought heavily both among themselves and against the British in the 19th century. More recently, their battle has been to reclaim land and escape poverty. In some districts Maori make up around half the population – 60 per cent in Kawerau, compared with 15 per cent in New Zealand as a whole, 56 per cent in Mangakino, 54 per cent in Opotiki and 36 per cent in Rotorua, heartland of Maori culture. The Maori cultural heritage and community spirit is very strong on and around its 35 marae, with important taonga at the museum, the famous school of carving (whakairo) and a strong tradition of ta moko (tattooing).

In between the more notable tourist areas are settlements such as Mangakino and Kawerau that grew up to service the industries of the region and are now struggling to survive. **Mangakino**, north of Taupo, was built in 1945 to house the workers on a series of hydroelectric schemes along the Waikato River; when the dams and power stations were finished it declined, with virtually zero employment. Now its residents are locked in battle with a developer who has bought the entire village for a pittance and is trying to sell it for a fortune as a scenic holiday village. **Kawerau** is another town that was built from scratch, in 1953, for workers at a huge pulp and paper mill, many of whom came from overseas – the USA, Britain and Scandinavia – imbued with optimism. Fifty years on it has high levels of unemployment and not much else to offer – apart from the proud boast that it is New Zealand's second largest user of electricity, contributing in excess of NZ$1 billion to the New Zealand economy per annum and the jumping-off point for visits to the picturesque **Tarawera Falls**. It might not be your first choice for relocation, but you can never tell which will be New Zealand's next renaissance town – or property-developer's dream.

# Gisborne

The Gisborne region is one of New Zealand's smallest and least populous, covering not quite five per cent of the country's land mass and home to just over one per cent of its population. The fin of Maui's fish, the region borders Hawke's Bay to the south and the Bay of Plenty to the northwest; it stretches from just north of Morere thermal springs and Mahia Peninsula in the south to include the East Cape and Potaka township to the east of Opotiki. The major town is **Gisborne** (population 30,000), with outlying townships including Ruatoria (about 900 people), Tokomaru and Tolaga Bays and Te Karaka (populations of approximately 550, 750 and 580 people, respectively).

The region is best known to the outside world as the setting for the film *Whale Rider*. The film was shot at **Whangara**, just north of the regional capital, where, legend has it, Ngati Konohi ancestor Paikea landed after riding from Hawaiki on the back of a whale. Around 45 per cent of the region's population is of Maori descent, giving it the highest proportion of persons of Maori descent anywhere in New Zealand, and Gisborne and the East Coast are among the few places in the country where Maori is commonly spoken as an everyday language. Throughout the district there are more than 100 marae, representing the predominant tribal groupings of Ngati Porou to the north and Aitanga A Mahaki, Rongowhakaata, Nga Ariki and Ngai Tamanuhiri to the south of the district. East Coast Maori are descended from Paoa of the Horouta and Kiwa of the Takitimu waka (canoe), who landed here as part of the migration from Polynesia in the 1400s.

Maori people of the district continue to adhere to their historical values and sense of origin, including the Maori language (te reo) and a collective approach to land ownership and social solidarity. The district has for some time been the cradle for Maori leaders, from the outlaw warrior Te Kooti – who hid out in the inaccessible Urewera Ranges to the west of the region, from where he swept down to massacre the population of Matawhero, including small babies who were tossed in the air and caught on the points of bayonets, in 1868 – to opera diva Dame Kiri Te Kanawa.

Of the remaining population, around 53 per cent describe themselves as being of European descent, and just two per cent are of other nationalities. Along a beautiful coastline with several good surfing beaches are one or two places of note to Pakeha history too. **Young Nick's Head** is named after Captain Cook's cabin boy on the *Endeavour*, who was the first to sight land. It was sold recently, amid furore, to an American. Cook made his first landing here, in what he named Poverty Bay after local Maori proved inhospitable. Cook anchored at **Tolaga Bay** in 1769 and again in 1779, filling his water casks at Cook's Well in **Cook's Cove**.

The East Cape is the first place in the world to see the dawn each day, and from a visitor's point of view the region is attractively underdeveloped – largely because Maori trusts own much of the land. The wine industry is slowly fermenting here, in a region otherwise reliant on agriculture, horticulture, forestry, fishing and associated industries (one of New Zealand's first freezing works – which made the export of meat and dairy products possible – was in Gisborne). These export industries have made the region vulnerable to the strong New Zealand dollar, but construction, retail and hospitality have benefited from strong domestic demand. Gisborne, which has a ramshackle charm that has attracted property-buyers seeking undiscovered locations, nonetheless has a higher than average level of unemployment. It is also a very long way from anywhere else (over three hours' drive to Napier, over four to Rotorua or Tauranga).

# Hawke's Bay

Long known as the fruit bowl of New Zealand, Hawke's Bay has reinvented itself over the past generation as a wine region to rival Bordeaux and a 'lifestyle destination'. No one talks of anything but wine, and there's not much to do on your day off except tour the vineyards sampling winery lunches – and of course the wines; some of them are very good ('magnificent, simply magnificent', gushes one connoisseur of the Te Mata Coleraine cabernet/merlot). The region is popular with British immigrants for its quasi-Mediterranean climate and laidback way of life. You can eat and drink outdoors from September to May. It's definitely low-stress.

Hawke's Bay's earliest colonial settlers established massive sheep stations, and 'old', landed Hawke's Bay society is still snooty (contrary to popular opinion, New Zealand has an entrenched class system; at one grandiose summer function, bagpipe players appeared on the roof of the mansion, declaiming the ancestral origins of the family in 13th-century Scotland). These days, however, sheep farmers are cashing in on the land by subdividing it for 'lifestyle' developments or turning it over to vineyards. The wine industry has brought a huge injection of new money and new blood into the area, with some ostentatious developments to glorify the new, mostly foreign, owners – Craggy Range Winery Vineyard (American-owned) and Elephant Hill Estate and Winery (German-owned), to name just a couple. Sophisticated tastes in wine have brought with them a food revolution. For the discerning palate, there are any number of locally produced Epicurean delights, from freshly caught fish to raspberries, tayberries and loganberries, apricots, peaches and nectarines, asparagus and sweetcorn – all available for a short, sweet season only. With some high-class chefs around, you can eat like a queen. It's hard to know which ingredient crowns Hawke's Bay with smugness.

Surprisingly, for what feels like a rural region, the three bay cities – Napier, Hastings and Havelock North – make up the fifth most populous conurbation in the country (after Auckland, Wellington, Christchurch and Hamilton). In the old sheep-station and orchard days, **Hastings** (pop. 70,000) used to be the smartest of the three – where the farmers' wives would go for a day's shopping. These days, while it still services the rural industries (if you need a new tractor, go to Hastings) and is home to what is now the bay's only hospital, it has an underprivileged underclass which makes the shopkeepers surly: in their eyes you're a shoplifter unless you prove otherwise. A flat, sprawling town, it is nonetheless home to a sumptuously restored opera house and a public art gallery, not to mention the regional showgrounds. Some of the suburbs are attractive, with still affordable colonial villas.

The pseudo-village of **Havelock North** is where a lot of the flash money is now – but it also has the highest levels of credit card debt in New Zealand. It keenly promotes its village atmosphere, with one or two quaint shops and cafés along the shopping streets that radiate off its central roundabout, which is laid out in a flower shape that can only be appreciated from the sky – presumably to please the residents of the swanky **Havelock Hills**, one or two of whom travel mainly by helicopter. Some of the nicest wineries with eateries are sited on the sunny north-facing slopes of the Te Mata Hills, among the 'luxury lifestyle' homesteads. From the top of Te Mata Peak you get spectacular views of the fruit-growing plain.

**Napier** (pop. 55,000), for years a sleepy seaside resort, has a good share of the action now. It's the only one of the three bay cities with its own Marine Parade and boardwalk, flanked by the National Aquarium, Marineland dolphinarium, Ocean Spa hot and cold pools, museum and art gallery, as well as the famous Art Deco architecture and a 1950s reinforced concrete cathedral. The colonial town was razed by an earthquake in 1931, which you can find out all about in a film at the tiny museum. The 'quake didn't discourage the town planners and developers, who rebuilt the city in Art Deco style – flat, stucco buildings with decorative borders, painted pretty pastel shades. On any day of the week you can see gaggles of tourists taking the Art Deco walk, gawping at the buildings, and once a year Napier stages an Art Deco weekend, for which the populace turns out in flapper dresses and blazers to picnic and dance. Much of the best architecture is in fact pre-earthquake, and can be found on **Napier Hill**, the city's most desirable residential zone.

Whether you choose to settle in one of the three main cities or their suburbs; in one of the seaside settlements at **Te Awanga**, **Haumoana** or **Waimarama**; by the river in the hamlet of **Clive**; on a lifestyle block up the **Esk Valley** or along the **Tukituki River**; among the vineyards at **Maraekakaho**; at the northern end of the bay in remote **Wairoa** – one of New Zealand's most Maori towns, famous for its cinema (the largest in the country) and a jumping-off point for the scenic Mahia Peninsula, Lake Waikaremoana and the Urewera Ranges – or further afield in the Central Hawke's Bay towns of **Waipukarau** or **Waipawa** – grand in their glory days as service towns for dairy farmers, but still awaiting their renaissance (surely not far off) – Hawke's Bay is extremely liveable. It has a good balance of open space with essential services – schools, shops and healthcare – as well as a small but thriving art scene and a couple of good bars and restaurants in Napier's Port Ahuriri. On the downside, it's not the most scenically spectacular part of the country: there's almost no native bush or forest, the cultivated countryside is inaccessible and many of the beaches are shingly, with dangerous rip tides that make them no good for swimming or surfing. While historically the Ngati Kahungunu iwi and the colonial settlers got on well, today the region is conspicuously white and culturally uniform.

Economically Hawke's Bay is thriving. Its main industries are pastoral farming, horticulture and viticulture, fishing, food processing, forestry and wood processing and tourism, with some light industrial manufacturing thrown in for good measure – although all anyone talks about is winemaking.

The region is crying out for doctors, nurses and teachers, and workers in all the building and related trades to keep up with the demand for new housing, and there are plenty of opportunities in tourism and the wine industry, too. The economy of the region is expected to slow, however, due to the strength of the New Zealand dollar (affecting exporters) and a slowdown in the arrival of new immigrants. Unemployment rates across the Hawke's Bay region tend to be slightly higher than the national average, and are particularly high in Wairoa.

# Taranaki and Waikato

## Waikato

The Waikato Region cuts a broad swath across the North Island, from the forested coves of the Coromandel Peninsula in the east through lush farmlands to Raglan's famous surf beach in the west. The mighty Waikato River, its flow now interrupted by a series of dams, feeds fertile pastures that were fiercely battled over by the British and Maori in the 1860s. It was here in the 'Kingitanga' that some Maori tribes got together to proclaim a king in 1856. The colonists, unwilling to see some of the best land in the country lost to their control, took this as a cue to crush the people and seize the land – leading to deprivation, loss of mana and longstanding grievance. The Maori king, Te Arikinui Tuheitia Paki, still resides at **Ngaruawahia**, in the Turangawaewae Marae. The largely rural region also takes in the industrious, workaday city of Hamilton – the country's fifth largest metropolitan area – and Cambridge, an English-inspired town of tree-lined streets famous for its horse studs. In fact 75 per cent of the region's population is urban. The only real tourist attraction in the west of the region is the Waitomo Glow-worm Caves.

The rocky coves and sandy beaches of the forested **Coromandel Peninsula** come to life over the Christmas holidays, when the red flowers of the pohutakawa trees line its roads; the rest of the year, although it is only an hour away from Auckland, the peninsula is the preserve of alternative lifestylers and artisans – the nearest you'll get to the South Island in the North Island. From the gold-mining town of Thames, at the foot of the peninsula, it's a short drive to **Coromandel** township, another town redolent of the region's pioneering gold-rush days in the 1850s. From there north it's all gravel roads through national park, dotted with DOC campgrounds. The east coast, from Whitianga to Waihi, is more developed in patches with seaside baches being replaced by grander developments. **Waihi** is where the real gold was found in 1878, and still has a profitable mine. **Whangamata** has a good surf beach. The flat **Hauraki Plains** to the southwest are best known for bird-watching at **Miranda**.

**Hamilton** (population 100,000 and growing fast) is proud of its zoo and its formal gardens, and also has the excellent Waikato Museum, crammed with taonga of the Tainui people, but it's not likely to be anybody's first choice either to live in or to visit – unless they're en route to Ngaruawahia to see the Queen at her annual regatta, or to **Raglan** in search of the surf on an *Endless Summer* trip. Nonetheless it is the centre of the dairy industry and agricultural research, and home of a university and polytechnic. The names of places around Hamilton, such as Meremere, Rangiri and Orakau, are remembered for the battles that took place there after the invasion of Waikato by British colonists in the 1863 Waikato War, in which more than 1,500 people died. Now they sit quietly amid prime dairy land. Fifteen minutes' drive south of Hamilton, **Cambridge** is famous for its horse-breeders and village-green Englishness. To its northeast, **Matamata** is another horsey town, now more famous as the home town of Hobbiton, created for Peter Jackson's *Lord of the Rings* on a farm nearby. South from Cambridge you reach the dairy-farming service town of **Te Awamutu**. To its west, on the coast, **Kawhia Harbour** is where the waka of the Tainui people landed from Hawaiki in the 14th century.

If you carry on south from here you enter the **King Country**, where Maori king Tawhiao took his family and followers into internal exile from 1860 until 1884; for 20 years it was a no-go area for Pakeha, and still has a stronger Maori presence than the rest of New Zealand (Maori make up 21 per cent of the population across the region, compared with the national average of 14 per cent). **Otorohanga** ('Oto'), which has reinvented itself as the capital of Kiwiana (New Zealand kitsch), is the access point for the Waitomo Caves (marvellous for glow-worms if you can stand the paraphernalia of tourist caves). Carrying on south you reach **Te Kuiti** (where you can see Te Kooti's carved Te Tokanganui-o-noho Marae) and **Mokau**, small rural service towns in the midst of beautiful farmland. Further inland is **Taumaranui**, another quiet town, at the edge of the Tongariro National Park. All sorts of workers are in demand in Waikato; it may be the only region where you'll find jockey, stud groom and stallion master as well as ski and snowboard technicians on the list of skills needed.

## Taranaki

A bump jutting into the sea south of Waikato, the Taranaki region shares much of that region's colonial history and its fertile farmlands. Taranaki's most famous landmark is **Mount Taranaki** (or **Egmont**; 2,518m or 8,260ft), a dormant volcano which was the setting for *The Last Samurai* (2003), starring Tom Cruise. The mountain rises in a perfect cone shape above **New Plymouth**, the region's biggest town (population 50,000) and one of the first major colonial settlements in the country, founded by the New Zealand Company in 1841. Today, the town is best known as the home of the Govett-Brewster Art Gallery, which features most of the abstract animation and kinetic sculptures of Len Lye, and the Puke Ariki museum, which has an extensive collection of Maori taonga. The snow-topped summit of Taranaki, in **Egmont National Park**, is popular with walkers and skiers (depending on the season) and brings plenty of rain to the lava-rich agricultural and dairy land. It last erupted 350 years ago.

### *Painting Mount Taranaki*

Mount Taranaki famously appears in the painting *Taranaki* by British immigrant artist Christopher Perkins, a definitive work of New Zealand's cultural nationalist period in the 1930s. It depicts the volcanic cone in the 'hard, clear light' that poet and critic A. R. D. Fairburn defined as typical of New Zealand and that so influenced its landscape painters. A generation later Toss Woollaston redefined the mountain's image in fluid, expressionistic, earthy tones in his *Taranaki*. More recently, artist Judy Darragh has taken a stab at the clichés of New Zealand landscape painting with her *Taranaki*, a deliberately 'bad' landscape painting on a tablemat, framed with kitsch plastic ferns. True to his more earnest form, the grand old man of New Zealand painting, Colin McCahon, inscribed Maori language, genealogy and history on the land in his *Parihaka Triptych* – a depiction of the Maori pacifist stronghold of Te Whiti and Tohu, razed by colonial troops in 1881. (Parihaka is just inland from Hawera, on the coast south of Mount Taranaki.) Sympathetic to Maori history, McCahon was nonetheless a Pakeha, and his version of the events at Parihaka was later challenged by Maori artist Selwyn Muru.

The New Zealand Wars of the 1860s were at their nastiest in Taranaki. When the New Zealand Company settlers arrived in the 1840s, they found the area practically deserted, as tribes from the Waikato had driven out the Taranaki Te Ati Awa tribe. Colonists rushed to claim the land, but when the dispossessed tribes returned from exile they contested the sale of their land to the Pakeha. After the Kingitanga was founded in 1856, the British abandoned their policy of negotiations for land sales and went to war. Taranaki chiefs had not even signed the Treaty of Waitangi, and war lasted for 10 years. Just as the war was ending in Waikato, followers of the Pai Marire (or Hauhau) sect took up weapons against the colonial forces – giving the British an excuse to intervene and crush the 'rebellion', following a brutal scorched-earth policy. Land confiscations provoked a further round of fighting in 1868. When Maori forces dispersed, the war came to an end and non-violent Maori resistance to European occupation took its place at Parihaka. The prophet leaders Te Whiti and Tohu were arrested and exiled in 1881, after British troops stormed the pa only to be met by singing children.

Nowadays the area relies heavily on its farmers. The economy has also been given a boost by the Maui natural gas field in the South Taranaki Bight. It's a good place to look for work if you're a petroleum industry specialist.

## Manawatu-Wanganui

This largely rural region encompasses the spectacular Tongariro National Park, including the ski slopes of Mount Ruapehu, the Tararua Ranges and bleak inland settlements like Woodville and Pahiatua, the rolling farmlands of the coastal districts, the picturesque Whanganui River with the charming old town of Wanganui at its estuary, and the region's main town, the unprepossessing **Palmerston North**.

Poor old 'Palmy' does have its good points: it is home of the second largest university in the country, Massey University, and has a thriving student scene (although TV adverts focus on the low rents to attract students); The Square, laid out in 1866 at the town's heart, attracts visitors with its formal gardens, fountains and memorials, while neighbouring George Street has some interesting boutiques and cafés; the Te Manawa centre combines a museum of Maori taonga, a contemporary art gallery and a hands-on science centre under one roof ('life, art and mind'); and looming over the city is the southern hemisphere's largest wind farm, an impressive agglomeration of windmills. Nonetheless, first impressions of the town are reminiscent of some of the worst of British town planning of the 1960s, ring road and all.

Other parts of New Zealand's self-styled 'River Region', squashed between Taranaki to the north, Wellington, Wairarapa and the Kapiti Coast to the south, Hawke's Bay and the Bay of Plenty to the northeast, can make only one claim: that they are conveniently located to reach other parts of the country, traversed by State Highways 1 and 2 – the main north–south trunk roads. Visitors will speed through grim **Dannevirke** and **Norsewood** as fast as they can, and it would take quite some incentive to move here from the other side of the world. Take a detour down some of the side roads, however, and you may be mesmerised by the rolling hills of the sheep farms and the grand station houses.

Tourists flock to the **Tongariro National Park** summer and winter, for walking, white-water rafting, trout fishing or skiing on Mount Ruapehu. It's one of the North Island's most scenically spectacular areas, and well developed for outdoor activities. It even has some grand winter sports resort hotels, such as the Grand Château Hotel at Whakapapa. If you're a working holidaymaker, there could be worse places to look for seasonal work.

While the central plateau is now the tourist destination of the region, once upon a time it was the **Whanganui River** that attracted tourists. Plied by steamboats from the 1880s, by the early 1900s as many as 12,000 tourists a year were chugging up and down the 'Rhine of Maoriland' in paddle steamers. It's very unspoilt: soldiers returning from the First World War were rewarded with sections of land on the upper reaches of the river above Pipiriki, which proved impossible to cultivate and were soon abandoned. It's still a stunning drive up the Whanganui River Road, passing the carved niu poles of the Hauhau at Maraekowhai.

**Wanganui** town sits comfortably at the estuary of the river amid the rolling farmlands of the coastal plains. It's an attractive, unshowy, historic town. With Maori living here since the 14th century, it was first colonised by the overflow from the New Zealand Company settlements in Wellington after 1840. Local Maori were incensed by the theft of their land, and fought it bitterly; in the end the dispute was settled by arbitration and Maori–Pakeha relations remained good here throughout the Taranaki Land Wars. More recently, in 1995, Maori claimed the Moutoa Gardens as Maori land and occupied the park for four months; after a legal battle that went to the High Court, the claim was over-ruled. As well as some historic buildings, Wanganui has one of the best regional museums, crammed with Maori taonga including a carved waka, and the Sarjeant Art Gallery, with one of the best collections of recent New Zealand art (although the controversial mayor is trying to sell some of it).

The coastal districts of **Rangitikei** and **Horowhenua** are rich dairy and pastoral farmlands that more than anywhere else in New Zealand resemble the English countryside. In February 2004, however, they were devastated by floods that washed away people, cows, sheep and farms as six times more than the average monthly rainfall fell.

## Wellington and the Wairarapa

Some denizens of Wellington love it for its village atmosphere, others hate it for its claustrophobic setting and society; the two are, of course, flipsides of the same coin, and for many it's a love-hate thing. For a national capital, Wellington is definitely small (population 412,300), and surprisingly inaccessible. It is easy to feel hemmed in in Wellington, as much by its topography as by its social groupings: the first settlement to be established by the New Zealand Company, the land around Port Nicholson (as it was then known) was mis-sold to colonists off the map as flat sections, when in fact it rises steeply from the harbour. Victorian and Edwardian wooden villas still perch precariously on the hillsides, reached up or down steep flights of steps or even by individual cable cars (a nightmare to carry your weekly shopping up and down, and there's no online shopping with deliveries here) – a testament to the determination of the first settlers to make the most of the opportunity they had purchased for themselves. The insidious cliquishness of its professional middle classes can make you want to climb the walls in the same way that Katherine Mansfield's did in the early years of the last century. As one writer (Damian Christie, *Metro* magazine) put it recently, if you are a native Wellingtonian you are doomed to bump into your old schoolmates and their mothers daily (with less and less to say to them each time), and if you're single it's hard not to date your best friend's ex. If *The Truman Show* matches your fantasy of a perfect life, you've nothing to complain about here.

But maybe this is giving the wrong impression of the world's southernmost capital city, with only two roads in and out, one a terrifying single-lane mountain pass road over the Rimutakas into the Wairarapa, the other twisting northwards along a similarly scary corniche road up the Kapiti Coast; an airport with a runway too short and a prevailing wind too strong for international flights (no wonder most international businesses have simply relocated to Auckland); and a ferry crossing to the South Island over the Cook Straits, so perilous that even Odysseus would flinch to cross them. It is cursed by a southerly wind that causes rattling-window phobias and sends its inhabitants scurrying indoors at the slightest twitch of the barometer. On the other hand you can walk everywhere.

As the seat of government, the home of parliament and public service, it is the most political and perhaps the most serious of New Zealand's cities. Less money-obsessed and more bureaucratic than Auckland, it moves at a slower pace. Its arty types are of the homespun variety, compared to Auckland's commercial artists. Outside government administration, the majority of Wellingtonians are employed in services such as business and finance, retail and hospitality, health and education, communications and film and television. The construction industry has been booming here too. More people work in Wellington than in the rest of the country (69 per cent) and more of them are in professional, managerial and clerical jobs than elsewhere. Like other parts of the country, the Wellington economy has been given a boost by the number of people arriving from overseas; many expat New Zealanders also come home to roost in their youthful stomping grounds in Wellington. Business and consumer confidence are high, fuelling an optimistic atmosphere in the capital.

Desperate to be the 'cultural capital', Wellington is the home of the Museum of New Zealand Te Papa Tongarewa – an interactive behemoth of national identity from visual arts and Maori taonga to wildlife (does a *papier mâché* wild boar that grunts when you push a button define anyone's identity?) – as well as the Royal New Zealand Ballet, New Zealand Symphony Orchestra, New Zealand Opera, Chamber Music New Zealand and New Zealand School of Dance. It's one of the few places in New Zealand where you'll see theatre; it has a number of good independent bookshops and is home of the National Archives and Library, including the Alexander Turnbull collection of colonial documents; it boasts interesting art galleries as well as the City Gallery, which hosts interesting contemporary exhibitions, and the Dowse, museum of applied arts; and – when you've had enough of culture as even Wellingtonians do – it's where many rugby internationals are played. Peter Jackson and most of New Zealand's film studios are based in 'Wellywood' (although most advertising and TV production take place in Auckland). When it runs out of homegrown entertainment, Wellington hosts the biennial international arts festival, which brings plenty of performing artists in.

In the cultural interstices, Wellington is packed with shops, cafés and restaurants (it has the highest number of restaurants per capita in the world). And while most bars and other venues are crammed into a few streets in the city centre, you can easily get to one of the bays for a breath of fresh sea air. While some of the capital's best residential areas are on the waterfront or inner city hills – **Mount Victoria**, **Thorndon**, **Oriental Bay**, **Roseneath** and **Kelburn**, for example – much of the population lives in the **Hutt Valley**, **Porirua** and up the

**Kapiti Coast**, where the city has been squeezed through narrow valleys and out the other side. Luckily, Wellington is the one place in New Zealand with a good commuter train network, which links these outlying suburbs with the centre. Golden sands and more bracing winds characterise the Kapiti Coast, where the tiny holiday baches of yore have been replaced by dense suburban sprawl, especially popular with retired people.

If you take the alternative route out, you find yourself in the rural **Wairarapa**, where one-horse towns such as **Martinborough** and **Greytown** have enjoyed a renaissance since the wine industry moved in and the region gained popularity with weekending Wellingtonians; they are now crammed to the gills with twee boutiques and eateries.

# South Island

## Marlborough

Marlborough is the jumping-off point for the South Island for travellers from the North, signalling a change of pace: as soon as the Wellington–Picton ferry leaves the perilous waters of the Cook Strait behind for the meandering Queen Charlotte Sound – a prelude to the remote coves and inlets of the **Marlborough Sounds** – you enter a region of great natural beauty. The 'Mainland' as a whole is more rugged and much more sparsely populated than the North Island. (It's also much whiter: there are many fewer Maori, and few Pacific Islanders at all, while Asians are concentrated in Christchurch, where the Cantabrians beat them up.) The deep, convoluted waterways and coasts of the Sounds are a favourite with foreign tourists and New Zealand holidaymakers for walking, kayaking, fishing or just plain hiding-away. The warm, sunny climate here (miraculously sheltered from the southerlies that batter Wellington across the water) also makes Marlborough the country's main wine-producing region. Many of the best-known export wines come from here, especially sauvignon blancs such as Cloudy Bay.

The charmless ferry port of **Picton** is the logistical centre for exploring the drowned valleys of the Sounds, along walkways, by boat or on the few roads: many of the islands and secluded bays can be reached only by water. West from Picton along the famously scenic Queen Charlotte Drive, **Havelock** is another tourist base, renowned for its green-lipped mussels. South of Picton, **Blenheim** is the urban centre of the wine industry, which is concentrated on the slopes of the Wairau Valley. The base for wine tourists, Blenheim (population 20,000) has a thriving restaurant scene. Further down the dramatic east coast is **Kaikoura**, famed for its crayfish (kai means food, and koura means crayfish) and as the departure point for whale-watching boats.

In Marlborough, 94 per cent of the population is European (compared with 80 per cent for all of New Zealand). The South Island was never heavily populated by Maori, but warrior chief Te Rauparaha and Ngati Toa wiped out most of the Ngai Tahu tribe here after being driven out of Waikato and down the west coast of the North Island by a confederation of tribes. His tactic of bloodshed, among other things, provoked the British into formalizing their relationship with New Zealand at the Treaty of Waitangi (1840). Not long after, his nephew Te Rangihaeata massacred a group of settlers with a fraudulent claim to land in the Wairau Valley.

Most jobs in Marlborough are either in agriculture (including viticulture) and fishery, or in tourism.

# Nelson and Tasman

**Nelson** is New Zealand's number one expatriate region. It boasts the most sunshine hours anywhere in the country and golden sandy beaches; three popular national parks – Kahurangi, Nelson Lakes and Abel Tasman – are accessible and beautiful. The attractive old town of wooden villas and the sprawling settlements along the coast are home to a liberal-minded arty-crafty community, while the back country is cultivated with vineyards and orchards. This heady combination has conspired to turn Nelson into one of New Zealand's real-estate hotspots, with the value of beachfront properties, lifestyle blocks and colonial cottages rising by 30 per cent or more in the last few years (although here, as elsewhere, prices have now stabilised).

Maori tribes settled the Nelson area from the 16th century on. Ngai Tumatakokiri were the supreme tribe here until the 18th century, when they were wiped out by Ngai-apa from Wanganui and Ngai Tahu. Between 1828 and 1830 Ngai-apa were practically wiped out too, by armed tribes from Taranaki and Wellington. When the New Zealand Company founded a settlement at the mouth of the Waimea River in 1840, there were no Maori left here. The colony nearly foundered while land entitlements were being disputed, and was further demoralised by the massacre of 22 men including Arthur Wakefield, brother of the Company's founder, by Te Rangihaeata at Wairau Valley. Further gloom followed the bankruptcy of the Company in 1844, and it took a second wave of German immigrants to kick start the region's economy. Today, a high proportion of German and Dutch people still lives in the region.

**Nelson** town (population 52,500) has preserved many of its original houses, including a row of restored workers' cottages from 1863–7 (South Street) and one or two grand colonial-era villas such as Italianate Melrose House, as well as the many old houses that have been converted into boutique B&Bs. The Suter Art Gallery here is the oldest in New Zealand (founded by Bishop Suter in 1899), with a small but good collection of New Zealand art, from early colonial paintings to works by Toss Woollaston and Colin McCahon. It also functions as a full-blown arts centre, hosting exhibitions, music and drama. The annual World of Wearable Art Award raised the profile of the region's fashion-designers-cum-artists, attracting around 15,000 people for a week-long annual carnival of clothes dressed up as artworks, until it became a victim of its own success and was relocated to Wellington. Nelson is enlivened annually by an arts festival and a jazz festival too. For the rest of the year residents find their thrills at the weekly Saturday market, with stalls selling arts and crafts and local organic produce.

Set in the midst of orchards, vineyards and market gardens, smack bang on the sea and with its own breweries, Nelson is an excellent place to eat and drink – everything from freshly fished scallops, oysters and mussels to deep-sea fish served with local or Marlborough wines – an Epicurean paradise. It's also a great place for serious vegetarian food, which means plenty of choco-lates and cakes too. Along the coast, the tiny quayside settlement of **Mapua**, and **Motueka**, the last stop before Takaka Hill, are charming little places to eat, drink and live, with more potters, weavers, painters, sculptors and jewellers. While as much of the coast is being developed as is physically possible, if you travel a couple of miles inland there is still space for 'lifestyle' living. The great thing about Nelson is that while it is sunny, by the sea and slightly alternative, it's also big enough to have an arts scene, decent schools and a hospital – while more remote and rugged landscapes are only a short drive away.

**Tasman** is like an extreme, isolated version of Nelson out on a limb. It's just over Takaka Hill from Motueka, but the two-hour-long drive through cloud, up and down a narrow, winding pass road, makes all the difference to the atmos-phere on the other side. As you drive down the hill you see **Golden Bay** stretching out in front of you like a lush promised land; the rainfall here is several times that of Nelson, creating a humid, almost subtropical climate. It's a beautiful area, from the golden sands of forested **Abel Tasman National Park** to the bird sanctuary of **Farewell Spit**, the broad sands of **Wharariki Beach** and the Heaphy Track, which takes you through the **Kahurangi National Park** to the west coast. British, German and Dutch alternative lifestylers and craftspeople have taken over the area since the 1970s, living communally and growing organic vegetables in clearings in the resurgent native bush. Relations are sometimes strained with the old-style New Zealand dairy farmers who continue to farm here – although the region as a whole has an ecological bent. The main towns are **Takaka**, a one-street town with an organic store, whole-meal café, community gardens and supermarket, and **Collingwood**, with a dairy and a chocolate shop. This is the area to move to if you want to get away from it all, with a whole lot of other people who are doing the same thing. You'll need to be as self-sufficient as they are, however, as there's not much work around here. Access to schools and hospitals is limited too.

## The West Coast

The West Coast of the South Island, aka Westland, is notoriously wet – and lusciously beautiful. Despite the damp, it has a warm climate, enjoying as many sunshine hours as famously dry Canterbury on the far side of the mountain ranges. It's a narrow strip of land squeezed between the Southern Alps and the Tasman Sea, 600km (350 miles) long from Kahurangi Point in the north to Awarua Point in the south (greater than the distance between Auckland and Wellington), and no more than 70km (44 miles) wide at any point. The region takes in five national parks (Kahurangi, Arthur's Pass, Paparoa, Westland and Mount Aspiring), dripping rainforest, snow-topped mountain peaks and glacial valleys, rushing torrents and crystal lakes, rocky coast, primeval swamps, lagoons and ancient trees; the southern end is so unspoilt that it has been designated the Southwest New Zealand World Heritage Area. Most of the rest is spectacular too, with beaches, rivers and forests up and down the region the setting for adventure sports such as rafting, kayaking, hunting, fishing and tramping. In between are patches of farmland.

Westland is isolated – five hours' drive over Arthur's Pass or Lewis Pass to Christchurch, and three hours' through Buller Gorge to Nelson – with just a few small towns that service the tiny hamlets strung along the coast. It's sparsely populated too: with a land area of 23,000 square kilometres (9,000 square miles), it covers nearly 10 per cent of New Zealand, but its population of 30,000 is less than one per cent of the national total – and dwindling; it was one of the few areas to register a decline in numbers at the last Census. Its inhabitants, known collectively as Coasters, are 95 per cent Pakeha. They are less well educated (around 40 per cent have no qualifications, at all, and only 25 per cent have a university-level qualification) and earn less than the rest of the country. That said, the cost of living is lower too in this region, with land and property notably cheaper than elsewhere – particularly in comparison to inflated Nelson and Tasman, the region's northern neighbours. The small population means, however, that there is not a big choice of schools, pre-schools or doctors; you may have to travel for specialist medical treatment.

While the tourist attractions of the Coast are, justifiably, much hyped, and the area was chosen as the location for Gaylene Preston's 2003 film *Perfect Strangers*, out of the tourist season most Coasters live off farming and coal mining. In among the farmers, coal miners and tourist operators are enclaves of hippiedom, driftwood artists and craftspeople, greenstone, jade or nephrite carvers, potters and weavers. The country's best pounamu comes from around Greymouth; Ngai Tahu made the area their rohe after finding the stone in the 17th century. The section of the tribe who came to be recognised as the guardians of the West Coast pounamu were known as Poutini Ngai Tahu, but were cheated into selling the whole of the Coast to colonial agents for £300 in 1860. The tribe's claim to the Waitangi Tribunal was settled in 1997, with compensation – and has been one of the success stories of the tribunal. The area is famous too for its 1860s gold rush. Today you can see numerous historic gold mining settlements (Mitchell's Gully, Charleston, Gillespies Beach and Waiuta among others), and there are still active gold mines at Reefton and Ross. Hokitika was the treacherous gold-rush port, where ships went down at a rate of one every 10 weeks in 1865 and 1866).

At the northern end of the coast is **Karamea**, the exit point for the Heaphy Track, a sleepy end-of-the road dairying village which fills up with beachgoers in summer; visitors come here for the spectacular limestone formations (caves and arches) of Oparara Basin too. Down the bushy coast, **Westport** is a functional town without great charm. It has an opencast coal mine, a cement works, a commercial port from which the coal and cement are shipped, and a seasonal fishing fleet of 200 boats. Its other main business is manufacturing clothes for the Postie Plus chain. Roundabout, *pakihi* – dried-out swamplands with poor drainage – are being broken up to create fertile soil for horticulture: tropical fruits (tamarillo and passion fruit), blueberries and medicinal herbs are now being grown here. It's a region where old-style pubs still serve meat pies and beer, while down the road vegetarian cafés cook up wild mushrooms and organic salad. Despite the region's remoteness, high-speed Internet access, mobile phone coverage and even Sky Digital are available in most of it.

Along the rocky coast road south you reach the famous **Punakaiki** pancake rocks and blowholes, on the edge of the **Paparoa National Park**, before getting to **Greymouth**, the largest town of the region (population 13,500) – a gloomy place that feels like a way station, but it does have its own brewery (Monteith's). From here to Hokitika are more driftwood-piled beaches. **Hokitika** itself is the most attractive of the West Coast towns, a centre of pounamu carving and wild food. Heading on south to the Franz Josef and Fox glaciers, you enter dense rainforest around **Pukekura**, where there is a turn-off to **Okarito**, a wild coastal settlement of 30 people where Keri Hulme, author of *The Bone People*, lives; Okarito's ancient lagoon and swamps inspired the novel. The glacier towns are little more than tourist villages for glacier visits, but the countryside around is studded with deep, clear lakes. Last stop along the coast is the Haast region, an unspoiled ecology of rainforest and wetlands, kahikatea swamp forests and sand dunes, populated by rare native birds.

**Jackson Bay** is at the southern end of the road, a gloomy little fishing hamlet where several attempts to establish immigrant settlements failed. If you turn inland at Haast, a long, mountainous road eventually takes you to Wanaka and Queenstown.

# Canterbury

The broad Canterbury Plains are prime New Zealand farmlands, to the west of which rise the pinnacles of the Southern Alps – most spectacularly Mount Cook and Tasman Glacier, with Lakes Tekapo and Pukaki at its feet. **Christchurch** (population 340,000), the South Island's main city, is the capital of this region. Long characterised by the old-fashioned snobbery of its longstanding denizens, the original station owners, it has embraced modernity in the form of trendy cafés, bars and restaurants and groovy boutiques – although it is less cosmopolitan in its ethnic mix than any of the northern cities. It is not rare to hear reports of Asian immigrants being beaten to a pulp by white youths after Saturday night drinking binges in the city centre. This most English of cities boasts art galleries, wooden villas and Victorian Gothic architecture, and is within easy reach of Akaroa, a French settlement on the dead volcano of Banks Peninsula, and the vineyards of Waipara. Canterbury's dry climate contrasts with that of its West Coast neighbour: prevailing winds bring rain clouds in from the Tasman Sea, which drop the rain when they hit the mountain ranges.

The snooty English character of Christchurch is not accidental. The town was founded in 1850 as an ordered Anglican settlement that would mirror the class structure of the old country. The gentry were given the best farmland, while the lower classes were encouraged to immigrate as labourers. The landowners soon became rich on wool, and made Christchurch as English as they could: it has a Gothic Anglican cathedral, British street names and punts on its river, the Avon. While that old élitism does persist in suburban villas with English-style gardens, the 21st-century city has begun to forge a more New Zealand identity. The Canterbury Museum, for a start, displays mainly New Zealand artefacts such as carved pounamu, and Christchurch Art Gallery regularly features contemporary New Zealand artists. The Centre of Contemporary Art is even more up-to-the-minute, exhibiting the works of innovative young artists, and the Arts Centre hosts performances of every genre, while the country's largest marae, Nga Hau e Wha, offers a Maori cultural experience.

Especially around 'the Strip', the city is crammed with cafés and restaurants, many competing to provide the best modern New Zealand cuisine with fresh local produce. You can hear live music at many of the bars in this area too, and if you want to shop you'll have no problem parting with your money at fashion boutiques, arts-and-crafts shops or Ballantynes, a real old department store. Christchurch is a good place for children too; it's close to the sea and surrounded by gentle countryside, wildlife reserves and walking trails. **Lyttelton Harbour** is where you'll find the city's historic port (where the first European settlers arrived in 1850).

If Christchurch is oh, so English, coastal **Akaroa** is like a French provincial village. Inland, ski slopes are only a couple of hours' drive away. And unlike the rest of the South Island, Christchurch is easily accessible. International flights arrive and depart at its airport, as do domestic flights to most other parts of the country. It's not too long a drive north to Blenheim and Picton on mainly straight, flat roads, south to Dunedin, or over the ranges to Greymouth on the West Coast or Queenstown in Otago.

In the north of the region are the **Waipara Valley**, Canterbury's main wine-producing area (Waipara Springs, Pegasus Bay and Canterbury House are some of the best-known vineyards) and **Hanmer Springs**, the South Island's main thermal resort. From here you can head into the mountains over the Lewis Pass. West of Christchurch is Arthur's Pass, the other route over the mountains to the West Coast, and the **Arthur's Pass National Park**, with some serious tramping routes and mountain ascents. South of Christchurch, the flat coastal plain is relatively built up as you head to the small towns of **Temuka** and **Timaru**. Temuka is best known in New Zealand for its pottery, while Timaru is the port for the South Canterbury agricultural region. It has one of the South Island's best public art galleries, the Aigantighe ('at home'). The only downside of the east coast is that most of its beaches are not safe for swimming; an exception is Caroline Bay.

Inland is **Mackenzie Country**, the area you commonly see in TV adverts featuring New Zealand's 'high country'. It's sheep-grazing land, overlooked by the snow-capped peaks of **Aoraki/Mount Cook National Park**. Lake Tekapo, and the region as a whole, are a foretaste of the Queenstown and Wanaka area: deep lakes, high mountains and all those daredevil outdoor activities for which New Zealand is famous: trekking, mountaineering, skiing, fishing and boating. The national park itself is part of the Southwest New Zealand World Heritage Area (along with Fiordland, Mount Aspiring and Westland national parks). It has most of New Zealand's highest mountains, including Mount Cook, known to Maori as Aoraki ('cloud-piercer'), at 3,755m (12,316ft) the highest in Australasia. It's where Sir Edmund Hillary and Tenzing Norgay cut their teeth for Mount Everest. Short walks are possible even for the inexperienced, but anything longer needs mountaineering experience – and even so people regularly go missing on the mountain slopes. The Hermitage, New Zealand's most famous hotel (built in 1884), is the poshest place to hang out and look at the mountains.

# Otago

Otago splits neatly in two: coastal Otago, including North Otago, Dunedin and the Otago Peninsula; and Central Otago, including the mountain resorts of Queenstown and Wanaka. On the coast, Dunedin, the Edinburgh of the southern hemisphere, was settled by Scottish Presbyterians in 1848, and still reflects its Gaelic roots in its stern Victorian public buildings (this is the only region to build in stone). It has one of New Zealand's best universities (Otago) and a lively, student culture to go with it, as well as the high culture of academic institutions, museums and art galleries. Its peninsula is a haven for wildlife-watchers – penguins galore. Inland Queenstown and Wanaka, by contrast, are the action stations par excellence of the country, set on the shores of deep lakes at the foot of high mountains. Central Otago is fast becoming one of New Zealand's top wine regions, too, benefiting from the warm summers east of the main ranges. Otago as a whole has some of the greatest climatic extremes of the country, with temperatures ranging from −18°C (0°F) in winter to 35°C (95°F) in summer. On the whole it's dry, though.

If you can stomach – or indeed relish – the Gaelicness of **Dunedin** (a statue of Robert Burns guards its centre), it is one of New Zealand's most cultured and lively cities for its size (its resident population of 111,000 is swollen by 20,000 students during the academic year). Its history is florid: the Maori tribes of the peninsula, Ngai Kahu and Ngaimamoe, feuded into the 19th century, when whaling communities brought diseases that did away with most of the rest of them. Presbyterian settlers arrived at Port Chalmers in 1848 to establish an ideal community, but cast aside puritanism as gold was discovered and the province became rich and influential. The gold didn't last long, but today the town is flourishing again. The gold rush era is reflected in the solid stone Victorian architecture of its public buildings and the rambling wooden villas on its hillsides. Its Public Art Gallery has one of the country's best collections of New Zealand art. As well as a host of lively cafés, bars and restaurants, drinking holes and indie music venues, Dunedin has its very own surf beaches at St Clair and St Kilda. And just down the road is the wildlife area of **Otago Peninsula**.

North Otago has a character of its own. **Oamaru**, the area's biggest town, was settled by Europeans in 1853, became rich on meat shipping and built some imposing buildings in Gothic revival and neoclassical Italianate styles out of local limestone on the proceeds. It's where Janet Frame (*An Angel at my Table*) came from, and still has a reputation for its arts. The agricultural hinterland is also known for its potatoes (Oamaru jersey bennies). Heading inland, the valleys around Cromwell, Alexandra, Clyde, Palmerston and the Clutha District were all once goldmining hotbeds, and the towns still have a pioneering gold rush atmosphere. The inland plains and valleys of this rugged plateau are now largely given over to orchards.

**Queenstown** is New Zealand's self-proclaimed action capital. A booming resort town, it is the centre for bungee jumping, jet boating, white-water rafting, river surfing and white-water sledging, canyoning, skydiving, skiing, even mountain biking and walking – and a hectic nightlife. None of the activities come cheap, and the cost of living is high too (property here is very expensive for New Zealand). Queenstown is brash, but its more sophisticated restaurants and boutiques attract a classier type too. And the area is gaining a reputation for its wine industry: Peregrine, Chard and Gibbston Valley are three of the best-known pinot noir wine producers here.

All these added attractions can stand in the way of the fact that Queenstown is located on the shores of beautiful **Lake Wakatipu**, in a stunning mountain setting at the foot of the Remarkables. Away from the hurly-burly, you can reach more remote valleys of the region by road, or by foot on walking trails such as the Routeburn Track. North of Queenstown, Wanaka has all the same beauty, with fewer gold-digging tour operators – although it may well go the same way as its brasher neighbour. Situated on the shores of Lake Wanaka, it offers most of the same action sports as Queenstown, but is a little more inaccessible.

# Southland

You'll probably know Southland from photographic calendars of New Zealand. The primordial landscapes of Fiordland, in the southwest, are some of the most photographed in a much-photographed country: forested mountains plunge straight down into deep fiords in this inaccessible region – another piece in the jigsaw of the Southwest New Zealand World Heritage Area. But dripping, lichenous Milford and Doubtful Sounds are not all there is to Southland: urban Invercargill, on the central plain, isn't top of anyone's list to live – although it has most of the region's population – but the hills and dunes of the Catlins in the southeast are quietly beautiful too. The region has two drawbacks: the climate, which is not only cold but also wet – 6m (236in) annual rainfall round the fiords – and the plague of sand flies (little nippers) that accompany the rain.

The **Fiordland National Park** is an essential stop on any tourist itinerary of the South Island, but not much of the southwest is inhabited, or inhabitable. The most direct route to **Milford Sound** is on foot, over the Routeburn Track from the Queenstown side of the Humboldt Mountains, but the more common approach taken by tour buses and tourists in cars is via **Te Anau** – the main settlement of the Fiordland region. Situated on the shores of glacial Lake Te Anau, the town is largely a jumping-off point for the spectacular drive down to Milford Sound, for the walking tracks of the region and for Queenstown-style adventure tourism. It's growing, however, with subdivision set back only temporarily by a powerful earthquake in 2003. **Manapouri**, 20km (12½ miles) south of Te Anau, is another tourist base for the region, on the shores of its own lake – famous as the catalyst for the green awakening of the 1970s (*see* p.20). It is the jumping-off point for **Doubtful Sound**, eco-tourism and more tramping.

**Invercargill** (population 50,000) is the main farm-service town of the deep south, orderly and grim – although it is giving itself new life by luring students to the polytechnic with free tuition. With many of its old pubs closed, it doesn't even have much to offer in the way of wining and dining. (For a long time this part of the country, settled by Scottish immigrants in the 1850s and 1860s, was dry.) The port of Bluff, 30km (18½ miles) south of Invercargill, is a sad industrial town that makes Invercargill look cheerful. It's best-known for its oysters. **Gore**, northeast towards Dunedin, is still smarting from the moniker 'gay-man's Gore' given to it by comic duo Havoc and Newsboy on a televised road trip through New Zealand. If you're gay and you think you've just stumbled on your new home, stop there: Gore's not it. Another farm-service town, its inhabitants are happiest trout-fishing, line-dancing or singing along to country music – although the town has a fine art collection in its Eastern Southland Gallery, with works by Dunedin artist Ralph Hotere and Rita Angus, as well as international art stars.

**The Catlins**, in the southeast, have far more appeal. Not as intractable as the southeast, the forests and bays of the Conservation Park, from Waipapa Point to Nugget Point, are nonetheless remote. With podocarp forests of kahikatea, totara and rimu stretching down to sand dunes populated by seals and penguins, it's a fabulous area to visit for the gentler sort of camping or farm-stay-based tramping holiday. There's not much civilisation though, in the form of banks, petrol stations and shops, so the closest you're likely to get to living here is **Balclutha**.

Another place you're more likely to visit than to move to is **Stewart Island**, New Zealand's 'third island', across the Foveaux Straits south of Bluff; it's a remote conservation area, with one tiny settlement at **Oban**.

# New Zealand Today

New Zealand today bears only a passing resemblance to the 'Britain of the South Pacific' it once so strongly resembled. More than 150 years after its colonial foundation, it is still negotiating its bicultural (Maori-Pakeha) identity, even as it becomes more multicultural. Culturally, it has already moved on from the nationalistic assertion of its difference from the colonial mother country into more international art forms – although with a distinctively New Zealand voice. It has a political system based on the Westminster model, but with creeping changes such as the introduction of proportional representation transforming political debate; the word 'republic' is even mentioned in public, and with more conviction since the legal system cast off the Privy Council in London as its ultimate court of appeal. The media face the same problems they do everywhere, however – foreign ownership, a predominance of imported material (especially on TV) at the expense of local talent, a fading public service ethos – but with a limited market that restricts creativity and diversity.

At the time of writing, the country is enjoying a long economic boom, although it is susceptible to knock-on effects from any global downturn; it relies heavily on exports, and imports of oil, so remains linked to economic cycles. In some ways, however, it benefits from its geographical remoteness and political neutrality on the international scene; its image as a 'clean, green' safe haven has attracted new immigrants, and with them property speculation and investment.

# Major Political Parties and Alliances

New Zealand is a modern parliamentary democracy. Its style of government still follows the Westminster cabinet model, but with important distinctions. The national government comprises a single legislature, the House of Representatives, which is elected every three years rather than the five-year cycle customary in the Westminster system.

New Zealand governments from the Second World War until the late 1990s alternated between the Labour (more or less left-wing, sometimes socialist) and National (right-wing, conservative) parties. In 1996 a new electoral system known as MMP (mixed-member proportional) was introduced to countervail the effects of repeated swings from left to right and back again – which had left the electorate disenchanted with politicians, politics and the political system as a whole. The German-style system of proportional representation, which replaced a classic 'first-past-the-post' system, was voted in by a referendum in 1993. Under this new system, 62 MPs represent General Electorates, seven Maori Electorates, and a further 51 are voted in from party lists to make up the total of 120 MPs in parliament. Although there was some initial scepticism over the manoeuvrings of parties to form coalition governments, by its third test in 2002 the MMP system was broadly considered a success; the 2005 election was very closely fought by Labour and National, leading to some undignified behind-the-scenes deal-making, most notoriously the appointment of gaffe-prone Winston Peters, leader of the ultra-minority New Zealand First Party, as foreign minister in return for his support of the Labour government.

## The Labour Party

The Labour Party, which first came to power in 1935 and governed through the war years until 1949, initially wore a socialist mantle (in fact it started life as the Socialist Party). By the time it was swept to power by the Depression, Labour no longer planned to smash capitalism, but wanted to make capitalism work better. It wanted to ensure that in a country with the resources of New Zealand nobody would have to go hungry, or without work, education or healthcare. It won the 1935 election in a landslide with 55 seats (out of 80) and a powerful mandate for change – promising to 'erect the new socialist state that will once again cause New Zealand to inspire the world'.

Labour introduced social security to the country in the form of a cradle-to-grave welfare state. To start off with, a Christmas bonus was issued to the unemployed, old age pensions were restored and increased, secondary schools were made free of charge, a 40-hour week was brought in for some workers and a minimum wage introduced based on the income required to support a married couple and three children, and a state housing scheme was launched. In 1938 the Social Security Act gave the country a free health system and further extended pensions. The social blueprint of the Labour movement was fulfilled, and Maori in particular benefited. Maori in fact supported Labour parliamentary candidates for three decades after 1935, in an alliance with the Maori Ratana movement.

By 1984, however, when Labour came to power for the fourth time, the party was wearing the boot on the other foot. Following an unexceptional period in office 1957–60, by the 1970s Labour had become the flower-power party. It withdrew New Zealand troops from Vietnam, protested French nuclear testing in the Pacific, cancelled an apartheid Springbok tour and flirted with communal land management (ohu) – but all its 1960s aspirations were dampened by the oil crisis, which ended another brief period of Labour rule (1972–5). But in the 1980s Labour finally said goodbye to its ideological origins and brought in a programme of monetarist reform to counteract recession that inspired Margaret Thatcher (at the opposite end of the left–right spectrum).

The youthful government of David Lange abandoned the interventionist, big-spending policies of many of its predecessors on both right and left. It recognised that the welfare state which it had pioneered 50 years earlier was unaffordable, especially in an era of economic downturn. Finance minister Roger Douglas pioneered a new set of reforms: public services were sold or charged with making a profit; agricultural subsidies were phased out; finance was deregulated; a sales tax was introduced; and income tax rates were halved. The bitter pill worked – inflation was reduced, and economic growth increased – but at a social cost that many Labour supporters and even cabinet ministers found unacceptable.

By the time the 1987 stockmarket crash took the shine off the economic achievements of 'Rogernomics', the Labour government was so divided that prime minister Lange resigned and the party was unable to win another election. No government since has attempted to reverse the monetarist trend, but since 1999 the Labour coalition government of Helen Clark has been revisiting some of the social policy issues that first defined the party. As the party in power at the time of writing it is the hardest to define – it is dealing with real policy, not slogans – but Clark has established a statesmanlike reputation overseas, despite accusations at home that her government focused on 'trivial' issues such as a Civil Union Bill to allow gay marriage and an excess of political correctness. Especially on racial issues (*see* 'The Treaty of Waitangi Revisited', pp.82–6) it has struggled to find a centre path that does not send moderates into the arms of right-wing conservatives at the same time as failing to appease Maori radicals. In the 2005 election it lost votes, despite economic prosperity, as National hijacked the pro-business ticket. It has 49 MPs in the 2005–2008 parliament.

## The National Party

The National Party, which has held the balance of power for the remainder of the post-war years, has never strayed far from its conservative origins. 'If you want to condense our policy,' soon-to-be prime minister Sidney Holland told an audience in 1948, 'it is the private ownership of production, distribution and exchange.' The party's programme was aimed primarily at businessmen, farmers and their supporters. The National government of 1949–57 soon made its mark in the waterfront dispute of 1951, in which it went head to head with the militant unions of the Trade Union Congress. Wharfies (dock workers) went on strike for a 15 per cent pay increase, and were sacked for refusing to work overtime. The National government clamped down harshly when the union refused arbitration, banning publicity of the dispute, penalizing those who helped the strikers' families, and bringing in the military to keep the wharves working. The strike, or lockout, lasted 151 days – and strengthened National's hold on power. National also showed itself keen to back the United States in combating communism at this time – both abroad (Korea) and in McCarthy-style probes at home.

National's next stint in power lasted 12 years (1960–72), with farmer Keith Holyoake as prime minister. Apart from his political longevity, Holyoake became renowned for his 'mannered façade, fruity voice and booming bonhomie' – but he kept the party in power on a 'Steady Does It' slogan. He saw National as the natural party of government and his role to maintain the status quo – a successful policy in an era of economic prosperity. In 1965 he committed troops to Vietnam on the basis of 'forward defence' (keeping enemies away from New Zealand), collective security (recognizing that New Zealand could not defend itself without allies such as Britain and the United States) and co-operation with Australia. It was a policy which divided the nation, but did little to dent National's position over the next seven years.

The next National government, Robert Muldoon's of 1975–84, is best remembered for its 'Think Big' strategy, devised by Muldoon, who chose to be both prime and finance minister. It was the last interventionist, big-spending government, imposing a wage and price freeze, controlling rents and trying to force down interest rates, as well as instituting a superannuation regime that paid out 80 per cent of average salaries to the retired. Muldoon ultimately lost out to the monetarism of Labour and Rogernomics (*see* p.64). When National resumed power in 1990, under Jim Bolger, party boundaries had become blurred: National carried on with monetarist reforms, reducing welfare spending, increasing pharmaceutical charges and charging market rents for state housing. Between 1996 and 1999 National led a wobbly coalition government with few conspicuous achievements, other than the country's first woman prime minister, Jenny Shipley.

The National Party, now led by John Key, a self-made millionaire who grew up on a housing estate in Christchurch, claims to 'seek a safe, prosperous and successful New Zealand that creates opportunities for all New Zealanders to reach their personal goals and dreams'. Its manifesto states: 'We stand firmly against political correctness and strongly for personal freedom and responsibility.' The anti-PC claim cocks a snook at Labour, perceived by critics on the Right as pandering excessively to the socially, economically or racially underprivileged. The party bemoans 'the reality that traditional Kiwi values are being destroyed by a government-funded culture of welfare dependency'.

In the run-up to the 2005 general election National campaigned on an economy, education, welfare, security and race relations ticket; it is the last two that grab the headlines. Reclaiming the Right's self-image as the natural home of law and order, the party asserts that, 'When people step over that line which forms the boundary between honest and criminal activity, between civilised behaviour and that which preys on the community, they should expect a forceful response. We stand entirely in support of the victims of criminal acts, and immovably against the criminal.' In the contentious area of Pakeha–Maori relations (*see* 'The Treaty of Waitangi Revisited', pp.82–6), the party maintains that 'We need to head off the dangerous drift to racial separatism. We must deal, fairly and finally, with historical grievances, but then ensure that all New Zealanders, of whatever race or creed, are treated equally before the law. Settlements of historic claims have created a backward-looking grievance industry. We must look to the future, not the past. As Governor Hobson said in 1840, "we are one people now".' In 2005–2008 National had 48 MPs, lagging behind Labour by one.

## The Minority Parties

Since the 1993 decision to introduce the mixed-member proportional (MMP) electoral system, several smaller parties have sprung up, wielding the power in coalition-building to form minority governments. The major minority parties are currently Progressive, ACT, the Greens, New Zealand First, Maori Party and United Future.

**Progressive** is the heir to the Alliance, a social democratic left party which took over where the Labour Party left off in the 1980s: former Labour MP Jim Anderton left the party over its monetarist reform programme, which he viewed as inimical to Labour values, and founded a socialist grouping to represent those values. The Alliance as such was formed in 1991 'to fight against the New Right capture of both the Labour and National parties' and claims 'to have been instrumental in blunting the privatisation agenda that laid waste to New Zealand's social and economic infrastructure during the 1980s and 1990s.' In 1996, 13 Alliance MPs were elected to Parliament and three years later, after the 1999 election, the Alliance entered into a coalition government with Labour. After internal dissension, Alliance was replaced by the Progressive Party at the 2002 election; following the 2005 election the party, led and solely represented by Jim Anderton, formed the minority partner in the Labour Progressive coalition government. The Progressive agenda is based on a raft of issues based on the welfare state as part of a continuing New Zealand tradition; one success it has notched up is paid parental leave for mothers (and fathers).

**ACT**, which calls itself the Liberal Party, was founded in 1994 by Roger Douglas (of 'Rogernomics' fame) and Derek Quigley as the Association of Consumers and Taxpayers. The association was originally intended by its founders to promote sound social and economic policy as a lobby group, but in 1995, with MMP looming, the political party ACT New Zealand was formed in order to carry these ideals into Parliament. Richard Prebble became leader in March 1996 and the party gained eight seats in the 1996 election, expanding this representation to nine seats in 1999, and falling back to eight in 2002, and just two in 2005, after Rodney Hide replaced Prebble as leader. ACT's main principles are that: 'People are important, not money or institutions. Power should be put back into the hands of people by taking it away from politicians and government.' Broadly speaking, it stands for individual freedom and responsibility, embodied in free market consumer choice, as the driving force for society. It is opposed to 'open-ended welfare that diminishes dignity and individual enterprise'. One of its main campaigns is for a reduction in legislation.

**NZ First** is the 'patriotic' party of former National MP Winston Peters, who was dismissed from cabinet in 1991 after prolonged disagreements with the leadership over economic and fiscal and foreign ownership policy issues, and effectively kicked out of the party in 1992. He stood as an independent candidate in 1993, gaining 90.8 per cent of votes in his old constituency, and set up the NZ First Party later the same year. The core of his message is that, while the New Zealand economy may be booming, ordinary New Zealanders are not benefiting. He is particularly opposed to the asset-stripping of New Zealand, through the sale of land and industry to foreigners. Nearly 50 per cent of the New Zealand share market is overseas-owned, he notes; none of New Zealand's exports or imports is carried on a New Zealand-owned vessel; while New Zealand wine is world class, most of the wineries are owned by foreigners; and most of the foreign investment that other political parties are so keen to pull in is in the form of 'direct takeover' – with the net result that most of the profits leave the country, he concludes. A controversial but to some charismatic leader, Peters is rarely out of the headlines with his rabble-rousing talk. In the 2005–2008 parliament, NZ First had seven MPs, and Peters scored a triumph by negotiating the role of foreign minister for himself in exchange for support of the Labour Progressive coalitions.

The **Green Party** of Aotearoa New Zealand has been a strong ideological force in the country since the 1970s, but only since the introduction of MMP has it gained a parliamentary presence. It campaigns on a raft of unsurprising issues: GM-free food production, protection and conservation of the environment and renewable sources of energy. While the party's leader, Jeanette Fitzsimons, is widely liked, the outspoken, dreadlocked 'crusty' MP Nandor Tanczos – waging a single-handed campaign for the legalisation of cannabis – to many represents the most irritating side of Green activism. In the 2005 parliament, the Greens held six seats.

**United Future**, led by Peter Dunne, believes broadly speaking in freedom and responsibility based around the family, functioning in an open market economy. One of its mantras is to speed up the settlement of Waitangi grievances. It had two MPs in the 2005 parliament and a 'confidence and supply' agreement with the government.

The new **Maori Party**, founded in 2004, has emerged at the other end of the Waitangi spectrum – out of opposition to the Labour coalition's Seabed and Foreshore legislation (*see* pp.82–6). In the 2005 parliament, it has four MPs, led by Labour defector Tariana Turia, backed by well-known urban Maori campaigner Pita Sharples. The party is in opposition to the Labour-led government.

# Religion

## Christianity

The European colonisation of New Zealand was characterised by Christian missionary activity, but New Zealand today is not a religious society. The Anglicans arrived first – in the 1820s – rapidly followed by Presbyterians, Methodists and Roman Catholics. Since the 1880s the Church of the Latter Day Saints (Mormons) has had a small but significant presence, alongside the Salvation Army, Baptists, Congregationalists, Quaker Brethren and several other minor denominations.

The four major Christian communities claimed the allegiance of nearly 90 per cent of the population in 1926. Fifty years later this number had fallen by a fifth – and of those claiming a religious affiliation on Census forms, few were actively practising according to Census statistics (Presbyterians made up 18 per cent of the total population, but head counts by the Presbyterian Church revealed that only 2 per cent of the population were regular churchgoers). This trend has continued into the 21st century. The relevance of mainstream religions since the Second World War has been eclipsed by materialist secularism, with only around 10 per cent of New Zealanders religiously active – although many more will still turn to the Church for the rites of passage: 'hatch, match and dispatch'. At the same time, smaller religious bodies have expanded in both number and adherents – notably the Mormons and some Charismatic groups – and there are also growing (although small) non-Christian religious communities: the Orthodox Church has become established, as well as a Jewish community, Sikhs, Hindus, Buddhists and Muslims. The fastest-growing group in New Zealand, however, is that with no stated religion.

New Zealand now is a society based on religious pluralism; it is hard to say if it is even fundamentally a Christian society. Historian W. H. Oliver has suggested that 'the Christianity which characterises the bulk of the New Zealand people is a vestigial sort which is manifested fitfully in moral attitudes rather than in explicit beliefs or overt behaviours'. How much New Zealand's moral and social values derive from Christianity remains open to debate. At state level there has always been religious neutrality – as an antidote to the rivalry that existed among settler faiths in the early days. And while New Zealand reflects in its ethos much of the Christian past of its European ancestors, it is more secular than most of western Europe. Its foundation on several different Christian traditions has meant that New Zealand has always effectively been pluralistic, and the last century has seen the decline of large national religious institutions and the proliferation of small religious groups.

The most striking feature of modern religion – in New Zealand as elsewhere in the West – is that each individual is freer but also bears more responsibility for 'working out his own salvation in fear and trembling' (St Paul) or to 'work out your own salvation with diligence' (Buddha). Few in the modern era are able to accept the 'answers' of religious authorities to the dilemmas of human existence, with the result that religion is more and more tailored to the individual in belief and lifestyle. This phenomenon is particularly marked in New Zealand, which only established its Christian foundations in the 19th century, when the Enlightenment had already started to bring 'spiritual unsettlement' and a questioning of Christian doctrine. The late 20th century saw a move away from institutionalised religion to a more diffuse mystical and personal tradition centred on concepts of a pervasive life force as opposed to the one God – a change that has coincided with the revival of traditional Maori spirituality with its belief in a diffuse deity (atua).

Historically, the colonists' conviction of the superiority of white Protestant civilisation led them for a long time to look to Britain as the source of religious scholarship and spiritual leadership. Church buildings followed the style of Victorian Gothic or neoclassical architecture – with the exception of simple wooden rural churches, and the Rangiatea church at Otaki, which took on a Maori idiom. Among Pakeha, New Zealand Christianity varied little from its British models. New Zealand Protestantism's colonial dependence reflected the dependence of society as a whole, and as links with Britain have been slowly severed, so the New Zealand Churches have slowly developed their own ethos. The Methodist (1959), Presbyterian (1966) and Anglican (1977) Churches all ordained women to their ministry before their British counterparts. Contemporary Maori preaching, too, can be an interesting blend of European style with the style of Maori oratory and a fondness for allusion, illustration and vivid pictorial imagery.

## Maori Variants on Christianity

Maori variants on Christianity have been influential over the 150 years since the Europeans first arrived with Bibles. While early missionaries had some success in converting Maori tribes, in several instances the new Christian teachings were amalgamated with existing Maori beliefs – and the pantheon of Maori gods – to form syncretic religions. The most famous sects include the Papahurihia, which sprung up in the Bay of Islands in the 1830s, identifying strongly with the Israelites of the Old Testament as a disinherited but chosen people promised deliverance and fulfilment by God; a handful of followers of Papahurihia, who called himself Te Atua Wera – the fiery god – are still to be found in the Hokianga. The Pai Mairire sect, which wove Biblical and Maori elements into rituals that included incantation and dancing around a traditional niu pole, took on a highly political and warriorlike role in the New Zealand Wars of the 1860s – despite the name, which means 'good and peaceful'.

One or two of these Maori millenarian sects still exist as practising religions. The Ringatu Church, founded by Maori warrior Te Kooti Rikirangi in the late 19th century, has around 6,000 adherents, mostly in the Bay of Plenty and Ureweras. The Ratana Church, founded by Tahupotiki Wiremu Ratana, a Taranaki farmer, in the 1920s, made a profound impression through its 'deep psychological appeal to the Maori mind, with a lure of nationalism and the promise of redress of the wrongs suffered by the Maori people'. Ratana emphasised the abandonment of traditional beliefs. It claims around 35,000 members today, mainly from Taranaki to Northland.

Right-wing sects and Catholicism have proved more resilient to secularisation than the Protestant denominations. Over the past decades there has appeared within the historic Churches in New Zealand a movement of spiritual renewal which has led some to claim that it is God's answer to the spiritual and moral bankruptcy of the nation. Charismatic renewal has risen from obscurity to a recognisable force. Pentecostalism – Churches such as the Apostolic Church with their emphasis on 'baptism of the Spirit', 'gifts' of healing and 'speaking in tongues' – has grown in respectability and acceptability, and renewal movements have become active in the mainstream Churches too. The movements appeal to a freer expression of the emotions as part of religious experience, and the need for a sense of community not embedded in ossified religious institutions; Maori adherence is strong. Sectarianism has also thrived over recent years. Mormon ideology in particular offers a substantial appeal to ethnic minorities, its popularity among Maori due in part to a personal, face-to-face approach in the initial proselytizing stage.

## Jews and Other Faiths

New Zealand has a very small Jewish community, of fewer than 5,000 people, with three Orthodox synagogues (in Auckland, Wellington and Christchurch). Although the country has seen similar waves of Jewish migration to elsewhere (from the Russian pogroms and Nazi persecution), Jewish immigrants have tended to move on – to the United States, Israel or Australia. A move away from orthodoxy, combined with intermarriage and assimilation, have led to dwindling numbers of practising Jews, although this has been balanced to some degree by the conversion of spouses, observance of religious festivals and a return to rituals such as bris (circumcision). Julius Vogel, a notable 19th-century prime minister of the country, was Jewish, but the community has developed no particular power base or intelligentsia and remains marginal.

Waves of immigration from the Indian subcontinent, Southeast Asia and the Middle East have also brought Muslim, Sikh, Hindu and Buddhist communities to New Zealand, generally small and self-contained.

# Family and the Role of Women

Women's status in New Zealand society is ambivalent. On the one hand, New Zealand pioneered many women's rights; on the other, macho pioneering values are deeply entrenched. New Zealand women scored some notable firsts: New Zealand was the first nation in the world to give women the vote (1893); the world's first woman doctor (1896) and practising woman lawyer (1897) were New Zealanders. Women were ordained to the Protestant ministries in New Zealand long before their counterparts in Britain, and New Zealand appointed the world's first female bishop in 1990. And yet the cult of women as home-makers – bearing and rearing children, cooking and cleaning – is persistent, offset by the stereotype of men as tough guys on the rugby pitch and hard drinkers – decent blokes and good mates, but no softies. Women's domain is the kitchen, men's the garage; women bake scones, men erect fence posts; women volunteer in the community, men run businesses – although more and more women are becoming successful businesswomen in New Zealand today.

Women immigrants were brought in by the shipload in the late 19th century to balance the numbers (in 1871, New Zealand had 66 per cent men to 34 per cent women; in 2001, women outnumbered men by 110 to 100), to break up the male culture of labour and drink, and to civilise and domesticate the frontier men. New Zealand men are still resisting the effeminate influence. 'New Zealand women were brought up to be farmer's wives, they ate porridge, beef and dairy products and accepted sexual repression as a normal part of growing up. New Zealand men were rugged individualists who could turn their hand to anything, even women. They only thing they could not satisfy were their wives so they drank a lot, went to the races and the rugby and complimented each other on how great New Zealand was at showing the rest of the world how to play sport. Sex was a necessary evil, except when they talked about it with their mates. They accepted their repression stoically, because that is how men were supposed to act,' Maori woman film-maker Merata Mita has observed.

At the time of writing, three of New Zealand's top four constitutional positions are held by women (the governor-general having been recently replaced by a man): the prime minister (the second successive woman), the attorney-general and the chief justice. Eight out of 26 government ministries are headed by a woman; women are fairly well represented in parliament (40 MPs out of 120 in the 2005 parliament – 30 per cent, ranking New Zealand high in the world league tables for parliamentary balance) and slightly less well in the upper echelons of the law (35 woman judges to 135 men – just over 20 per cent). At the same time, women are under-represented overall at the top levels of public service, in all decision-making bodies and in the higher ranks of private corporations (ever since former Telecom CEO Teresa Gattung was forced to resign after admitting phone charges were made as complicated as possible to confuse the customer), and many of the issues that have dogged feminist debate for a century or more remain unresolved.

The amount of time women spend on unpaid work (mainly in the home) and the right to equal pay for equal work continue to nag. Equal pay for women was already a topic of discussion in the 1890s and has been campaigned for ever since: 'Are they 80 per cent efficient?' one frustrated woman worker asked in 1944. Yet in the early years of the 21st century New Zealand women earn on average just 78.7 per cent of the pay of their male counterparts, at hourly rates of 84.8 per cent of men's. 'Occupational segregation by gender' (women working in undervalued occupations – or women-dominated occupations being undervalued) may have something to do with the pay differential: the most common occupations for New Zealand women are as teachers, nurses and carers, or in hotels, bars, restaurants and shops. Many women take on clerical roles, but women are less likely than men to be legislators, administrators and managers. The working patterns of women may affect pay too: over 30 per cent of working women work part-time.

A recent government report to the UN, however, noted the continuing 'residual' or unexplained pay gap – evidence of more subtle discrimination related to the predetermined roles of women and men, or linked to women's continuing low expectations. Women comprise almost half of the labour force, but receive less income than men by about NZ$10,000: the median income for women is NZ$14,500, compared with NZ$24,900 for men. Women's earnings are lower than men's from the outset, with even younger (childless) women tending to earn less than men (the median income for 20–29-year-olds is NZ$3,100–NZ$7,100 less than men) – suggesting that women or their employers still see their careers as a brief interlude before they start a family – while 35–39-year-old women (who are most likely to be looking after children) receive NZ$17,300 less than men. In all these comparisons, Maori women are even less well off than their Pakeha sisters.

While New Zealand did its feminist dash in the 1970s, consciousness-raising and all, these days there's not much talk of feminism and the 'growth of the whole, individual person'. A number of women's and feminist issues have gained public and official recognition at the same time as real movement towards gender equality has proved elusive. Abortion, contraception and divorce have been more or less dealt with, and the objectification of women sidelined as an issue (who protests about Miss World and the cosmetics industry now?), but campaigns for pay equity, better provision of childcare, paid parental leave and so forth continue – embodied in a contemporary discourse of 'work–family balance'. In 2002 legislation was finally introduced to enforce paid parental leave for mothers, bringing New Zealand into line with the rest of the West – although not all would agree that the entitlement is enough. New mothers are entitled to 14 weeks' government-funded paid leave up to full earnings or a maximum of NZ$391.28 a week if they have worked for the same employer for at least six months previously. Employers are also required to keep positions open for a 52-week period of unpaid maternity leave, and the government offers means-tested childcare subsidies for up to 37 hours a week.

At the same time, the hot potato of equal pay for work of equal value has still not been addressed in law. While the Equal Pay Acts of 1960 (public services) and 1972 (private sector) made it illegal to pay women and men different wages for the same job, legislation introduced in 1989 by a Labour government to enforce more widespread equality of pay was promptly repealed by an incoming National government in 1990 before it could be put to the test. More recent legislation to address barriers to equality in employment (the Employment Relations Act 2000) through collective bargaining, which requires employers and employees to act in good faith, and re-unionisation, seem unlikely to bring drastic improvement to existing disparities. Ironically, New Zealand's first Labour government (1935), which was seen as a champion of women's rights, enshrined the notion of the male breadwinner supporting the female home-maker in the country's first minimum wage – calculated as the sum needed for a man to support his wife and three children. When women entered the workforce it was assumed they were not taking on this responsibility; there is still an underlying assumption that women are just earning a little extra – for themselves or the household – and the career system is still geared to the male life-cycle – a 40-hour week for 40 years, which takes no account of time spent in child-rearing. So just how much child-rearing are New Zealand women doing? Along with the rest of the West, New Zealand is barely replacing its population. In 2002, 64 countries had rates below the theoretical replacement level of 2.1 births on average per woman, with another 25 countries just on or over this level. New Zealand's fertility rate is 2.05 children on average per woman, with urban women having fewer children than rural and small-town women, and European women reproducing least (1.83 children on average), just less than Asian women (1.88), Maori women more (2.79) and Pacific islanders most (2.84). The most common family type is still a couple with children, but single-parent families are on the increase.

According to 2001 Census figures, in that year there were also 1,356 same-sex couples with children (960 female, 396 male), and 3,714 same-sex couples without children (1,878 female, 1,836 male). While New Zealand society has historically tended to homophobia (think of those stereotypes, male and female), the Women's Liberation movement of the 1960s and 1970s brought lesbians stridently out of the closet and gay men rode the crest of the liberation wave. Homosexuality is well established in law, most recently by the Civil Union Bill (2004), which allows same-sex 'marriages' (although the bill deliberately avoided that word); de facto same-sex relationships are already legally recognised in many areas (immigration, property). Nonetheless, homosexual relationships are likely to find a more tolerant culture in the cities than out in the back country.

# Media

## Newspapers

All New Zealand's larger towns and cities have daily newspapers. The dailies of Auckland, Wellington and Christchurch have a quasi-national status, and can be bought in other parts of the country, while those of the smaller centres have a distinctly regional feel and are distributed only within their own publication area.

Auckland's paper, the *New Zealand Herald*, claims to have the highest circulation; its coverage is targeted at the country's largest and most commercial city. Wellington's paper, the *Dominion Post* (circulation 90,000), is the most authoritative on government affairs. Christchurch's paper, the *Press* (circulation 90,000) is the most read paper in the South Island.

All these papers combine local and regional news with national and international reports (mostly syndicated from the British and American press or news agencies), business, sport and features, and publish 'big' Saturday papers with lifestyle sections. The regional dailies, which are mostly evening papers, publish a similar mix, but with much greater emphasis on local news and issues.

By international standards, the breadth and depth of reporting is limited. Major news stories around the world are reported, but it is hard to get a full and balanced picture of world affairs from the New Zealand press. Most editorial, op-ed analysis and commentary is on national issues, and writing is often lively.

There are three national Sunday papers, also modest in size and scope when compared with British or American Sunday papers. The main Sunday broadsheet is the *Sunday Star-Times*, complete with glossy supplements that take the average reader 49 minutes to read. The new *Sunday Herald* now competes directly with it. The *Sunday News* is New Zealand's weekly 'sports and entertainment' tabloid.

Following recent mergers and buyouts, most New Zealand newspapers are owned by one of two Australian media groups. The *Herald* is owned by APN News and Media, an Australian media organisation which also owns the *Listener* – a widely read national, weekly current affairs and entertainment magazine – and the iconic *NZ Woman's Weekly*.

Most of the rest – including a raft of regional dailies from the *Waikato Times* to the *Southland Times* – are the property of Fairfax NZ, subsidiary of an Australian company in which Rupert Murdoch has a stake. Fairfax also owns magazines including *NZ House and Garden*, *Truck Trader* and *Fish and Game NZ*. A few papers, such as the *Otago Daily Times*, remain independent. None of the press, however, shows a strong political bias.

The two main New Zealand Internet news sites are **www.nzherald.co.nz** and **www.stuff.co.nz**, associated with the APN and Fairfax stables, respectively.

## Case Study: From Metropolitan Metro to Colonial Dominion

Guy Somerset, books editor of the *Dominion Post*, moved to New Zealand because house prices in the southeast of England were so high that he and his wife, Linley, could not afford a home for their family even if they both worked full time. 'Houses were just too expensive,' says Guy, who commuted daily from Brighton to his job as deputy arts editor at *Metro* in London. Once Guy added the travel time on to the long working hours, he had no time to see his children either. 'So the other, major reason we're here is the amount of time I can give to my family,' says Guy, who calculates that he gets an extra 15 hours a week family time (it takes him 10 minutes to travel from suburban Karori to the newspaper's office in central Wellington).

Getting established here was a step-by-step process for the Somersets. At first, Linley stayed in a bach on Lake Taupo, with children Laura (then 2) and Kit (6 weeks old), while Guy worked shifts as a sub-editor at the *Dominion* (as it was then). When the subbing shifts turned into a permanent job, the Somersets found a house in Wellington. 'Property was not as cheap as we'd hoped – we moved from one boom to another – but we still found a much better house here,' says Guy, who definitely feels it has been a good move for the children. 'Wellington's a decent-sized city, with parks and playgrounds, a good kindy [kindergarten] system – and no waiting lists.' And New Zealand's deserted beaches more than make up for the lack of the historical and cultural attractions of Europe, which the children would be too young to enjoy.

Guy finds working in newspapers here less stimulating than in the UK, as the market is smaller and the press more parochial – but he is realistic about his own career too. 'There are more interesting, better-paid media jobs in Britain,' he says, 'but I wouldn't necessarily be doing them.' He adds that, while journalists are well paid only at the top levels in Britain, in New Zealand, journalism is poorly paid at all levels. 'There is no top,' he says. 'But at least you don't have to give up your life for the slog.' As the books pages Guy edits have a local bias, Guy has had to do a bit of a crash course on New Zealand literature – but that's what journalism is all about. 'It's a very enjoyable subject,' he adds.

'From a strictly journalistic point of view, Auckland would have been a better place to settle – it's where the best media jobs are – but then it would have been back to square one with the traffic and the house prices.'

# Radio

While the New Zealand press may be found limited, public service Radio New Zealand is excellent. The two main state-owned stations are **National Radio**, which broadcasts mainly news and current affairs programmes, and **Concert FM**, which specialises in classical music (check the *Listener* or **www. radionz.co.nz** for frequencies and programme times).

National Radio's four main news programmes are comprehensive and author-itative. *Morning Report* with Geoff Robinson and Sean Plunkett is an agenda-setting news programme which goes 'behind the headlines' on national and international stories (rather like the *Today* programme on BBC Radio 4). *Midday Report* offers extended news reports and comment. *Checkpoint*, the drive-time programme, has won several awards for presenter Mary Wilson and her team's treatment of major news stories. *Late Edition* rounds up all the news at the end of the day.

On top of these, the daily series *Worldwatch* contextualises significant inter-national news, while weekly current affairs programme *Insight* takes an in-depth look at one topical issue. Magazine programmes *Nine to Noon* with Kathryn Ryan, *Saturday Morning* with Kim Hill and *Sunday Morning* with Chris Laidlaw range from hard news to lifestyle issues. These and other programmes also look at Maori affairs, business, sports, science, books, films and so on, and are interspersed with music, comedy and drama (often from the BBC). Jim Mora adopts a cosy approach to *Afternoons* and Barry Crump gives a more youthful twist to *Nights*.

There are also several Maori language radio stations, and about 120 private radio stations, which broadcast mostly popular music.

## Television

Most television is as bad as the press is indifferent and the radio is good. New Zealand has five free-to-air television channels, and between them they broad-cast 75 per cent imported material, with 14 minutes of commercials in every hour. State-owned **TV One** broadcasts a mix of British and local drama – including favourites such as *Coronation Street* – documentaries and sporting events and plenty of house, garden and cookery shows. **TV2** (also part of TVNZ) broadcasts popular New Zealand programmes such as the soap *Shortland Street* and recent cult viewing *Eating Media Lunch* and *The Insiders' Guide to Happiness*, and well-known American shows such as *The Sopranos*. **TV3** also broadcasts sports and high-rating American programmes such as *Oprah Winfrey*. **TV4** is a pop music channel. **Prime TV**, owned by Sky, broadcasts docu-mentaries and nature programmes (bought in), comedies such as *Seinfeld*, and a range of imports from *Eastenders* to *The Late Show with David Letterman*.

Glad as you may be to find the *Antiques Roadshow*, the latest BBC costume drama or crime series and global fodder such as *Pop Idol* or *The Simpsons*, your couch potato pleasure will be seriously marred by the frequency and duration of commercial breaks – especially in prime-time films, where it often feels as if you will never reach the climax.

TV One and TV3 broadcast competing hour-long news programmes daily at 6pm (*One News* and *3 News*). The news agenda on both channels is mainly national – often topped by a car crash or boating accident – with sports reports taking up a good third of each programme. Viewers are kept hanging on until the end by the all-important weather forecasts, just before 7pm. The rivals are distinguished mainly by the international reports they buy in to cover world events from the BBC and American networks. Prime TV also has a half-hour news programme, *Prime News* – 'First at 5.30'.

At 7pm TV One and TV3 go head-to-head again on 'in-depth' current affairs with *Close Up*, fronted by veteran political commentator Mark Sainsbury, and *Campbell Live*, best known for its presenter's casual greeting to viewers – 'Hi, guys' – delivered in a throaty baritone. TV One and TV3 show competing weekly current affairs programmes on Sunday evenings: *Sunday* and *20/20*. Both combine locally produced reports on topical national issues – often interesting and well-presented – with syndicated American and British TV reports. A weekly documentary slot on TV One, *DNZ*, examines such perennially hot topics as the culture of drink in New Zealand society.

A recent newcomer is **Maori Television**, a government-funded service, which broadcasts seven and a half hours a day in te reo Maori, with a remit to revitalise Maori language and culture. As well as Maori news, and the Maori outlook on other news, it shows educational programmes for children, youth music programmes, and lifestyle programmes such as *Marae DIY*. It is currently available only on UHF frequencies or via satellite.

On satellite, **Sky Television** has a wide reach with its usual mixtures of films, sports and so on. **Telstra Clear** runs a cable TV channel screening sports, music, cartoons and the like.

# The Economy

New Zealand has a mixed economy, which operates on free market principles, with sizeable manufacturing and service sectors complementing a highly efficient agricultural sector. The economy is strongly trade-orientated, with exports of goods and services accounting for around 33 per cent of total output. Energy-based industries, forestry, mining, horticulture and tourism have all expanded rapidly over the past two decades. While pastoral agriculture and commodity exports remain of vital importance to the country, the significance of the service sector relative to primary production and manufacturing continues to grow.

Over the last two decades the New Zealand economy has changed from being one of the most regulated in the OECD (the Organisation for Economic Cooperation and Development) to one of the most deregulated. The stated aim of the minority Labour-led coalition government elected in 2002 was to foster the transformation of New Zealand into a leading knowledge-based economy with high skills, high employment and high value-added production.

# Background

## 1945–60

New Zealand emerged from the Second World War with an expanding and successful agriculture-based economy. In the 1950s and 1960s – a period of sustained full employment – gross domestic product (GDP) grew at an average annual rate of 4 per cent. Agricultural prices remained high, due in part to a boom in the wool industry during the Korean War. However, even during this period there were signs of weakness. In 1962, the Economic and Monetary Council advised the government that between 1949 and 1960 New Zealand's productivity growth had been one of the lowest among the world's highest-earning economies. In the late 1960s, faced with growing balance of payments problems, successive governments sought to maintain New Zealand's high standard of living with increased levels of overseas borrowing and increasingly protective economic policies.

## The 1970s

Problems mounted for the New Zealand economy in the 1970s. Access into key world markets for agricultural commodities such as butter, lamb and wool became increasingly difficult (due largely to EU and American protectionism; New Zealand is still sore at having been cast off by Britain when it joined the European Union). The sharp rises in international oil prices in 1973 and 1974 coincided with falls in prices received for exports. As in many OECD countries, policies in New Zealand were principally aimed at maintaining a high level of economic activity and employment in the short term. High levels of protection of domestic industry had undermined competitiveness and the economy's ability to adapt to the changing world environment. The combination of expansionist macro-policies and industrial assistance led to macro-economic imbalances, structural adjustment problems and a rapid rise in government indebtedness. After the next major shift in oil and commodity prices in 1979 and 1980, New Zealand's position deteriorated further.

## The 1980s

From 1984 onwards, the direction of economic policy in New Zealand turned away from intervention towards the elimination of many forms of government assistance. Under the guidance of Labour minister of finance Roger Douglas, the country abandoned social democratic Keynesianism for New Right monetarism. On the macro-economic level, since the 1980s policies have aimed at achieving low inflation and a sound fiscal position, while micro-economic reforms have been intended to open the economy to competitive pressures and world prices. The reforms of 'Rogernomics' included the floating of the exchange rate; the abolition of controls on capital movements; the ending of industry assistance; the removal of price controls; deregulation across a number of sectors of the economy; the corporatisation and privatisation of state-owned assets; and labour market legislation aimed at facilitating more flexible patterns of wage bargaining (de-unionisation).

The application of pure neo-liberal economic theory – broadly continued by successive governments of both left and right – has been proclaimed an international success story. The 'New Zealand experiment' has been cited as a global model, spawning imitators around the world (notably Margaret Thatcher in the UK and Ronald Reagan in the USA). Critics in New Zealand, however, have lamented the social costs of unfettered market-led liberalism since its introduction to the country, while the deregulated global economy itself has been increasingly under fire. Some New Zealanders have begun to demand alternatives to the free market agenda that has come to rule their lives; a satisfactory 'third way' has yet to be found.

## The 1990s to the Present

New Zealand's relentless pursuit of free market principles since the 1980s has exposed a remote country of four million people to the full impact of international market forces – treating its social, political and cultural life as irrelevant. While the 'national interest' had been redefined in the 1980s to mean making business more competitive in the international marketplace, for many ordinary New Zealanders this change has represented a threat to identity, jobs, communities and the right to control their own lives. One direct result of the relaxation of foreign investment rules was the sale of state assets such as telecommunications, forests and the post office to foreign companies; while much of New Zealand is now foreign-owned, the absence of any requirement for major foreign investment (except in land) to meet a 'national interest' test continues to grab headlines. Unease over the concept of 'economic sovereignty' for New Zealand is exacerbated for Maori by the unresolved seizure of 'capital' by colonists over a hundred years earlier.

Over the last two decades, the New Zealand economy has changed from being one of the most regulated in the OECD to one of the most deregulated. The minority Labour-led coalition government first elected in 1999 and elected for a third term in September 2005 states that it aims to continue the transformation of New Zealand into a dynamic knowledge-based economy and society, underpinned by values of fairness, opportunity and security.

The New Zealand economy grew strongly over the 1990s, with the exception of a period over 1997 and 1998 in which the economy was affected by the twin shocks of the Asian economic downturn and consecutive summer droughts. Following this period, the economy has performed strongly, apart from a short weaker period during 2001, which the economy quickly recovered from, with a combination of two good agricultural seasons, relatively high world prices for

New Zealand's export commodities, a low exchange rate over 2001 and 2002 and a robust labour market contributing to strong income flows throughout the economy. Over 2002 to 2004, growth in GDP was in the range of 3.5 per cent to 4.5 per cent, peaking at 4.6 per cent annual average growth in December 2002. This period of strong growth included a period in which the economy was subject to several negative temporary events. These included travel disruptions and uncertainty due to the conflict in Iraq, the outbreak of Severe Acute Respiratory Syndrome (SARS) in Asia, and the effects of dry weather on hydro-electricity production and farm output.

More recently, growth has eased as a result of high oil prices and interest rate increases, with the economy flat in the second half of 2005. There was a slight recovery during the first half of 2006, with annual average growth slowing to 1.4 per cent in the year to 30 September 2006, down from a recent peak of 4.4 per cent in the year to December 2004. Growth is forecast to remain relatively subdued in the short term as households go through a period of consolidation before an export-led recovery leads to growth increasing to trend levels of around 3 per cent in 2009 and 2010.

The slowing in growth over 2005 was largely driven by the external sector. A relatively high exchange rate and some relatively poor agricultural production seasons resulted in weak export growth, while a strong domestic economy contributed to considerable growth in import volumes. Recently, however, growth in the domestic economy appears to have eased with weakness in the household sector as growth in private consumption and residential investment slow. This has led to a significant slowing in import volume growth and has seen some rebalancing towards net exports following strong increases in agri-cultural production. Annual Consumer Price Index (CPI) inflation increased to 4.0 per cent in the June 2006 quarter, largely driven by high petrol prices and a continuing strong housing market, before reducing to 2.6 per cent in December 2006. Lower petrol prices were a dominant factor in the decline in inflation in the December quarter.

## Latest Snapshot and Outlook

At the time of writing, a strong labour market and high world prices for New Zealand's commodity exports are providing a boost to domestic spending, although a slowdown in GDP growth is predicted. At the same time, declining net migration, rising interest rates, the high level of the exchange rate and high oil prices all provide downside risks to the outlook.

In 2008 the unemployment rate is 4 per cent, the lowest since 1987 – the growth in employment reflecting demand for labour in response to the strong growth of the New Zealand economy. The fall in unemployment means that it is becoming increasingly difficult for firms to find labour, which is likely to lead to increases in wages as firms seek to retain staff. It may also encourage firms

## Economic Indicators

New Zealand's Ministry of Economic Development prefaces its 2007 biennial summary of economic indicators with the observation that 'A country's well-being is determined by a wide range of factors, from its material living standards to the nature and quality of its social and environmental situation' – a sure indicator that it is doing better in the former than the latter. Indeed, the report goes on to note that New Zealand ranks more highly in the OECD on quality of life indicators than on the two narrower economic measures: gross national income (GNI) per capita (what New Zealand earns) and gross domestic product (GDP) per capita (what New Zealand produces).

• While New Zealand's GDP per capita has been growing faster than the OECD average, the level of GDP per capita remains lower. While it has higher than ever employment, it suffers from relatively low labour productivity, and while investment has been high in some areas (plant and machinery, business and housing investment), government investment has fallen drastically since the 1980s, saving rates are low and the sharemarket is small.

• New Zealand lags behind the OECD in investment and innovation, although research and development rates are growing.

• New Zealand's share in world trade is a staggering 0.36 per cent; imports and exports make up a surprisingly small percentage of GDP. Levels of inward investment and immigration are high, while outward investment is rock bottom.

• New Zealand's university graduation rate is one of the highest in the OECD, but there are still significant numbers of people at the lowest levels of literacy and numeracy.

• The quality of much of New Zealand's infrastructure (transport, ICT) is low.

• New Zealand ranks second in the world for ease of doing business.

• New Zealand's tax burden as a tax-to-GDP ratio is average (35 per cent).

• New Zealand's macroeconomic foundations (GDP growth, inflation, interest rates and exchange rates) are volatile.

to look for new investment to increase production. Business investment has already expanded strongly over recent years, although residential investment and the heated housing market have now begun to slow.

Oil price rises and the continuing high level of the exchange rate (the NZ dollar recently hit a record high of US$0.81) continue to provide some potential downside risks to the outlook. Resource pressures are an additional risk to the outlook, with labour becoming increasingly hard to find and signs of inflation rising. Growth is likely to slow as higher interest rates, declining net migration and a likely end to recent large increases in the terms of trade all begin to slow domestic activity.

At the time of writing, New Zealand economists are debating the likelihood of recession along with the rest of the world. Their predictions are no more conclusive than those of their British and American counterparts. What they see is the global credit crunch, a high kiwi dollar, high interest rates and a falling share-market. One doom-and-gloom-monger warns that conditions are similar to those preceding the 1998 recession: against the worsening global backdrop, the local housing market is weaker than expected, consumer confidence is in decline, and drought and power crises are expected. 'Slowdown' or 'soft landing' are still the preferred terms for what is not yet a recession. Optimists point out that Asia and Australia are now twice as important as the USA and Europe as trading partners, so New Zealand may be buffered against the worst effects of the crunch. With good export prices for its commodities, New Zealand is enjoying the most favourable terms of trade in 34 years; let's hope it can make the most of them.

# Internal Issues

## The Treaty of Waitangi Revisited

The issue that most divides New Zealand today is the process of land settlement and redress between the Crown (symbolically representing Europeans in general) and Maori, initiated by the Waitangi Act of 1975. Initially designed to deal with injustices in contemporary dealings, under the terms of the 1840 Treaty of Waitangi, the act acquired much greater scope and significance in 1985 when it was made retrospective. The floodgates were opened to claims of unfair land grabs and the seizure of customary resources perpetrated by Europeans since the earliest days of British colonisation. Twenty years on, the process is to many beginning to seem very drawn out, as it becomes ever more complicated and contentious, with Maori tribes claiming rights to everything from oil and gas reserves to air space. For many Pakeha, too much has been conceded, while for many Maori the redress has not been enough. The function of the claims process as a 'truth and reconciliation' commission has yet to reach its cathartic final stages.

The main areas of grievance, as outlined by the Waitangi Tribunal, which researches claims, and the Office of Treaty Settlements, which negotiates the claims on behalf of the Crown, are specific. They claim that:

- **the Crown unjustly confiscated land in the 1860s, at the end of the New Zealand Wars (land confiscations were retributive, and prime farming land was seized, irrespective of the role played by tribes in the wars).**

- **the Crown sold or leased Maori reserves to settlers.**

- **the Crown claimed that it had bought land that tribes did not think they had sold.**

- the Crown bought land from Maori who did not have the right to sell it (the last two often compounded by the inter-relationship between tribes).
- the Crown did not protect access to Maori burial grounds and other sacred sites.
- the Crown granted title to the New Zealand Company or to settlers who had not legitimately bought land.
- Maori land was taken for public works, but not used for them.
- Native Land Court rulings resulted in large-scale alienation of Maori land.

Settlements involve a formal apology from the government for wrongs committed; commercial redress (most often in the form of cash payouts rather than land, most of which is no longer in Crown hands); and cultural redress (for example access to traditional food sources, recognition of traditional place names, or a say in the management of resources on Crown land). By March 2004, 1,054 claims had been lodged with the tribunal, relating either to specific pieces of land or generic government policy. Many claims, however, relate to the same group of people or events; when all similar claims have been lodged, they are grouped together as District Inquiries and dealt with as one. Settlements are negotiated – where possible – at the 'large natural group' level (iwi) and once a claim has been settled no more claims are possible in that area – in theory, at least. In practice, hapu (sub-tribes) may disagree about claims and choose to act independently of each other, and the settlement of South Island claims with Ngai Tahu has recently been disputed by other tribes who feel they lost out. The tribunal aims to report on all claims in the next 10 years, and expects all claims to be settled in the next 10–15 years – although many see these targets as optimistic.

The question over who should own the foreshore and sea bed and what ownership means is the one that has most divided New Zealand in recent times. It has drawn a declaration of civil war from a prominent Maori academic, while Pakeha have fretted that they will no longer have access to beaches for fishing, navigation and recreation; rights to the seashore draw out particularly emotional reactions. Confusion over the debate starts with what the terms actually mean: in fact, the area under discussion is from the high-tide mark down, and claims cover customary rights of access, ownership and custodianship. At the time of writing, hearings are still under way over proposed legislation, which envisages that the coast and sea will be in trust with dual ownership between Maori and the Crown as 'public domain'.

The sea bed and foreshore debate has raised issues of foreign, private and public ownership as well as customary Maori interests and by-now traditional Pakeha use of the beaches too. This area of claims follows a major settlement by the Waitangi Fisheries Commission in 1992, which gave Maori a NZ$150m payout and a 20 per cent quota of fishing catches, followed by a similar settlement for aquaculture (marine farming) – one of the most significant settlements in a process which has seen more than NZ$675m paid out in redress so far. Another contentious area of settlement has been Crown-owned forestry land, claimed by Maori when the state attempted to sell it in 1988; profits from these commercial forests are now paid into a trust intended to pay for the final settlement. Other substantial settlements have been to the Tainui (NZ$170m) and Ngai Tahu (also NZ$170m) tribes.

The Ngai Tahu settlement in the South Island is an example of a claim that has functioned as it should. On a wall of the tribe's headquarters hangs a document of formal apology by the New Zealand government for the wrongful alienation of Ngai Tahu land in the 19th century, signed by the prime minister of the day. The apology followed a finding by the Waitangi Tribunal that the claim by Ngai Tahu to the greater part of South Island was legitimate. But, that being acknowledged, Ngai Tahu said they recognised the place of many other settlers who had come subsequently to New Zealand, and did not want all of the land for themselves. Instead an agreement was reached whereby the Crown allocated NZ$170m to Ngai Tahu, money which has been invested in health, education, housing and the general well-being of the tribe. (Tainui, on the other hand, have come under fire for mismanaging the money settled on them.) Ngai Tahu were also affirmed as the guardians of 130 species of native flora and fauna and of sacred sites such as Aoraki/Mount Cook. The mountain was deeded back to Ngai Tahu, who then formally returned it to the nation. A basic dynamic of human relationships underlies this process: a wrongdoer acknowledges and repents of a wrong, and makes appropriate reparation; the act of repentance in turn frees the wronged party to act generously and, in a spirit of reconciliation, a new partnership is established.

Unfortunately this is not the tone of much of the debate about the work of the Waitangi Tribunal. Barely a day passes without a newspaper story about a claim, pitting Pakeha against Maori, right-wing against left-wing, them against us. While few fair-minded persons can take issue with the conclusion that the original Waitangi Treaty was a deal in which Maori interests were not protected, and that those interests mostly were not protected until recent times and that recompense is due, many dispute the terms of renegotiation. To some it appears more of a reinterpretation of the treaty than an attempt to ensure its terms have been impartially applied.

The 'principles' of the treaty are much cited, even in the legal context – but no one really knows what they mean, even though the ambiguous 'principles' have been enshrined in various pieces of legislation relating to the environment, conservation, education, building permits, the arts and genetic modification. Others argue with the fundamental process of historical revisionism involved in casting today's values back on the actions and behaviour of the nation's forebears. One historian has talked of a 'retrospective utopia'; the treaty is being re-examined as if it, and the actions consequent on it, had not taken place in a historical context. Would it ever have been possible to fulfil the treaty's undertakings, especially within the norms of the time? To which those actively involved in the judicial process respond that it is not an attempt to establish an objective history, and that the use of history as legal evidence inevitably leads to distortion.

Underlying the subtlety of some academic debate on the orthodoxy of Waitangi Tribunal history is a feeling that the treaty has come to be seen by many as a one-way street, a document that enables Maori to claim and receive apologies and compensation from a largely Pakeha government without reciprocation, let alone thanks. Since the expansion of the tribunal's brief 20 years ago to include claims from the past, there has been a claim-and-settlement process which inevitably casts the ancestors of today's Pakeha as villains and of Maori as victims. It does not matter whether the claims are justified – as most of them are. Pakeha are required to carry a moral burden. The moral climate for Pakeha is worsened by some Maori leaders saying they do not belong here, their culture is elsewhere and describing up to eighth-generation non-Maori as settlers or strangers.

Has the whole legal process, designed to redress the imbalance in power in earlier negotiations, descended into a cynical 'treaty industry'? Are claims to the country's oil and gas reserves (ultimately rejected by the government, contrary to tribunal recommendations) and air space over certain lakes (under discussion) opportunistic attempts to jump on a 'gravy train' by groups who see no limit to what they can gain from redress? And has the tribunal itself, which started off as a fact-finding body, become an advocacy body for Maori claims, as much of the press argues? Has the settlement process become a 'grievance industry', which prevents New Zealanders, and Maori in particular, developing a 'culture of aspiration'? The Waitangi Tribunal process is one from which the National Party of Don Brash, as well as Winston Peters' NZ First, have gained much mileage. Brash's rhetoric has focused on 'one rule for all in a single nation state', the treaty standing for unity not 'division' fomented by the actions to bring Maori out of dispossessed poverty. He argues that both Europeans and Pakeha were motivated by self-interest in 19th-century dealings, and that it is not the fault of today's generation that one group was stronger than the other (and therefore arguably took advantage). The original Waitangi Treaty was badly drafted and ambiguous, he argues, and should no longer be taken as the basis for New Zealand's constitution. 'The Treaty of Waitangi should not be used as the basis for giving greater civil, political or democratic rights to *any* particular ethnic group,' Brash says, adding that the settlement of historical grievances in the treaty process should be separated from social welfare issues (discrepancies in wealth, housing, education and health). Throwing a final hot potato into the hangi, Brash states that there are now very few New Zealanders of pure Maori ethnicity, and asks why the country should be bogged down in compensation based on self-determined ethnic identity.

A more balanced stance might be to say that, in the treaty debate, Pakeha must acknowledge and right past wrongs, and also acknowledge how vital

Maori culture and vision are to New Zealand's future. For their part, Maori must acknowledge the place of Pakeha and the value of Pakeha culture and institutions. The original treaty was about citizenship as well as property rights, but article three paved the way for the affirmative action that gets under the skin of so many Pakeha; you cannot have equal citizenship for Maori without special treatment (in the form of health and education funding, as well as Waitangi compensation). The day when New Zealanders can see themselves as one people, with common interests, can only come when the Maori sense of injustice has been fully recompensed. But many on both sides of the debate will be happy to see the end of a process that often divides, polarises and separates.

# Culture and Art

There are two entangled strands to contemporary New Zealand culture, reflecting the nation's dual identity. The dominant thread is literature, visual arts, film, music and performing arts that have emerged out of colonial New Zealand's quest for an identity – European in origin, distinctively New Zealand in its late 20th-century manifestations and increasingly international in the new millennium. The other thread is traditional Maori arts and crafts, song and dance, which have undergone a renaissance in recent decades. Increasingly, however, Pakeha creators have appropriated Maori themes and imagery, and Maori creators have chosen to work within Pakeha structures – a blurring of boundaries symptomatic of the country's attempt to forge a bicultural identity for the 21st century.

While the European settlers did their best to obliterate Maori culture in the first hundred years or so of colonisation, it took them at least that long to start developing their own cultural identity. It was not until the inter-war period that writers and artists began to express a New Zealand aesthetic in their work, and not until the 1970s that film-makers and musicians adopted their own New Zealand idiom. Having passed through a phase of 'cultural nationalism', many New Zealand creators are now more interested in relating their work to the international scene than in dwelling on a strictly local reality. Nonetheless, familiar themes (the landscape, 'man alone') and styles (often Maori) do continue to give the work of contemporary practitioners a particularly New Zealand flavour, while urban culture and the multiculturalism brought by new waves of immigration add spice.

## Literature

New Zealanders are avid readers: around 40 per cent of men and 60 per cent of women say that they read a book regularly, and the excellent public libraries issue 38 million books a year – roughly 10 per person. As well as the specialist university and government department libraries, there are four open to the public – the National Library, Alexander Turnbull Library, Parliamentary Library and Hocken Library – with a New Zealand emphasis in their collections. One sign of how seriously New Zealanders take their books is a recent spate of thefts from libraries and antiquarian booksellers by a well-organised book-snatching ring. But with all this reading, what are they writing?

Two early European chroniclers of the New Zealand experience stand out: **Lady Barker**, who published her spirited account of *Station Life in New Zealand* in 1870; and **Samuel Butler**, a Bach-playing sheep farmer who satirised colonial New Zealand's Victorian manners and mores in *Erewhon*. A more straight-forward account of Butler's views of New Zealand can be found in his *A First Year in Canterbury Settlement* (1863) – 'a spiritual journey from the confines of civili-sation to high places occupied by a handful of men'.

## Early 20th-century Writers

One of the first writers to abandon the romantic idealisation of the New Zealand landscapes and society was short-story-writer **Katherine Mansfield**. Like others of her generation, she left the country of her birth for London (in 1908) in search of bohemia and a more sympathetic readership. Her career blos-somed enough to get up the nose of Virginia Woolf with the publication of stories including *The Garden Party* and *The Colonel's Daughters* – evocations of middle-class Edwardian life – until she died from TB in 1923. She is now one of New Zealand's most revered, albeit expatriate, writers. **Jane Mander**, who lived in London and New York from 1912 to 1932, wrote half a dozen novels including *The Story of a New Zealand River* – reviewed with hostility in New Zealand at the time for its 'immoral content', but now reclaimed as a classic. The poet **R. A. K. Mason**, a contemporary who stayed behind, became so disillusioned with the lack of receptive readers that he pitched unsold copies of his first book of poems, *The Beggar*, into the sea; his reputation, too, has become established over time, and he is now widely regarded as New Zealand's 'first wholly original, unmistakably gifted poet'.

## 'Cultural Nationalists' and the 1950s and 1960s

By the 1930s several distinctively New Zealand voices were making them-selves heard, among them poets **Allen Curnow** ('Always to islanders danger / Is what comes over the sea') and **Denis Glover** ('I do not dream of Sussex downs / or quaint old England's quaint old towns – / I think of what may yet be seen / In Johnsonville and Geraldine'), and fiction-writer **Frank Sargeson** (*A Man and His Wife*). Sargeson, the country's first 'professional' writer (from 1931 until his death in 1982 he lived in an isolated bach, making a living from his writing), introduced the New Zealand vernacular to English literature, in an *œuvre* that eventually totalled more than 20 books of novels, stories, plays and memoirs.

This generation of writers came to be known as the '**cultural nationalists**', seeking a 'New Zealand-centred truth' apart from the British colonial dependency and rugged landscapes. The Christchurch-based **Caxton Press** played a key role in bringing the innovative writing of the 1930s and 1940s to a wide audience: seminal publications of the 1940s included *Beyond the Palisade*, the first volume of poems by precocious Dunedin writer **James K. Baxter**, who later gained a reputation as a visionary. Janet Frame later wrote of feeling that she had found her true family among these writers in *Speaking for Ourselves*, a collection of stories edited by Sargeson, and *A Book of New Zealand Verse 1923–45*, edited by Curnow. She was not alone: the influence of this group has been not just on the literary scene, but also on New Zealand's broader quest for an identity.

Sargeson became a mentor to two subsequent generations of writers, among them **A. P. Gaskell**, **Greville Texidor**, **John Reece Cole**, **David Ballantyne**, **Maurice Duggan**, **Kevin Ireland**, **Maurice Gee**, **C. K. Stead** and **Janet Frame**. Among these diverse writers, one culturally defining theme emerges: the man or woman at odds with his or her environment, physical or human. John Mulgan's single novel, *Man Alone* – a classic story of man against the elements – is regarded as the seminal work of Kiwi identity, while Frame's autobiographical trilogy, *An Angel at My Table*, chronicles the fate of an imaginative girl in small-town 1950s New Zealand, labelled mad for her difference. Needless to say, after a period in a psychiatric hospital, Frame went on to become one of the sacred cows of New Zealand literature.

## The Late 20th Century

By the 1970s, not only New Zealand's two home-grown publishers but also the local offices of London-based publishers were publishing New Zealand writers in force. Among writers who began prolific careers in this decade were poets **Bill Manhire**, **Ian Wedde**, **Lauris Edmond** and **Sam Hunt**, and fiction-writers **Owen Marshall**, **Elizabeth Smither** and **Fiona Kidman** – establishing that it was possible to build a career in New Zealand based on serious writing – while **Barry Crump** established a reputation for comic popular fiction with *A Good Keen Man*. Around the same time, Maori writers began to find their own voice. Poets **Hone Tuwhare** and **Alistair Campbell** and fiction-writers **Patricia Grace** (*Mutuwhenua the Moon Sleeps*), **Witi Ihimaera** (*Whale Rider, Bulibasha, Tangi*) and Booker prize-winning **Keri Hulme** (*The Bone People*) have all been pivotal figures in a 'Maori renaissance'. Grace's first stories were criticised for the strange constructions she used to create a voice for the English spoken by Maori around her. Ihimaera's early work explored the alienation of young Maori caught between traditional tribal and modern urban culture, while in his later works he has turned his focus to gay experience (*Nights in the Gardens of Spain*). Hulme has used fiction to explore her mixed Maori and European whakapapa.

More recently, **Alan Duff**'s *Once Were Warriors* exposed the violence underlying urban life for many socially deprived Maori.

## The 21st Century

In the last few years, New Zealand writing has been dominated by graduates from a creative writing course at Victoria University (Wellington), run by Bill Manhire. The work of these up-and-coming writers tends to be published in the faculty magazine, *Sport*, and by the Victoria University Press – a conveyor belt of 'spectacular babies' writing formulaic books marketed by their authors' looks, critics snipe. Among those who have come under fire for their success are **Emily Perkins** (*Not Her Real Name, Leave Before You Go* and *The New Girl*), **Catherine Chidgey** (*In a Fishbone Church, Golden Deeds*), **Elizabeth Knox** (*The Vintner's Luck, Black Oxen*) and **Damien Wilkins** (*The Miserables* and *Little Masters*). Another criticism is the tendency of these writers to move rapidly from personal, local stories to generic international tales – but maybe this is a sign that New Zealand has found the confidence to assume a postmodern, global, literary identity.

# Film

Any film-goer could be excused for confusing New Zealand with Middle Earth since the three-years-in-a-row release of **Peter Jackson**'s blockbuster, Oscar-winning *Lord of the Rings* trilogy. While Jackson's latest, mainstream work has brought commercial success and international renown to the New Zealand film industry, he started his career with three cult comedies, the schlock horror *Bad Taste*, *Meet the Feebles* ('the Muppets meet *Blue Velvet* in Hell') and zombie splatterfest *Braindead* – before making *Heavenly Creatures*, based on the true story of two matricidal teenage girls, featuring a young Kate Winslet. While his next venture (*King Kong*) was strictly Hollywood in genre, it was made in New Zealand using local expertise and talent.

**Jane Campion**, New Zealand's most successful film-making 'export', has taken her talent overseas instead, moving at the same time away from the New Zealand stories that typified her early work. *In the Cut*, her latest offering, is a New York-set, darkly 'feminist' thriller in which the director fixates, with consummate visual style, on her abiding fascination with female masochism – a theme less violently visited in her adaptation of *The Portrait of a Lady* and her romantic Victorian pioneer masterpiece, *The Piano* – while her earlier works examined the awkward reality of 1950s provincial New Zealand: writer Janet Frame's emerging creativity in a time and place where it was perceived as insanity (*An Angel at My Table*) and the unsettling account of a young woman's uncomfortable relationship with her boyfriend and disturbed sister (*Sweetie*).

Jackson and Campion may have hogged the international limelight recently, but New Zealand feature-film-making first took off in the 1970s with productions that have gained an enduring place in New Zealand popular culture and a reputation for independent film-making that has launched many of its authors into mainstream US production. Among the low-budget trailblazers were **Roger Donaldson**'s nihilistic action-thriller *Sleeping Dogs* – energised by the blood, sweat and tears that went into making it happen – and *Smash Palace* – one of local cinema's finest hours and the springboard for the director's career in Hollywood. **Geoff Murphy**'s comic hit *Goodbye Pork Pie* – a classic road movie about two dope-smoking desperados on a road trip in a stolen yellow Mini – helped despatch its director to Hollywood too, after a local attempt at the sci-fi genre (*The Quiet Earth*) and another shot at the fugitive theme (*Never Say Die*).

Other notable films of the era include **Sam Pillsbury**'s *The Scarecrow*, a fine adaptation of the classic New Zealand novel (by Ronald Hugh Morrieson) about a crazed killer who instils fear and paranoia in a small rural community (Pillsbury's finest hour); **Vincent Ward**'s mesmerising debut feature *Vigil*, in which a young girl's idyllic lifestyle is disturbed when her father dies and an enigmatic stranger arrives in his wake – set against the magnificent and atmospheric backdrop of New Zealand's Southern landscape – and *The Navigator*, in which a group of 14th-century Cumbrians mine their way to contemporary New Zealand; **Ian Mune**'s *Came a Hot Friday*, in which Maori comedian Billy T. James stars in a yarn about a pair of inept bookmakers, and *End of the Golden Weather*, a delightfully nostalgic tale of a young boy's last summer holiday in 1930s New Zealand – ranked at the summit of local cinema output; and **Tony Williams**' *Solo*, a moody drama in which a lonely fire patrol pilot balances his life with that of his introverted son and a mysterious lady hitch-hiker (emotional isolation is the theme).

**Gaylene Preston**'s 1980s thriller *Mr Wrong*, in which a young woman acquires a Mark 2 Jaguar that appears to be harbouring the ghost of a past owner, and warm-hearted comedy of misfits *Ruby and Rata*, launched a prolific and successful career making New Zealand films, from *Married* – in which newly-weds cope with sex roles and a communication breakdown one day in mythical New Zealand suburbia, shot with a hand-held camera and an eye for the amusing – to acclaimed documentaries about New Zealand women (*Bread and Roses*, *War Stories*) and most recently *Perfect Strangers* – a thriller of possessive love, set on the rugged coastline of New Zealand's West Coast, that changes tack midway into blackly comic territory. Many film-makers have been attracted to 'psychodrama' as a genre – adopted by women interested in challenging the male gaze such as **Alison Maclean**, in her Gothic horror *Kitchen Sink* (among other works). Some of the most prominent innovators of the 1980s were gay film-makers such as **Peter Wells**, who has explored gay themes using a 'non-verbal visual language' in films such as *Foolish Things*, *Little Queen* and *Desperate Remedies* – an audacious, decadent soap-opera which proudly flaunts its contempt for traditional local film-making with drugs, kinky sex, prostitution, jealousy and bribery all rearing their dubious heads from under a shroud of luxuriant costumes and set design.

## The Depiction of Maori on Film

Several recent film-makers have explored Maori reality on film, in films which have achieved international acclaim. **Niki Caro**'s recent Oscar-nominated *Whale Rider* is a stirring adaptation of Witi Ihimaera's novel about a young girl's struggle to win the approval of her patriarchal grandfather and fulfil her destiny as a tribal leader in a small community on the East Coast of the North Island, which weaves a contemporary story with Maori myth, faith and heritage to demonstrate how the past impacts on the present and the path ahead. A decade earlier **Lee Tamahori**'s film adaptation of the Alan Duff novel *Once Were Warriors* brought the poverty and violence of dispossessed urban Maori to the screen. Maori experience has long been a favourite theme of New Zealand film-making – bringing with it a bitter polemic on the ownership and exploitation of the image. **Geoff Murphy** followed his comic tale of hoons on the run with a light-hearted revisionist quasi-Western set in the New Zealand Wars, *Utu* (revenge). **John Laing**'s *Other Halves* and **Mike Walker**'s *Kingpin* also portrayed urban and young Maori life with serious concern – also from a Pakeha point of view.

The film that revolutionised the depiction of Maori on film was *Tangata Whenua – The People of the Land*, a six-part television documentary made by Maori film-maker Barry Barclay, which for the first time gave Maori people some control over their own image. Barclay went on to direct classic feature films *Ngati* and *Te Rua*, and the documentary *The Neglected Miracle*. **Merata Mita**, at the vanguard of Maori woman directors, and an articulate spokeswoman, has commented that while Pakeha film-making circles around the notion of the white man or woman at odds with his/her environment, with his/her country and himself/herself – a 'colonial syndrome of dislocation'– Maori film is driven by 'identity, resolution and survival'. Her film *Mauri*, the documentary *Patu!* – a record of the bitter social division around the 1981 apartheid South African rugby team's tour – and *Bastion Point–Day 507* – which portrays the end of the most famous of Maori land protests – all take up these themes. Mita's documentary feature *Mana Waka* assembled centennial footage of the making of a waka (ceremonial canoe) for the 150th anniversary of the Treaty of Waitangi in 1990.

Many of the very first locally made moving pictures showed Maori scenes – such as canoe hurdle racing at Ngaruawahia, recorded in 1899 – although Maori people regarded the 'capturing' of their image with some suspicion from the outset. **James McDonald** filmed Maori tribal customs as ethnographic material for the Dominion Museum between 1918 and 1923, creating an important archive. Early foreign film-makers exploited the 'native' people, in films such as Frenchman **Gaston Méliès'** melodramatic *Hinemoa, How Chief Te Ponga Won His Bride* (1912), and American **Alexander Markey** was sent by Universal Studios to make a romantic drama about the Maori people in the 1920s – but he displayed such arrogant insensitivity that he was forced to leave the country without finishing the film. Pioneering New Zealand feature film-maker **Rudall Hayward** directed classic Western-style films *The Te Kooti Trail* and *Rewi's Last Stand* (1940) – pioneer times through Pakeha eyes, but filmed with respect for Maori courage and integrity – and in 1972 made a more biculturally complex documentary-feature, *To Love a Maori*. **John O'Shea**'s Pacific Films production company broke new ground in the 1950s, not just in the portrayal of Maori-Pakeha relations, but in its attempts to establish a modern New Zealand feature-film industry. *Broken Barrier*, another film by Pakeha about Maori, exposed the racism encountered when a Pakeha man forms a relationship with a Maori woman. O'Shea went on to make *Runaway* (1964), an allegorical film about the possible future of New Zealand once its ties with Britain were severed, and a comedy pop musical, *Don't Let It Get You*.

## Experimental Film

New Zealand has not been without its experimental film-makers either. The grandfather of New Zealand art film – who did most of his work in Britain and the United States, but bequeathed his collection to a foundation at the Govett-Brewster Art Gallery in New Plymouth, allowing him to be reclaimed as a national hero – was **Len Lye**. His early work combined elements of modern art with Maori, Aboriginal and Samoan tribal art – to the bewilderment of critics. Throughout his career he remained a true original, pioneering 'direct' film-making (images scratched directly onto celluloid) and kinetic sculpture. By the 1960s a whole host of experimental artists and film-makers were queuing up to step into Lye's shoes: well-known names include Tony Williams (*The Sound of Seeing*), **Geoff Steven** (*But Then*), **Martyn Sanderson** (*A Stitch in Time*), the **BLERTA** collective, which combined music and performance with films, and experimental video artists **Philip Dadson** (and the **From Scratch** collective) and **Leon Narbey**. More recently, music video has been one of the most experimental areas of commercial film-making, while much art film has moved into art galleries and alternative contexts (such as Merylyn Tweedie's Popular Productions).

## Visual Arts

The visual arts in New Zealand have followed a parallel path to New Zealand literature. In the first hundred years of European settlement, paintings of the landscape romanticised and 'sold' the country. Some paintings functioned as advertisements for new immigrants, such as the scenes of coastal settlements by **Charles Heaphy** and **William Fox**. Others like **John Bar, Clark Hoyte** and **John Gully** brought the western European Romantic tradition to the rugged landscapes of the interior. **Gustavus von Tempsky** focused on overblown depictions of Maori warriors, while at the turn of the century **Gottfried Lindauer, Charles Frederick Goldie** and **Louis John Steele** depicted 'the last of the old type of better Maori' in portraits of noble, dignified elders. In the 1890s **Petrus van der Velden**, **Girolamo Pieri Nerli** and **James McLauchlan Nairn** brought new ideas of Realism, Impressionism and a looser style of *plein-air* painting to the New Zealand landscape. The next generation of artists, including **Frances Hodgkins** and **Raymond McIntyre**, was so influenced by these imported hints of modernism that they left New Zealand for the more sympathetic environment of Europe; Hodgkins left in 1913 and by the 1920s had established a reputation as a British avant-garde painter.

New Zealand painting as an expression of national cultural identity began to take off in the 1930s, with the work of a group of painters now labelled the regionalists (or nationalists). British immigrant teacher **Christopher Perkins** urged the artists he taught to develop their own national school based on local subject matter and the harsh, clear lighting he saw as typical of New Zealand; his iconic painting *Taranaki* supplied a model of regionalist realism: stylistically it has the graphic qualities of a Japanese print, while symbolically the cone-shaped mountain with its head in the fertile clouds of Maori lore feeds the dairy industry at its foot. Affinities can be found in the work of **Rata Lovell-Smith, Rita Angus** and **Doris Lusk**, artists preoccupied with place and local identity, expressed through concern with realist depictions of typical small-town and rural scenes. Angus's *Cass* is perhaps *the* classic of this genre, with its rural railway station and telegraph poles set against the foothills and peaks of the Southern Alps. For these painters and generations to come, the words of critic A. R. D. Fairburn on the New Zealand landscape were like a scripture: 'There is no golden mist in the air, no Merlin in our woods, no soft, warm colour... Hard, clear light reveals the bones, the sheer form, of hills, trees, stones and scrub.'

In a later realist revival, **Don Binney** drew upon the inter-war realist tradition to make new, sharper images of motifs like coastal landscapes, incorporating flattened, outlined forms of native birds above the land; his works have a distinctive graphic quality which clearly draws on the hard-edged clarity of Angus' works. Related to Binney's work is that of **Robin White**, whose early painting is stylistically close to his; like him, she often used precise contours so that her forms have an unusually sharp focus; unlike him, she often introduced figures into her compositions, imbuing them with a social content now very clearly of its time – typical suburban or rural women. This realist strand in New Zealand painting continues in the works of **Grahame Sydney, Glenda Randerson, Peter Siddell, Karl Maughan** – who has made his name with mural-esque paintings of flower gardens – and others.

## Colin McCahon

While the regionalists went in one direction to create a cultural identity for New Zealand, the country's most influential artist, Colin McCahon, followed a more modernist line. Artists **John Weeks** and **Louise Henderson** were among the first to bring the formalist concerns of modern art to the country, in Cubist-style works. But of the pioneers of modern art in New Zealand, **Sir Mountford Tosswill (Toss) Woollaston** has a position of greater prominence. He was influenced by another British immigrant teacher, **Robert Field**, who brought a Fauvist use of colour and a spatial awareness that owed much to Cézanne. Woollaston found inspiration for his art in the ordinary rather than the grand landscape, and in uncompromising formal treatment of the figure – flattened and primitive. His fluid, expressionistic, earthy-toned *Taranaki* is a contrast to Perkins' (*see* p.93), which shows off Woollaston's exceptional painterly qualities.

Colin McCahon, now widely regarded as New Zealand's most important modern painter, reflects many theoretical aspects of modernism, but with a very personal interpretation; his work defies categorisation. Misunderstood by many as an élitist whose work is hard to get a grip on, he aimed to communicate with the 'ordinary people' with whom he was happiest hanging out down the pub. Maybe his reputation for difficulty was earned by his preoccupation with religious and moral issues, given substance in a sombre palette symbolically related to notions of good and evil. Landscape is a constant reference throughout McCahon's painting, a metaphor for the relationship between God and man; his early works evolved his own kind of regional landscape. Works like *Takaka Night and Day* share the realists' formal interest in the stark New Zealand landscape, but his pronounced use of light and dark adds a spiritual dimension. In his later works the use of religious imagery and text makes this more overt. McCahon was among the first Pakeha painters to recognise that the land of settlement was not empty, by inscribing Maori language, genealogy and history on the land in paintings like *Parihaka Triptych*. Large works like *The Northland Panels* reflect McCahon's experience of Rothko's large-scale sublime paintings.

At the time that McCahon was exploring the spiritual profundities of the land, contemporaries **Gordon Walters** and **Milan Mrkusich** were pioneering abstraction in New Zealand. Walters took the 'primitive' imagery of rock paintings and the traditional Maori motif of the koru (a fern leaf) as the basis for his abstractions (*Te Whiti*). Mrkusich experimented with grids of colour and later with gestural painting and pure formalism. Other abstract painters include **Don Peebles**, **Melvin Day** and **John Drawbridge**. **Ralph Hotere**'s style of minimalist abstraction has a pronounced political and social consciousness, revealed in imagery by symbolic blackness, the use of materials such as corrugated iron, poetry and Maori texts which draw attention to the environment.

# Since the 1980s

Since the 1980s, New Zealand art has fragmented into different strands. **Rudolf Gopas**, **Philip Clairmont** and **Tony Fomison** have been at the forefront of a neo-expressionist tendency taken up and turned inside out by **Jeffrey Harris**, **Pat Hanly** and **Philippa Blair**. Other painters have moved into more contemporary forms of abstraction, among them **Gretchen Albrecht**, **Ian Scott**, 'abstract expressionist' **Allen Maddox** – who has devoted his career to a single grid motif painted with emotive immediacy – and the painterly surface of the grids of **Geoff Thornley**.

In the postmodern age, figurative painting, appropriation of images from the mass media and pastiche of high art have emerged. Artist **Billy Apple** played with the exchange between artist and patron in a series called *Sold*. **Richard Killeen** plays with figurative imagery in a varied and thought-provoking way; the works for which he is most well-known are cut-outs, which are a mix of figurative and non-figurative 'signs' cut out of aluminium, which can be assembled in any composition. **Dick Frizzell** is another artist who has brought humour to his art, drawing on low-art sources such as fish-can labels and cartoon characters in his painting; in his *Tiki* series, he has even dared to debunk Maori imagery. The deadpan realism of his landscapes is conceived in the same ironic way. **Paul Hartigan** has also based his work on low-art imagery such as neon signs and tattoos, even satirizing the pretentiousness of postmodern theory in a series of neon works called *Art Speak*.

**Denys Watkins** is another painter who has moved between genres and types of imagery. **Bill Hammond** has become popular for his surrealist-style paintings, while **Gavin Chilcott** uses an eclectic range of imagery in a playful way that alludes to the glossy materialism of the 1980s and 1990s, in which everything is reduced to an artificial convention of taste. Further artists of note, although with a shifting place in the critical hierarchy, include **Jane Zusters**, **Tony Lane**, **John Reynolds** (who writes and doodles on paper or canvas supports, alluding to low-art sources like graffiti and hand-written signage) and **Peter Gibson Smith** (with a series of paintings of bookspines on wooden supports, assembled into mural-sized works; the works are researched and assembled with the help of a computer, but made with the old-fashioned media of egg tempera on gesso).

Relatively few women artists have made it to prominence in the New Zealand art scene. The women's movement of the 1970s to some degree redressed the imbalance, and helped to bring recognition to artists like **Jan Nigro** and **Jacqueline Fahey**, not necessarily working within the male modernist mainstream. The feminist dimension of Fahey's work can be seen in paintings such as *Merry Christmas*, which conveys satirically the multiple demands on a modern woman who must run a house, hold a job and yet escape the stereotype of the housewife bogged down with domesticity. Other artists whose work shows feminist leanings include **Carole Shepheard, Claudia Pond Eyley, Alexis Hunter, Maria Olsen, Julia Morison** and **Merylyn Tweedie**. These artists have variously used quilt and fabric design, domestic subjects, photographic narratives attacking the portrayal of women in the mass media, internal landscapes, archetypes and the Kabbalah to convey their artistic and in some cases feminist concerns. L. Budd, one of the multiple personas of Tweedie, has deconstructed the meaning of self-help books for women by cutting and layering the text. **Judy Darragh** has revisited the stereotypically picturesque, executing 'bad' landscape paintings on tablemats and mirrors, framed with kitsch plastic ferns (*Taranaki*).

## Maori Renaissance: Traditional Arts

In a sense it is illogical to talk about Maori arts separately from Pakeha arts. Many of New Zealand's best writers, film-makers, visual artists and musicians creating work within the dominant European cultural structures are of Maori ancestry or have explored Maori identity and representation in their work; others – whatever their origins – have appropriated Maori motifs, language and themes, layering them in works representative of a bicultural 'New Zealand' identity (*see* above). Overlapping with these 'mainstream' practitioners, however, many traditional art forms have been revived in what has been termed a Maori renaissance. By the time European settlers first arrived in New Zealand, the earlier Polynesian settlers had developed their own distinctive forms and styles of painting, carving, weaving, singing and dancing. Colonisation did its best to destroy this unique culture, but the revival of recent years has demonstrated that Maori arts never reached the primitive stasis that European ethnologists imagined, but have been continually evolving and innovating, partly in response to the influence of Western tools and ideas. Ironically it was a 1984 exhibition of Maori taonga (treasures) in the United States (Te Maori) that woke New Zealanders up to the riches in their own country.

The oldest existing Maori artworks are rock paintings found in the South Island, such as those at Waikari which depict stylised forms of people, dogs, birds and fish, drawn with charcoal and ochre. These paintings were superseded by the more decorative kowhaiwhai painting – usually abstract motifs and patterns – on elaborately carved meeting houses. The introduction of Western steel tools and milled timber brought innovation to this type of building and carving, centred on three main 'schools': Rongowhakaatu of Gisborne, Ngati Porou of the East Coast and Arawa of Rotorua. By the 1800s, Maori carvers were carving not only wooden buildings, but also tools, weapons and ornaments made of bone and pounamu (greenstone), and musical instruments. Maori taonga hold a very different symbolic value to Pakeha art objects, traditionally valued for what they represent and for the stories they carry, providing links with ancestry, with whakapapa and with the Maori spiritual world. Every object has mauri, or life force, and gathers stories over time.

## The Maori Tradition

The influence of Maori tradition on contemporary art and the relationship of Maori artists to the Pakeha art world is a complex one. Cultural borrowings have long gone both ways, from Maori use of the steel chisel to carve meeting houses in the 1840s (now considered traditional classics) to Air New Zealand's use of the koru in its logo, representing New Zealand to the world. While for many New Zealanders the 1984 Te Maori exhibition, at the Metropolitan Museum of Art in New York, opened their eyes to the wealth of historical taonga (treasures), te ao Maori (the Maori world) has long been in flux. Several

Several carving schools have been established to maintain and revive the skills of artisans, who once held a high rank in tribal communities. The most famous is the Rotorua Carving School, established under Apirana Ngata's Maori Arts and Crafts Act of 1926, part of a programme of cultural revival which led Ngata himself to publish a four-volume study of Maori waiata (song). Carvers from the school, and from the school established at Turangawaewae by Te Puea Herangi, were much involved in a revival of waka- (ceremonial canoe-) carving for the 1940 centenary of New Zealand's 'foundation', as well as numerous new meeting houses in the North Island. Ornamental pounamu is the most visible manifestation of Maori carving today. Other crafts that have been revived include flax weaving and the making of feathered cloaks and bags – all traditionally undertaken by women. While the moko (facial tattoo) once showed signs of disappearing, it is once again in vogue.

Outside the visual arts and crafts, Maori identity has traditionally found expression in an oral tradition of waiata (sung poetry) as well as in whaikorero (debate) and karanga (women's call of welcome). Maori creation, the activities of gods, migrations and tribal histories are all charted in oral tradition, while the cultural belief system and social structures have been upheld by a thriving oral literature. Many waiata have now been collected in print. A highly expressive form, waiata carries an inner ancestral depth in songs of love, war, jealousy and heroes. As well as voice, Maori musicians use a range of traditional musical instruments (taonga puoro) – revived since the 1980s by a group known as Te Haumanu (meaning both revival and breath of birds), which has recreated the instruments from museum artefacts, often recreating the sounds through the memories of elderly Maori. Each instrument has its own symbolic purpose, being played for special events such as childbirth, healing or death. The foundation of Black Grace, a group of Maori and Pacific Island dancers, in the 1990s, heralded a revival of dance in Maori tradition. A full range of traditional and new singing and dancing can be seen at annual Maori and Pacific Islands Performing Arts Festivals around the country, although you are most likely to see the haka – a warrior-like 'dance' – when the All Blacks play or on a visit to a marae or cultural centre for tourists.

artists since the 1950s and 1960s have chosen to explore their specifically Maori identity within the framework of contemporary practice. A leading practitioner is **Para Matchitt**, who has taken the war standard Te Wepu, with its imagery of pierced heart, triangle, crescent, six-pointed star and cross originally appropriated from playing cards and Catholic nuns, and reinterpreted it in wood. Pakeha artists have also paid mihi (acknowledgement) to Maori art in their work, with varying degrees of sensitivity: **Theo Schoon** and other 'primitivists', who found inspiration in rock paintings; **Gordon Walters**, much pilloried for his cold abstraction of a motif (the koru) imbued with significance – in contrast to Matchitt's use of the mangapore motif complete with its symbolism of survival; McCahon, who appropriated Maori beliefs as well as styles – but whose tribute to prophet Te Whiti lacks the cultural understanding of Maori artist **Selwyn Muru**'s (while Walters entitled a series of works 'Te Whiti' – after a street name where he grew up). Other artists dealing with Maori identity include **Robyn Kahukiwa**, **Emily Karaka**, **Kura Te Waru Rewiri**, **Diane Prince**, **Shane Cotton** (who has revisited the 'who owns the koru' debate), **John Walsh** and **Peter Robinson**, whose *Percent* paintings explored just how much of his identity was Maori.

In the 21st century, the New Zealand art scene is vibrant and diverse. The nationalistic concept appears passé, with most serious artists engaged in a postmodern discourse of representation mediating reality. Reputations come and go so fast that the best approach to identifying artists of the future is to check out commercial and public art galleries in Auckland, Wellington, Christchurch, Dunedin and the provincial centres.

# Music and the Performing Arts

New Zealand is not the obvious place to come for world-class or cutting edge live classical music, opera or ballet, although New Zealanders buy a lot of recorded music and are avid radio listeners (a 1987 survey showed that two-thirds of New Zealanders listen to music every day). The country does, however, boast one professional national orchestra – the **New Zealand Symphony Orchestra** – and major regional ones in Auckland, Wellington, Christchurch and Dunedin. The **New Zealand String Quartet** is the core of an active chamber music scene. 'Pro-am' opera (as well as musicals and drama) is regularly staged in the provinces, and the performing arts scene is given annual international injections of life by arts festivals in the big cities. Several top-level singers have originated in New Zealand – most famously soprano **Kiri Te Kanawa** and bass **Donald McIntyre** – and choral singing, with its origins in missionary hymn-singing, is one of the most popular forms of both amateur and professional music-making. The country can even claim a handful of 'classical' composers, starting with Victorian Romantic **Alfred Hill**. Home-grown composition came into its own in the 1930s and 1940s (in parallel with the first 'nationalist' writers and artists) with **Douglas Lilburn**, who cleared a path for the likes of **David Farquhar, Lyell Cresswell, Gillian Whitehead, Larry Pruden** and the more avant-garde work of **John Rimmer** (electronic instrumentation of natural sounds) and **Philip Dadson** (experimental performance music).

New Zealand does boast a world-class reputation for its popular music. In the 1950s and 1960s, **Johnny Devlin, Ray Columbus** and the Invaders, and **Max Merritt and the Meteors** brought rock and roll to the country. It was in the 1970s, however, that truly New Zealand bands took off, led by the uncompromisingly original **Split Enz** – still the best-known and best-loved local band – with their wild costumes and the songs of **Phil Judd** and brothers **Tim and Neil Finn**, and more alternative acts such as **Bruno Lawrence** and **BLERTA**. Since then, aided by independent recording studios such as Flying Nun, a more-or-less random selection of great NZ bands straddling several genres has included The Chills, **The Clean, Shihad, Straitjacket Fits, Crowded House, Moana and the Moahunters, The Muttonbirds, Dave Dobbyn, Don McGlashan, Shona Laing** and **Chris Knox**. The only downside to the New Zealand music scene is that once bands get successful they tend to take off for Australia or Europe in search of international stardom – with varying success. The most recent 'hit' export has been **The Datsuns**, a group of long-haired rockers from a small provincial town. Several bands have hit the big-time locally with home-grown reggae/dub – **Salmonella Dub, Black Seeds, Phoenix Foundation**. In another genre, virtuoso saxophonist **Nathan Haines** has made a name for his nostalgic style of jazz. Country music also has a following, especially in the South Island; the humorous **Topp Twins** are a household name.

## Comedy

There are countless honourable mentions that could be made, among them **Havoc** and **Newsboy**, aka Jeremy Wells and presenter of the satirical show *Eating Media Lunch* (now in its seventh series since 2003), but one comedy duo stands out: **Flight of the Conchords**, now starring in their very own HBO series with their very own brand of self-effacing Kiwi-ness and musical pastiche.

# Sports

Hordes of people fly halfway round the globe to tramp, ski, snowboard, jetski, wakeboard, kayak, sail, fish, hunt, dive, surf and bungee jump in New Zealand, so why not engage in a few adrenaline-pumping activities if you're planning to move there too? Team sports and the outdoors are what the country is best at, and its landscapes provide the perfect backdrop for releasing energy. From village-green cricket and local soccer and rugby to abseiling and paragliding, anything's possible. There are even one or two gentler open-air pursuits, such as bird- or whale-watching and rambling, for those who want to increase their vitamin D intake without bringing on a heart attack.

## Team Sports

Wherever you live in New Zealand there'll be a sports association that you can join to participate in rugby, soccer, cricket, netball and other team sports. If you're super-keen you'll get a chance to join the association committee too and sit in on endless discussions of toilet facilities, bar tariffs and waterlogged pitches. School-age children will automatically draw you in to spending Saturdays at the sidelines of the game, cheering on your hapless infant as he or she is pounded by kids five times his or her size, with thighs like kauri trees and not an iota of compassion for skinny, knock-kneed British kids. Some children love it, however, and before you know it you may find yourself washing club T-shirts and packing your little darling off to matches here, there and everywhere around the country. Adults can muscle in on a myriad of league teams too, which may involve deadly serious try-outs and frequent coaching sessions in the evenings as well as at weekends. If you're more interested in just kicking a ball around to keep the blood flowing, join a work team or get together with a group of mates and have a laugh.

## Water Sports

God may have created the seas for the fishes to swim in, but man has thought up a million other purposes for large expanses of water. Come summer, you'd have to take a pretty strong stance not to find yourself heading for beaches, lakes and rivers for a **swim**. The four biggest cities, Auckland, Wellington, Christchurch and Dunedin, all have their own beaches, and the fifth largest, Hamilton, is a short drive away from the famous surfing beach at Raglan. But most Kiwis, especially of the familial variety, will head away from home for at least some of the six weeks of summer (from Christmas until the end of January) for a seaside holiday. Traditionally this has taken place among groups of friends and extended family at baches – simple shacks that provide shelter in between picnics, barbecues and frolicking on the beach – or campgrounds. Increasingly over the past five to 10 years baches and municipal campgrounds have been sold for exaggerated sums to foreigners and wealthy city people in search of prime 'absolute beachfront' property. Beaches are now lined with flashy houses with tinted plate-glass windows, and remote beauty spots are restricted to the super-rich who can afford to stay in 'luxury lodges'. The traditional beach holiday does persist, however, thanks to a few sane people who have resisted development and the Department of Conservation's campgrounds.

If splashing around in the nearest river or jumping the waves is not quite enough for you, there are plenty of activities to spice up the waters: kayaking, waterskiing, wakeboarding, surfing, surfcasting, game-fishing, sailing, white-water rafting, diving galore. Take your pick.

While **surfing** is perhaps more quintessentially Australian, you can ride the crest of the wave in cooler New Zealand waters too. Raglan featured in that famous surf movie, and there are good surf beaches dotted around the coasts of both North and South Islands. Clockwise around the North Island from the northern tip of Northland, the best places to head for the surf are Whangamata in the Coromandel, Matakana Island and Mount Maunganui in the Bay of Plenty, Hick's Bay, Gisborne and Mahia Peninsula on the East Cape, Castlepoint and remote Tora on the Wairarapa coast, Lyall Bay in Wellington (right by the airport; surf to the sound of aircraft engines, *Apocalypse Now*-style), Fitzroy Beach in Taranaki, Manu Bay at Raglan, Piha and Muriwai Beach west of Auckland, and Ahipara Beach on the west coast of Northland. In the South Island, clockwise from Picton, the rideable breaks are at Mangamaunu and the Kaikoura Peninsula, Taylors Mistake and Sumner Bar outside Christchurch, St Clair Beach near Dunedin, Centre Island close to Invercargill, and Punakaiki and Tauranga Bay on the West Coast. Surf conditions at any time depend on winds, tides and currents; follow the guys with the surf boards strapped to their roof racks. For expert information consult **Surfing New Zealand, www.surfing. co.nz**, where you can find out about surf schools too. Easily accessible public beaches are patrolled by surf lifeguards in summer, but some of the best surf beaches are off the beaten track, and unpatrolled. You'll need a wetsuit to surf in New Zealand waters except for high summer in the north of the North Island.

**Kayaking** is a fabulous way to glide over the waters, reach hidden coves and inlets and observe birds and orcas. Coastal settlements have kayaking clubs, and more touristy places offer guided kayak trips, with boats and equipment provided. Abel Tasman National Park can be accessed by kayak across relatively shallow, calm waters. The lakes and sounds of Fiordland can be explored with a guide by kayak too, as can the Marlborough Sounds. In the north, the islands of Hauraki Gulf, the Bay of Islands and the Coromandel Peninsula are all well-explored by kayak too. You can also kayak on inland rivers and lakes, such as Lake Taupo, the Whanganui River, and many of the waterways around Queenstown and Wanaka.

Team New Zealand may have subjected the nation to a humiliating defeat at the 2002 Americas Cup in the Hauraki Gulf (when the team's boat sank), followed by an unsuccessful bid to reclaim the title in Valencia in 2007, but budding Russell Couttses are still **sailing** competitively or racing yachts around just for the fun of it. Most coastal towns with a harbour have a sailing club, which you can join to meet other sailors and get crewing. Junior club members can learn to sail and race dinghies most of the year. The Bay of Islands and

Auckland are the country's top sailing waters. **Windsurfing** is also popular on calmer waters.

One way to get close to marine life is to spend your time trying to catch it. **Fishing**, of one sort or another, occupies many a Kiwi weekend. If you want to catch your dinner cheaply, try surfcasting – fishing with a rod off the beach. It's certainly a pleasant way to while away the hours, even if the success rate is low for any fish other than the unjustly despised kawahai (a rather oily fish, best smoked). Hi-tech advances like the kontiki – a raft that you send out to sea on the end of a line – are more likely to catch you a haul of snapper or gurnard. If you're really flash, you'll go out on a boat. Many guys own their own, but you can also hire them for the day. The economics of your catch don't quite add up (you'd be better off buying fish and chips), but the sound of fat spitting in the deep fryer and crinkling newspaper can't quite match the experience of being out on the open sea with dolphins and sharks swimming around. If you're lucky you might even haul in a big yellow-fin tuna, kingfish or marlin. Surfcasting happens just about anywhere that sea meets land, but the best big-game-fishing areas are the Bay of Islands, Whitianga on the Coromandel Peninsula and around Whangarei in Northland. For freshwater fishermen, the lakes and rivers of both islands are well stocked with trout and, in the far south, salmon. The rivers around Lake Taupo are particularly famous for their trout. You can hire rod, reel and tackle in many places. To fish inland, contact the local Department of Conservation office or sports shop for a fishing permit.

For the less aggressive, **scuba diving** is the ideal way to see what's going on underwater without disturbing it. Again, the Bay of Islands, Hauraki Gulf, Great Barrier Island and Marlborough Sounds are popular dive sites, but the best of all are around the Poor Knights Islands, off the coast of Northland near Whangarei; for tourists of political subversion, the wreck of the *Rainbow Warrior* is nearby. These are just the top spots: you can dive just about anywhere south to Invercargill and the sounds of Fiordland.

You'll definitely have seen pictures of screaming, laughing tourists being carried down frothing torrents on **jetboats** or **white-water rafts**. There's an element of real danger, but in the hands of experienced operators the risks are minimised. (The flattest, safest rivers are given a 'grade' of I and the steepest, most risky are graded VI, with variations in between, so you can get an idea of what you're in for.) An archetypal activity of the Shotover and Kawarau rivers around Queenstown in the South Island, white-water rafting is something you can do on the upper reaches of many other South and North Island rivers including the Buller and Karamea rivers in the north of the South Island and the Tongariro, Wairoa and Rangitikei rivers in the central North Island. Excursions are usually by the day, including travel to and from the river launches. The flashest include helicopter drop-offs. **Jetskiing**, **waterskiing** and **wakeboarding** are other options for getting around on the water. If you can't identify a club, ask at sports shops.

# Land Sports

New Zealand is a surprisingly hard place to go for a quiet **ramble**: there's no network of established rights of way and land is either private, farmed and fenced, or too rugged to access; beaches and riverbanks are the best places for gentle walks. If you're keen on serious trekking, however, there are numerous magnificent trails through national parks. These routes are well-maintained by DOC volunteers, and punctuated by huts and campsites at convenient intervals. The only drawback with these superb walks is that the best of them are extremely well-trodden, even crowded; for some you have to book in advance so as to avoid walking in a crocodile. Nonetheless most of these walks do require a reasonable level of fitness and adequate preparation. This applies in particular to the more mountainous parks, where weather conditions are always uncertain and even experienced walkers and climbers frequently go missing. Some of the best-known tracks are the Milford, Tongariro Crossing, Routeburn, Kepler, Lake Waikaremoana and Abel Tasman, but there are many others too, through bush and forest. All provide an opportunity to observe wildlife first-hand, and walkers are asked to treat the environment with care.

For detailed information on where to walk, DOC publishes a range of leaflets and guides, and there are innumerable walking guides including the Lonely Planet *Tramping in New Zealand* book. Maps of New Zealand are disappointing if you're used to the Ordnance Survey, but Land Information New Zealand does produce some detailed topographical maps. If tramping's a little too tame for you, the Southern Alps are a haven for **mountaineering**. Check out the **New Zealand Alpine Club (www.alpineclub.org.nz)** for information. Guided walks across the Fox and Franz Josef glaciers are possible even for the relatively inexperienced. If your legs are aching at the thought of all that walking, you can always **cycle**; it's even possible to cheat on the mountains, and get dropped off at the top so you only have to do the downhill bit.

# Winter Sports

As the surfing, rafting, diving and kayaking season ends, the skiing and snowboarding season begins. It lasts roughly from June to October, and provides plenty of scope for **downhill** and **cross-country skiing, ski touring, heli-skiing** and **snowboarding**. The best way to get access to the snow as a resident is probably to join a ski club, although there are some commercial resort-type ski fields too. You can hire equipment and pay for ski passes by the day or season. In the North Island most ski slopes are around Mount Ruapehu. The top resorts are Whakapapa and Turoa, Tukino and Manganui on Mount Taranaki. South Island skiing is mainly around Queenstown and Wanaka, which also offer resort-style nightlife. The slopes are at Coronet Peak, the Remarkables, Treble Cone, Cardrona and Waiorau. There are other ski areas in South Canterbury (Ohau,

Mount Dobson and Fox Peak), Mount Hutt, Mount Potts, Porter Heights, Arthur's Pass and Craigieburn, Hanmer Springs and the Nelson Lakes region. The great thing about New Zealand is that you can reach the ski slopes for a couple of days from just about anywhere.

# Sky Sports

This would not be a guide to New Zealand if it didn't mention **bungee-jumping**. Head for Queenstown and join the queues to throw yourself off a bridge supported by a giant elastic band. **Skydiving** is another way to make a V sign at your own mortality, by hurling yourself out of a plane, which you can do around Taupo and Rotorua in the North Island and near Wanaka and Queenstown in the South Island (among others). **Paragliders** jump off various cliffs around the country too, including Queenstown and Te Mata Peak in Hawke's Bay.

# First Steps

04

New Zealand is in fashion. Flick through the pages of any glossy travel magazine and there it is, topping reader surveys of the best global destinations, alongside stunningly photographed feature articles on wine trails, or scenic treks in Fiordland. It's clean, it's green, it's '100 per cent natural' (or so the tourist board would have us believe). More than 15,000km (nearly 10,000 miles) of coastline, much of it spectacular and most of it unspoilt, plus lakes, fiords and mountains are the perfect setting for trekking, boating, whitewater rafting, fishing, whale-watching, even bungee-jumping – and all several thousand kilometres away from the overcrowding and stresses of life in built-up, polluted Britain.

But how does all this translate into real life? Much as some of us might wish it to be, for most of us life is not a beach. In fact, despite sheep-farmer stereotypes, more than 80 per cent of New Zealanders live in cities. While foreign millionaires rush to buy up prime coastal land for paradisaical playgrounds, and those who can afford it buy a few hectares (acres) near beauty spots to live in semi-isolated rural bliss (a mass phenomenon known in New Zealand as 'lifestyle living'), most of us still need work, shops, schools, doctors and hospitals, and some sort of community to settle into.

So what does New Zealand have to offer the average person looking for a better life? Since the earliest days of European settlement it has attracted Britons keen to find their own bit of space and opportunity – and this is still true. The living is (relatively) easy, New Zealanders are easygoing, nature is accessible and New Zealand in the 21st century has its own distinctive cultural identity too. The economy is thriving, skilled workers are in demand, business ventures are welcome, the cost of living is lower and property is still cheaper than in the UK (although wages are commensurately lower too). For British immigrants much is familiar, starting with the language, and if it seems a long way from home, the South Pacific also feels remote from terrorist threats and war.

# Why Live and Work in New Zealand?

## The Living Is Easy

The New Zealand lifestyle is famously relaxed and New Zealanders famously friendly. Wherever in the country you choose to settle, you will find the basic logistics of life are simply easier than in Britain. You are unlikely to have to travel more than 20 minutes to work unless you live in Auckland – or somewhere so remote that the drive down rural roads is a choice. Even in the bigger cities you'll never be far from countryside, of which there is lots (with roughly the same land mass as the UK, New Zealand's population is 4.25 million, compared with the 60 million people crammed into the UK). While the country's clean, green, '100 per cent natural' image may have been overstated (the last 150 years have seen the native ecosystem destroyed by high-intensity farming), there is still more than enough room for everyone (and a backlash against environmental destruction). You will never have the sensation of being unable to 'get away from it all' that you do in some parts of Britain, and everybody who moves to New Zealand from southeast England comments on how glad they are to be away from the traffic.

You might opt for 'lifestyle living' New Zealand-style: enough space to keep a few sheep and chickens and grow your own vegetables or, if you're more ideologically driven, a fully self-sufficient organic set-up. If, like the majority of New Zealanders, you end up living in town or in the suburbs, your weekends are still likely to include a trip to the beach, walking, fishing, boating or, for the more adventurous, high-adrenaline outdoor activities from kayaking, surfing, whitewater rafting, wake-boarding and kite-surfing to bungee-jumping. Even if you skip the sports, summer days will be wrapped up with a few beers and a barbecue. And in winter, most parts of the country are within reach of mountains for a skiing or snowboarding excursion. A typical New Zealand holiday is spent camping or staying in a bach (simple cottage) with a large group of friends and family – typically by the sea, or near a lake or river. (The number of incidents on the daily six o'clock news reporting people lost at sea or on mountain tops is testimony to the popularity of the outdoor life.)

As well as extensive national parks, where native New Zealand forest, bush and wildlife have been conserved or revived for recreation, the country has masses of farmland. Sheep stations, dairy farms, orchards and market gardens have now been joined by vineyards; all that agriculture – and the unpolluted seas – mean plenty of fresh local produce, from meat, fish and cheese, fruit and vegetables, to wine. If you're after something more sophisticated on a Saturday than a sausage sizzle on the beach, there are top-notch winery-restaurants in the wine-growing regions, a thriving café and bar culture in the larger towns and innovative 'Pacific Rim' or fusion cuisine just about everywhere.

If you are beginning to feel that the flip side to all this wholesome outdoors stuff is that there might not be much going on culturally, you will be pleased to discover that the contemporary cultural scene in New Zealand is lively – especially the visual arts, music, literature and film – and well spread around the regions. Although some of the major public art galleries are in the cities – Auckland, Wellington, Christchurch and Dunedin – others are dotted around the smaller regional towns: the Govett-Brewster in New Plymouth is one of the country's top exhibition spaces. There may be more venues for music in Wellington than elsewhere, but the Datsuns started off in Hamilton, and every summer brings rashes of open-air gigs and festivals. Local and international writers can be found in the excellent public libraries everywhere in the country. And while most small-town cinemas show mainly Hollywood films, film festivals with a strongly local bent tour the country too.

While its own culture is increasingly vibrant, diverse and self-confident, New Zealand is far removed from the traditional centres of culture; anyone used to imagining themselves at the hub of metropolitan life and consumer choice may find New Zealand sometimes rather parochial. You will occasionally get access to a more international arts scene at arts festivals, which bring performers from abroad; if, however, your perfect weekend is a chamber concert or avant-garde play and a stroll round an exhibition of Old Masters, the latest in European conceptual art or American modernism, you may find yourself frustrated – and it's too far from anywhere to hop on a low-cost flight for a stimulating 'city break'. But New Zealand's distance from Europe is its attraction too. The geographical remoteness of this South Pacific archipelago, added to its political neutrality on the international scene, make it feel like one of the safest places in the world to live. Even if it costs you around £1,000 a person for a trip 'home' (not worth undertaking for much less than a month), the Internet, e-mail and cheap phone rates make it easy to stay in touch with events on the far side of the world, and with friends and family.

## Cultural Difference and Public Life

For emigrants from Britain, there is the advantage of moving to a country where English is the main language, and which in many aspects mirrors the old country: the political and legal systems are closely modelled on the British systems, and business and finance run along similar lines. In many political and economic areas, New Zealand has in fact shown the mother country the way: New Zealand women got the vote in 1893, 25 years before their British counterparts; the country gained a 'cradle-to-grave' welfare state in 1938, with childcare benefits, pensions and a health service that provided the model for Britain's post-war reforms; it then showed Margaret Thatcher the way to dismantle social policy through economic monetarism in the 1980s.

The parliamentary system is modelled on the Westminster system, although New Zealand has done away with its upper house and since 1996 has elected its parliaments with a system of proportional representation (replacing the British-style first-past-the-post system). While the Crown is still represented in New Zealand by an appointed governor-general, the Queen's powers are limited. Unlike in Republican Australia, however, the word 'republic' is bandied about rather as Britons talk about doing away with the monarchy – enthusiastically until they realise that a US-style presidency could be worse. The legal system severed its links with the Privy Council in London, long its final court of appeal, in 2004, replacing it with a New Zealand Supreme Court, but to all intents and purposes institutional life has none of the baffling foreignness of, say, Italy, Spain or France.

As far as fitting in goes, New Zealand's British colonial origins make it unchallenging for Britons at the basic practical level – even if culturally New Zealand has been moving away from its 'Britain of the South Pacific' image over the last decades, recognizing at last that it is a bicultural state with a multi-ethnic identity. Maori culture has become more visible, and Pacific Island and Asian immigrants have brought new customs with them, too. But rugby and cricket – both British imports – are still fundamental to New Zealand life (soccer has never taken off in quite the same way, although you will hear the results of British league games on the radio, and see European championships on television). Subtle culture shocks might relate to the 'blokishness' at some levels of

## Case Study: Fated to Live in New Zealand

Gilda Swayn ended up in New Zealand 'by fate'. Her parents moved here some years ago, following her brother. When her father became ill in 1993 she came over to visit and 'loved it because you have so much space'. She kept coming back. Coincidentally, a good friend had moved here and, sadly, died. Barry called Gilda after the death, and kept calling until Gilda and Barry got married in 1997. 'I had already been divorced for some time and had no intention of marrying again,' says Gilda, 'but it was my karma to meet a New Zealander.' She has now been living here for seven years, and her daughter's family is trying to join her – although the family links have not been sufficient to procure them visas.

An energetic woman in her 50s, Gilda loves New Zealand – 'the lifestyle's a lot easier, it's more beautiful, cleaner, healthier, the weather's magnificent' – but has not found it easy to find her niche. Although she has worked all her life, and had a good job as a PA at Deutsche Bank in London, she could not find a job in New Zealand. 'I loved my job,' she says, 'and it was such a struggle finding a job here.' She tried all avenues – writing letters, knocking on doors, scouring the papers, agencies – and says she would have accepted any job, but was offered nothing. In the end a woman she met at a party said she could give her work at a bank. In the meantime Gilda had set up her own homestay business. 'I had to create something to keep my sanity,' she says. Having sold her house in England, she had invested in property – initially being duped by a real-estate agent into buying 'a nice house in the worst area'; she managed to sell it and did up a cottage for upmarket holiday rentals, using her 'flair' for home decorating.

There is lots that Gilda misses – although less over time. 'The initial two years were the most painful,' she says. Most of all she misses her daughter and grandchildren, but a close second is the buzz of city life, meeting her girlfriends and going out after work, and the shopping – although she adds that a lot has changed here in seven years, with new restaurants and shops opening all the time: 'There's so much more happening now, it's much more cosmopolitan.' She hasn't always found it easy to be accepted into her husband's family and circle of friends either, and has found that people are 'nice, loving and sweet, but not very accepting'. In compensation, she has taken up golf and plays regularly at the world-class Cape Kidnappers golf course.

New Zealand society, and the domesticity of many New Zealand women (men really do stand around the barbecue clutching bottles of beer and talking about speedboats and fast cars, while women chop salads in the kitchen and talk about babies and shower-cleaning products); however, these are balanced by a well-earned reputation for fairness and honesty. New Zealanders tend to be friendly, too, with little of the cliquishness that typifies British social life; you will be welcomed into the local community if you participate in sports, work or school events.

Be aware, though, that New Zealand society is very small for anyone used to the relative anonymity of life in Britain's big cities. Among a certain middle-class milieu, everybody knows everybody (not just in one area, but around the country – there's said to be one degree of separation, and when put to the test this has often been proven), and in any professional field, the same applies. Most towns are so small that you will bump into your bank manager at the swimming pool, share a nanny with your insurance salesman and bump into everyone you've ever met when your child is having a tantrum in the super-market. This can be good and bad: it's rather cheering to smile and wave to all your new best friends as you walk down the street; on the other hand people you barely know will soon get to know your darkest secrets...

New Zealand is a child- and family-friendly country, with children welcome everywhere and good education and healthcare services. Many expatriate New Zealanders return to settle down after seeking fame and fortune overseas, and there are many young families among new immigrants. There is a proliferation of pre-school childcare options, good 'kindies' (nursery schools) and primary schools and decent state secondary education. Further education may fall short of the high-calibre research that takes place in some British or American univer-sities, but it easily matches them at undergraduate level. Access to doctors and hospitals is better than in Britain, and standards of care in most cases higher – although there are more charges for treatment, and the New Zealand health service is struggling, like most in the developed world, to balance the principle of access for all with the increasingly expensive treatments available. Waiting times for surgery can be years long. It is worth bearing in mind that services in the more remote areas are few and far between: if you've set your heart on living in an idyllic rural location, it may turn out to be too far from medical care for a retirement paradise, or too far from good schools to raise a family.

## Economic Opportunity: Will You Be Better Off?

At the start of 2008 the New Zealand economy is still going strong, although the domino effect of the global credit crunch is starting to be felt. A clutch of New Zealand finance companies went bust in the second half of 2007, and the property market has cooled significantly. Ever higher petrol prices affect the cost of both imports (including basic foodstuffs such as bread) and exports, while internal fuel prices are inflationary. The New Zealand dollar has hit record high after record high, driven up by high interest rates (around eight per cent) that attract global 'carry trades' to a peak in early March 2008 of 81 cents (US) to the 'kiwi'. The high NZ dollar has hit exporters' profits – including those from tourism – hard; meanwhile imports have become cheaper, but goods brought in from anywhere other than China are still luxury items. Unemployment is around three per cent, and with such a tight labour market certain skilled trades and professions are endemically in demand – notably doctors, nurses and teachers; building and related trades are still in short supply, too, even though the property and construction boom has started to drop off (*see* **Working in New Zealand**, 'The Labour Market', pp.206–208).

At current exchange rates (at the time of writing £1 buys around NZ$2.50), the pound sterling still goes a relatively long way and the cost of living in New Zealand is moderately low. When you first arrive you will be struck by how cheap everything is: a cappuccino that cost you £3 in the UK will cost you NZ$3 in New Zealand; in the first week of your new life you may get a parking fine – for NZ$12, less than the cost of a London Travelcard (£5.90); cheap clothing stores abound, where you can pick up T-shirts for under NZ$10. Compared to a trip to Waitrose, a weekly shop at Pak'n'Save will seem a bargain – although there's less choice too. But your initial perception of how cheap everything is will soon wear off once you are immersed in the New Zealand economy and earning at local rates. In the June 2007 quarter, the average weekly income for all people was $667 ($832 for men and $510 for women), according to Statistics New Zealand. New Zealanders do, however, boast a high standard of living despite a relatively low GDP per capita. Working practices are similar to the UK (most people work a 40-hour, five-day week), with a minimum of regulation. Social security has been slashed since the 1980s, and taxes are lower than or comparable to UK rates – there is no capital gains or inheritance tax, the lowest income tax rate is 19 per cent, the top income tax rate is 39 per cent and goods and service tax (GST) is charged at 12.5 per cent (although petrol tax is exorbitant).

You are unlikely to get a highly paid corporate job in New Zealand, as the economy is too small to attract global big business, but you will find a positive 'can-do' approach to starting your own business. Although New Zealand is less egalitarian than it would like to think (there's an established aristocracy of large landowners and middle-class professionals), the man building a flash new house next door is more likely to have made his money setting up his own courier company or subdividing the old beachfront campground than from a golden handshake as CEO of a loss-making corporation. There is a much greater sense of opportunity than in Britain. Even if you don't make it big time you will probably have a better life here.

The country is keen to bring in investment, and the foreign millionaires who buy up wineries, beaches and beauty spots tend to be treated with adulation – even if it means selling off the family silver at internationally low prices. From the point of view of the small-scale migrant, if you are planning to sell up and move wholesale from Britain, any capital you can bring with you will go a long way to buying you a chunk of paradise. While housing prices soared in the early years of this century, they have levelled off recently. If you can afford a seaside property, 'lifestyle block' or old colonial villa in New Zealand now, you're unlikely to regret it in the long term.

A word of warning: it is expensive to travel home and, more ominously, to think of moving back to the UK. People who make the move often feel that they have burned their bridges – while selling a property in the UK might leave them with enough capital to buy a good house in New Zealand, if they want to do the reverse they may find themselves priced out of the market, and would find it hard to save enough money at New Zealand rates of pay to move back.

# Getting to New Zealand

Options for getting to New Zealand are restricted to the cheapest flights on offer at the time you wish to travel. It is well-nigh impossible to reach New Zealand as a boat passenger these days, unless on a cruise ship. If you decide, however, to ship your household and belongings, they will travel by container ship. Peak (most expensive) times of year for travel are between December and March (Christmas and the summer season), and again over the British summer holidays (July and August). The best prices are usually found by booking well in advance, although you may be lucky enough to get a cheap last-minute deal if you miss the boat with your advanced planning. Scheduled flights cost around £1,000 return, but cheaper fares can be found.

By all means research flights on the Internet, but a travel agent is still most likely to get you a good deal unless you have endless hours of patience. If travelling from London, pick up one of the free magazines for Australians and New Zealanders around Earl's Court (for instance *TNT*) or check magazines such as *Time Out* or Sunday newspaper supplements for agents advertising the best deals (usual caveats apply).

Flights go either east or west around the world from the UK. Either way the journey will take you more than 24 hours, including at least one stop-off. By the time you arrive, you'll be so disorientated by the time difference, jetlag and all those hours of restricted blood flow to brain and legs, you won't even know how long you've been travelling. Some people prefer to get it over with as fast as possible (the fastest option is Air New Zealand via Los Angeles, in 24 hours and 15 minutes); others, less hurried, choose to make the trip itself a feature of their move, buying a 'round-the-world' or similar ticket and travelling through Asia en route. Common routes are via Singapore, Dubai, Bangkok, Tokyo, Hong Kong or Sydney. Many these days feel that the safest option is not via the USA (where you may also have to undergo interminable security clearance procedures in transit). All international flights other than a few from Sydney arrive in Auckland or Christchurch; the airport at Wellington (the capital) is unable to accommodate long-haul planes owing to a short runway and strong winds.

# Airlines

## Air New Zealand
Flies daily London Heathrow to Auckland and Christchurch, via Los Angeles, in 24–26hrs; also flies via Singapore daily in association with Singapore Airlines.

- **New Zealand: t** 0800 737000, reservations call centre (freephone within New Zealand) **t** (09) 357 3000; **www.airnz.co.nz.**

- **UK:** Air New Zealand Travel Centre, Upper Ground Floor, New Zealand House, 80 Haymarket, London SW1Y 4TQ; reservations **t** 0800 028 4149 (freephone), **t** 0870 000 0123 (arrivals and departures), **t** (020) 8600 7600 (regional office); **www.airnewzealand.co.uk.**

## Singapore Airlines
Flies to and from Auckland and Christchurch via Singapore, in association with Air New Zealand. Flight times average around 28hrs.

- **New Zealand:** reservations (freephone) **t** 0800 808909; 10th Floor, West Plaza Building, cnr Fanshawe & Albert Street, Auckland, **t** (09) 379 3209 (ticketing), **t** (09) 256 6630 (airport); 13th Floor, Forsyth-Barr House, cnr Colombo and Armagh Streets, PO Box 13-514, Christchurch, **t** (03) 366 8099 (ticketing), **t** (03) 353 1950 (airport); **www.singaporeair.com.**

- **UK:** Zone E, Terminal 3, Heathrow Airport, Middlesex TW6 1NT, **t** 0844 800 2380, from within UK **t** (020) 8961 6993, **t** (020) 8750 2708 (ticketing), **t** (020) 8750 2718 (fares), **t** (020) 8745 4151 (flight information); **www.singaporeair.com.**

## Cathay Pacific
Flies to and from Auckland and Christchurch via Hong Kong.

- **New Zealand:** National Bank Tower, 11/F National Bank Centre, 205 Queen Street, 1313 Auckland, **t** 0800 800 454, **t** (09) 379 0861; **www.cathaypacific.com.**

- **UK:** Terminal 3 Departures, Heathrow Airport, **t** (020) 8897 9335 (flight enquiries), **t** (020) 8834 8888 (reservations); **www.cathaypacific.com.**

## Emirates
Daily flights from London Heathrow and London Gatwick to Auckland and Christchurch via Dubai and one or more stops in southeast Asia and Australia.

• **New Zealand**: Level 8, 45 Queen Street, Auckland, **t** (09) 968 2208; **t** 0508 EMIRATES (reservations), **t** 0508 364728 (reservations); **www.emirates.com**.

• **UK**: **t** 0844 800 2777 (reservations); **www.emirates.com**.

## Japan Airlines

Flights from London Heathrow to Auckland via Tokyo.

• **New Zealand**: **t** 0800 525 747; Jalpak International Oceania Pty Ltd, 12th Floor, Westpac Tower, 120 Albert Street, Auckland, **t** (09) 379 9906; Jalpak International Oceania Pty Ltd, 4th Floor, Clarendon Tower, 78 Worcester St, Christchurch; **www.nz.jal.com/en**.

• **UK**: Hanover Court, 5 Hanover Square, London W1S 1JR, **t** 0845 774 7700 (local call), **t** (020) 7618 3224; **www.uk.jal.com/en**.

## Thai Airways International

Flights most days from London Heathrow to Auckland via Bangkok.

• **New Zealand**: Level 8, Citybank Building, 23 Customs Street, Auckland City, **t** (09) 377 3886 (reservations); **www.thaiair.com**.

• **UK**: 41 Albermarle St, London W1S 4BF, **t** (020) 7491 7953 (sales and ticketing), **t** 0870 606 0911 (reservations); **www.thaiair.com**.

## Qantas

Flights from London Heathrow to Sydney, connecting with flights to Auckland, Wellington and Christchurch. It is also possible to fly from London to Bangkok or Singapore, connecting with Thai Airways or Singapore Airlines flights to Auckland. Alternatively, flies Auckland to Los Angeles, connecting with whatever flights are available from there to London.

• **New Zealand**: Qantas House, Ground Floor, 191 Queen Street, Auckland, **t** 0800 808 767 (freephone); **www.qantas.com.au**.

• **UK**: **t** 0845 774 7767 (local call rate), **t** (020) 8600 4300; **www.qantas.com.au**.

# Travel Agents

Check the travel supplements of weekend newspapers, listings magazines and the free press for antipodeans for agents offering good deals.

Travel agents who specialise in flights from the UK to New Zealand include:

• **Flight Centre**: **t** 0870 499 0040; **www.flightcentre.co.uk**. Around 60 agencies around Britain, including 22 in central London alone.

• **STA**: **t** 0871 2 300 040; **www.statravel.co.uk**. At least 47 branches around the UK, of which 12 in London, including: 74 and 86 Old Brompton Road,

London SW7; 117 Euston Road, London NW1, **t** (020) 7361 6161; Bristol **t** (0117) 929 4399; Leeds **t** (0113) 244 9212; Manchester **t** (0161) 834 0668; Oxford **t** (01865) 792800; Cambridge **t** (01223) 366966; Edinburgh **t** (0131) 226 7747.

Internet-only agents include:

- **www.cheapflights.co.uk.**
- **www.dialaflight.com.**
- **www.ebookers.com.**
- **www.flights4less.co.uk.**

# Removals and Relocations

If you're moving for good, or even for an extended period, you will probably want to pack up and ship out most of your belongings, too. A multitude of companies are keen to offer their services with everything from air freighting the stuff you will need in a hurry (over and above what you can take on a flight with you) to packing up the contents of your household and transporting more specialist items such as cars and fine art.

Most companies now offer more than a few cardboard boxes, a roll of packing tape and a packer – everything from counselling to childcare – but focus on the fundamentals: reliability, insurance, speed and cost. Remember to clarify details such as whether your goods will be shipped to your door at the other end, or can be stored until you find somewhere to live (and related costs). Be aware that container ships take around six weeks to sail around the globe.

Shop around and get two or three quotes. A trawl through the *Yellow Pages* or Internet will find a plethora of companies. Most will pay you a home visit to assess how much you have to ship – and do their sales pitch. Here are a few with reliable reputations:

- **Anglo Pacific:** 5/9 Willen Field Road, Park Royal, London NW10 7BQ, **t** 0800 633 54 45, **t** (020) 8965 1234; **www.anglopacific.co.uk.** Excess baggage, shipment of household effects and fine arts. Also offices in Manchester and Glasgow.

- **Crown Worldwide Ltd:** 19 Stonefield Way, South Ruislip, Middlesex HA4 0BJ, **t** (020) 8839 8000; **www.crownrelo.com.** Also has offices in Birmingham, Glasgow, Leeds, Aberdeen and in Ireland.

- **Dolphin Movers Ltd:** 2 Haslemere Business Centre, Lincoln Way, Enfield, Middlesex EN1 1TE, **t** 0800 032 9777 (freephone), **t** (020) 8804 7700; **removals@dolphinmovers.com, www.dolphinmovers.com.**

- **Excess International Removals:** 4 Hannah Close, Great Central Way, London NW10 0UX, **t** 0800 783 1085 (freephone), **t** (020) 8324 2066; **www.excess-baggage.com.** One of the largest. Container services, air

**freight and excess baggage. Also has offices at airports and railway stations country-wide.**

For removal firms within New Zealand, *see* **References**, p.266.

# Customs

Relocation and shipping companies will assist with the clearance of your goods through customs, but it's worth checking out New Zealand's customs regulations before you pack. You should be able to import all your household effects and a car free of charge as long as you intend to live in New Zealand, have been using all the items before your departure and are importing them for your own use. There may be a charge for any new, unused goods that you bring with you. Certain categories of goods are restricted – agricultural items (this includes food and plants), pets, medicines, weapons, money (over NZ$10,000 in cash) and pornography.

The most stringent aspect of customs clearance is agricultural quarantine (make sure you clean your shoes if you've been on a muddy walk before travelling and be prepared to answer questions about when you last went camping). You, or someone acting on your behalf, will need to be present to clear your shipment through customs. You will need to complete an Unaccompanied Personal Baggage Declaration, get agricultural clearance from the Ministry of Agriculture and Fisheries, get any special permits (such as a Police Permit to Import for firearms), produce your passport and an inventory of the goods shipped, and a Bill of Lading or similar shipping arrival papers (shippers should be able to do this for you).

Visit the New Zealand customs website, **www.customs.govt.nz**, for full details of prohibited goods, or items for which you may have to pay a fee.

# Red Tape

New Zealand lies somewhere between fortress America and the borderless European Union in terms of accessibility. The country welcomes new migrants – people who will contribute by bringing valuable skills or qualifications, setting up a business, or making a financial investment. It also offers opportunities for family reunification by allowing residents and citizens to sponsor family members for residence.

With its small population, low unemployment levels and strong economy, the country is keen to attract new short-term, long-term or permanent migrants, provided they can prove that they are able to contribute to the country through their skills, qualifications, experience, talents, business ventures or financial investment. Immigration is defined by the New Zealand government as a key source of talent, skills and investment, and a counterbalance to the emigration of native New Zealanders, especially those of working age. Students, young people, and the partners and family members of New Zealanders may also be able to move to New Zealand or stay there for extended periods with relative ease. Short-term visitors such as tourists and students are major foreign-currency earners for New Zealand.

To be granted the right to work or live in New Zealand requires a serious application supported by proof of your value to the country, or at the very least evidence that you will not be a burden on its state, and the process can be lengthy.

There are two main options when considering an application. The first is to apply for a work visa or permit (visas are granted outside the country, permits within), valid for up to three years initially and renewable indefinitely for further blocks of time. The second is to apply for permanent residence, which entitles you to live in New Zealand for as long as you want. (There are ways to turn a work permit into a residence permit too.)

Either way, there are three broad areas of eligibility: through what you can do, what you can invest financially, or your relationship to a New Zealander – i.e. talent, wealth, blood or love.

# Work Visas, Permits and Residence

With its small population, low unemployment levels (currently 3.4 per cent) and thriving economy, New Zealand is keen to attract workers to fill the shortfall in its own workforce. If you can demonstrate that you will benefit the country by your talents, skills, qualifications or experience, without taking work from New Zealanders, you are in a good position to get a visa or permit to work in New Zealand. Certain occupations are actively recruited – notably the medical, nursing and teaching professions and information technology experts (see 'The Long-term Skill Shortage List', p.122).

People with **exceptional talents** in the fields of sports, culture and the arts are actively encouraged to bring their talents to New Zealand, too. Other **skilled workers**, in areas including most of the building trades, among others, may also be permitted to work in New Zealand if there are specific jobs available which no New Zealanders are able to fill.

**Young people** and **family members of New Zealanders** may qualify to work in New Zealand without special skills.

Work visas and permits may be issued for up to **three years**, and extended for further periods of up to three years at a time.

If you have a job offer before you set out for New Zealand, you should apply for a work visa before your departure. If are already in New Zealand, you should apply for a work permit before you start work.

# Where to Apply for Visas and Permits

The latest information on visa and permit applications, fees payable and application forms can be found on the **Immigration New Zealand** website (**www.immigration.govt.nz**), or from one of the offices listed below.

## Visitor Visas

British citizens and passport-holders may visit New Zealand for up to six months without a visa. Residents and passport-holders of many other countries, including the European Union, the United States of America and Canada, can visit for up to three months visa-free; they must, however, provide evidence of onward (or return) travel and funds for their stay.

## Visa Applications (i.e. lodged in the United Kingdom)

- **Immigration New Zealand**, New Zealand House, 80 Haymarket, London SW1Y 4TE, **t** 09069 100100 (within the UK; calls charged at £1 per minute), **t** + 64 9 914 4100 (from outside the UK, 7am–7pm NZ time; standard overseas rates).

## Permit Applications (i.e. lodged in New Zealand)

- For all phone enquiries call the **National Call Centre, t** 0508 558855.

- **Auckland area and Northland**: for general enquiries call the National Call Centre, **t** (09) 914 4100 (from within the Auckland region) or **t** 0508 558855 (from outside the Auckland region). There are Auckland regional branches of Immigration New Zealand in central Auckland, Henderson and Manukau, which will process certain types of application in one day at the branch without appointment. This same-day service is only available for returning residents' visas, urgent travel, replacement labels (e.g. transfer of a visa from an old to a new passport) and confirmation of permit conditions. Branch offices are open Mon–Fri 8.30–3 only, and are closed on public hols.

- Auckland Central: Level 4, 280 Queen St, Auckland CBD, f (09) 914 4118.

- Henderson: 39 Paramount Drive, Henderson, Auckland, f (09) 969 3498.

- Manukau Branch: Level 2, Cogita House, 20 Amersham Way, Manukau City, Auckland, f (09) 914 4728.

For all other visas, permits and residence applications, send your forms and documents to: Immigration New Zealand, PO Box 76895, Level 3, 20 Amersham Way, Manukau City, Auckland.

- **Christchurch and upper South Island**: Immigration New Zealand, Level 1, Crystal Plaza, 73–5 Cathedral Square, Christchurch (open Mon–Fri 10–4); postal address: PO Box 22111, Christchurch, f (03) 963 7815.

- **Dunedin and lower South Island**: Immigration New Zealand, Level 6, Evan Parry House, 43 Princes Street, Dunedin (open Mon–Fri 9–3); postal address: PO Box 557, Dunedin, f (03) 955 7606.

- **Hamilton and upper central North Island** (phone numbers with the (07) prefix): Immigration New Zealand, Level 5, Westpac House, 430 Victoria Street, Hamilton (open Mon–Fri 9.30–3); postal address: Private Bag 3013, Hamilton, f (07) 957 3217.

- **Palmerston North and lower central North Island** (phone numbers with the (06) prefix): Immigration New Zealand, Level 4, State Insurance Building, 61–75 Rangitikei Street, Palmerston North (open Mon–Fri 10–3); postal address: PO Box 948, Palmerston North, f (06) 952 6910.

- **Queenstown**: Immigration New Zealand, c/o Work and Income Office, 9 Shotover Street, Queenstown (open Mon–Fri 9–3); postal address: PO Box 246, Queenstown, f (03) 441 2476.

- **Wellington and surrounding region**: Immigration New Zealand, Level 7, Regional Council Centre, 142–6 Wakefield Street, Wellington (open Mon–Fri 8.30–3); postal address: PO Box 27149, Wellington, f (04) 917 6640.

- **Business Migration Branch (all areas)**: Level 6, Aurora Chambers, 66 The Terrace, PO Box 3705, Wellington.

# Qualifying for a Work Visa, Permit or Residence

Anyone applying for a visa or permit to work in New Zealand is required to demonstrate good health, good character and good English (*see* p.129).

If you wish to live and work in New Zealand permanently, there are four basic options available when applying for a visa or permit:

• The **Skilled Migrant** category, for people who have the skills, qualifications and experience New Zealand needs.

• The **Work to Residence** category, which allows you to get a temporary work visa and/or permit as a step towards gaining permanent residence. Applicants may be qualified in occupations that are currently in demand in New Zealand, or may have an exceptional talent in sports or the arts.

• The **Residence from Work** category is for people who are already in New Zealand on a Work to Residence permit, and want to apply for residence.

• If you are a key employee of a business that is relocating its operations to New Zealand, you can apply for a work permit and later a residence permit under the **Employee of a Relocating Company** category.

You can also apply in the **Family** category or as an **investor**. If you wish to work in New Zealand **temporarily** there are three further options:

• Immigration New Zealand grants temporary work visas and permits to people who have a job offer from a New Zealand employer, people skilled in occupations that are currently in demand, people coming to New Zealand for a particular purpose or event, and people who want to gain work experience or work after studying in New Zealand.

• If you are aged between 18 and 30 you may be eligible to stay in New Zealand on a working holiday.

• There are several alternatives for people who want to do seasonal work planting, maintaining, harvesting or packing crops in the horticulture and viticulture industries.

## Skilled Migrant Category (SMC)

To apply for a visa or permit under the Skilled Migrant category you must be aged 20–55 and meet the basic requirements for good health, good character and good English. The application process is lengthy and you will be required to present sheaves of documents, as well as paying three fees (obviously subject to change, but currently totalling NZ$1,400) to support your application.

The aim of this category, from Immigration New Zealand's point of view, is to attract skilled workers to fill the gaps, long-term and immediate, in the labour market. The New Zealand government issues two lists of workers in short supply (updated twice a year): the **Long-term Skill Shortage List** – skills that the country will want to attract for the foreseeable future – and the **Immediate Skill Shortage List** – positions that are currently vacant and which employers have been unable to fill (*see* boxes, overleaf). It is safe to assume that skilled workers will always be in demand in the following areas: education, health and medicine, information and communications technology, agriculture and farming, and the engineering trades.

## The Long-term Skill Shortage List

Immigration New Zealand issues a biannual list of occupational groups in which there is an 'absolute (sustained and ongoing) shortage of skilled workers in New Zealand'. For updates to the list check the website, **www.immigration. govt.nz**. The list in 2008 includes:

- food technologists
- early childhood education teachers, secondary teachers and university lecturers
- veterinarians
- social workers
- auditors
- civil, electrical and telecoms engineers
- building foremen, surveyors, urban and regional planners
- medical specialists: anaesthetists, general surgeons, intensivists or ICU specialists, clinical cardiac and respiratory physiologists, pathologists, psychiatrists, radiation oncologists, radiologists, renal physicians, specialist physicians in palliative medicine, obstetric and gynaecological registrars, general practitioners (rural areas only)
- other medical positions: anaesthetics technicians, audiologists, cytotech-nologists, dieticians, medical laboratory technologists, medical social workers, midwives, nurses, occupational therapists, osteopaths, pharma-cists, physiotherapists, psychologists, radiographers and radiation therapists, sonographers, speech language therapists
- tradespeople: diesel mechanics, , motor mechanics, boat builders, cabinet makers, carpenter-joiners, electricians, fitter welders, fitter and turners, plumbers
- information technology professionals: in management and projects management, policy planning and research, systems analysis, systems development, technical advice and consultancy
- horticultural occupations: grower managers, orchard managers
- film animators
- chefs
- electronics (various roles)

Stage one is to submit an **Expression of Interest (EOI)**. This is a points-based initial assessment of your suitability as a migrant. It and other application forms can be downloaded and/or submitted online, **www.immigration.govt.nz**. Points are awarded for offers of skilled employment in New Zealand, qualifica-tions, past work experience, and factors such as age and familial ties.

### The Immediate Skill Shortage List

While the skills listed on the Long-term Skill Shortage List do not change much from year to year, the Immediate Skill Shortage List is short-term, specific and regional.

The list in 2008 includes: arborist, architect, autoglazier, baker, beekeeper, bicycle mechanic, bricklayer, broiler farm manager, crane operator, dentist, dispensing optician, drainlayer, engineering draughtsperson, fibreglass tradesperson, fire alarm technician, flat weaving specialist, florist, graphic artist, hatchery manager, IT specialist, jockey, licensed cadastral surveyor, marine laminator, optometrist, perfect binder, primary school teacher, radio frequency technician, scaffolder, shepherd, skydive tandem master, sommelier, stud groom (in season), turkey farm manager, winemaker, yacht rigger.

The Immigration New Zealand website offers a useful 'Self Assessment Guide for Residence in New Zealand'. Skilled employment and graduate or postgraduate qualifications clock up the most points (50 each), followed by youth (five points are deducted for every five years over 30) and work experience (five points are added for every two years' skilled employment). Bonus points can be gained for particular skills or a commitment to live in an underdeveloped area (outside Auckland). If you claim over 100 points you enter a pool of applicants for fortnightly selection; if you claim over 140 points, go straight to the next stage – an **Invitation to Apply (ITA)**.

At this stage you will be asked to submit supporting documents for your application: police and medical certificates (*see* p.129), proof of good English and evidence of a job offer, qualifications and experience to support your points claim. A full assessment will then be made of your suitability as a migrant (in the eyes of Immigration New Zealand); you may be invited to an interview. If your application is successful you will be offered a residence visa or permit; if it is borderline, you may be offered a nine-month Work to Residence visa or permit.

## Work to Residence Category

The Work to Residence category allows you to live and work in New Zealand for up to 30 months, with the possibility of ultimately gaining residence and living in New Zealand permanently. In order to gain a Work to Residence visa or permit you need to meet certain criteria, starting with good health and good character. You must also convince Immigration New Zealand that you intend to work in your permitted field and leave when your permit expires, if you do not gain residence, and you must be under 55.

If you meet these basic requirements, you may apply for your visa or permit under one of several different policies: if you have a job offer from a New Zealand employer and your occupation is on the Long-term Skill Shortage List; if you have a job offer from a New Zealand employer under the Talent (Accredited

## Occupational Registration

In New Zealand, registration is required by law in order to undertake employment as any one of the following: accountant, architect, barrister or solicitor, chiropractor, clinical dental technician, clinical dental therapist, dental hygienist, dental technician, dental therapist, dentist, dietician, dispensing optician, electrician, electrical service technician, enrolled nurse, line mechanic, medical laboratory scientist/technologist, medical laboratory technician, medical practitioner, medical radiation technologist, nurse and midwife, occupational therapist, optometrist, osteopath, pharmacist, physiotherapist, plumber, gasfitter and drainlayer, podiatrist, psychologist, real estate agent, cadastral (land title) surveyor, teacher, veterinarian.

The process of registration can be lengthy and expensive, requiring at least the presentation of a full documentary record of qualification and practice, in some cases the sitting of examinations and continuing competency tests, and in all cases a registration fee.

## Occupational Registration Authorities

• **Accountants**: Institute of Chartered Accountants of New Zealand, PO Box 11 342, Wellington, t + 64 (0)4 474 7840, f + 64 (0)4 473 6303, **www.icanz.co.nz**.

• **Architects**, New Zealand Registered Architects Board (NZRAB), PO Box 11 106, Manners Street, Wellington, 6142, New Zealand, t + 64 (0)4 471 1336, **info@nzrab.org.nz**, **www.nzrab.org.nz**.

• **Barristers and solicitors**: New Zealand Law Society, PO Box 5041, Wellington, t + 64 (0)4 472 7837, f + 64 (0)4 473 7909, **www.lawyers.org.nz**.

• **Chiropractors, dieticians, dispensing opticians, medical laboratory technicians, osteopaths, midwives, optometrists, podiatrists**: Registration Boards Secretariat, PO Box 10 140, Wellington, t + 64 (0)4 499 7979, f + 64 (0)4 472 2350, **www.regboards.co.nz**.

• **Dental/clinical dental technicians**: Dental Technicians Board, PO Box 11 053, Ellerslie, Auckland, t + 64 (0)9 579 7096, NZ freephone t 0800 620 066, f + 64 (0)9 525 1169, **www.dentaltec.org.nz**.

• **Dentists, dental therapists, dental hygienists**: Dental Council of New Zealand, PO Box 10 448, Wellington, t + 64 (0)4 499 4820, f + 64 (0)4 499 1668, **www.dentalcouncil.org.nz**.

Employers) work policy (i.e. your job offer is from an employer who has been accredited to recruit staff from overseas); if you have recognised talent or ability in the arts, culture or sports and it is deemed that your time in New Zealand will enhance the country's reputation, under the Talent (Arts, Culture and Sports) work policy; or if you want to establish a business in New Zealand, under the Long-term Business Visa/Permit category.

- **Electricians, electrical service technicians, line mechanics**: Electrical Workers Registration Board, PO Box 10 156, Wellington, **t** + 64 (0)4 472 3636, NZ freephone **t** 0800 661 000, **f** + 64 (0)4 473 2395, **www.ewrb.govt.nz**.

- **Engineers**: Institute of Professional Engineers New Zealand, PO Box 12 241, Wellington, **t** + 64 (0)4 473 9444, **f** + 64 (0)4 474 8933, **www.ipenz.org.nz**.

- **Medical practitioners**: Medical Council of New Zealand, PO Box 11 649, Wellington, **t** + 64 (0)4 384 7635, **f** + 64 (0)4 384 8902, **www.mcnz.org.nz**.

- **Medical laboratory workers, scientists**: PO Box 7242, Wellington South, **t** + 64 (0)4 801 6250, **f** + 64 (0)4 381 0270, **mls@medsci.co.nz**.

- **Medical radiation technologists**: PO Box 7242, Wellington South, **t** + 64 (0)4 801 6250, **f** + 64 (0)4 381 0270, **mrt@medsci.co.nz**.

- **Nurses**: Nursing Council of New Zealand, PO Box 9+ 644, Wellington, **t** + 64 (0)4 802 0247, **f** + 64 (0)4 801 8502, **www.nursingcouncil.org.nz**.

- **Occupational therapists**: Occupational Therapy Board of New Zealand, PO Box 10 202, The Terrace, Wellington, **t** + 64 (0)4 918 4740, **f** + 64 (0)4 918 4746, **www.otboard.org.nz**.

- **Pharmacists**: Pharmacy Council of New Zealand, PO Box 25 137, Wellington, **t** + 64 (0)4 495 0330, **www.pharmacycouncil.org.nz**.

- **Physiotherapists**: Physiotherapy Board of New Zealand, PO Box 10 734, Wellington, **t** + 64 (0)4 471 2610, **f** + 64 (0)4 471 2613, **www.physioboard.org.nz**.

- **Plumbers, gasfitters and drainlayers**: Plumbers, Gasfitters & Drainlayers Board, PO Box 10 655, Wellington, **t** + 64 (0)4 494 2970, **www.pgdb.co.nz**.

- **Psychologists**: NZ Psychologists Board, PO Box 10 140, Wellington, **t** + 64 (0)4 474 0742, **f** + 64 (0)4 472 2350, **www.psychologistsboard.org.nz**.

- **Real estate agents**: Real Estate Agents Licensing Board, PO Box 99 881, Newmarket, Auckland, **t** + 64 (0)9 520 6949, **f** + 64 (0)9 520 6995.

- **Surveyors**: New Zealand Institute of Surveyors, PO Box 831, Wellington, **t** + 64 (0)4 471 1774, **f** + 64 (0)4 471 1907, **www.surveyors.org.nz**.

- **Teachers**: New Zealand Teachers Council, PO Box 5326, Wellington, **t** + 64 (0)4 471 0852, **f** + 64 (0)4 471 0870, **www.teacherscouncil.govt.nz**.

- **Veterinarians, veterinary surgeons**: Veterinary Council of New Zealand, PO Box 10 563, Wellington, **t** + 64 (0)4 473 9600, **www.vetcouncil.org.nz**.

Each of these policies has certain requirements:

- **Long-term Skill Shortage List** work policy: a genuine, full-time offer of work for two years in an occupation on the LTSSL; suitable qualifications and experience for the job, and registration if required for your occupation (for example health workers, see box, above).

• **Talent (Accredited Employers)** work policy: similar to the LTSSL policy, except your job offer must come from an employer who has been pre-accredited to employ non-New Zealanders and your salary must be at least NZ$50,000.

• **Talent (Arts, Culture and Sports)** work policy: an exceptional talent in sports (e.g. being a national team player) or the arts that will enhance New Zealand's accomplishments and participation in your field; sponsorship by a New Zealand organisation of national repute.

For the **Long-term Business Visa/Permit** category, *see* 'Business and Investor Categories', below.

## Residence from Work Category

If you have been granted a visa or permit in any of the Work to Residence categories, you can apply for residence under the Residence from Work category after two years.

## Temporary Work Category

Various categories of people may be eligible for a temporary work visa or permit. Business travellers, international salesmen and diplomats need not apply. Those who may need to apply include: people taking up a job on the Immediate Skill Shortage List, or with an employer who cannot find a suitable New Zealander for the job; anyone visiting for a specific purpose or event (Specific Purpose or Event policy), for example preachers and missionaries, sports referees or coaches, dance or music examiners, flower show judges, performing artists and film-makers (if the unions don't object) and installers of specialist machinery supplied from overseas; students on work experience or wishing to stay on after completing studies in New Zealand; work exchange candidates; partners of New Zealand residents on a temporary visit; tour guides; Thai chefs, Japanese interpreters and the crew of chartered foreign fishing vessels.

### Working Holidays

New Zealand has reciprocal working holiday schemes with a clutch of countries around the world, from Argentina to Uruguay. There are unlimited places for young Britons, aged 18–30, to stay for 12 or 23 months. Conditions apply, including good character and good health, adequate funds to holiday more than work (NZ$350/month) and a return ticket, and a commitment not to enter full-time work or become a prostitute, and to pay tax on your work. Working holidaymakers are encouraged to work in seasonal agricultural, horticultural and viticultural jobs. The Immigration New Zealand website lists some useful resources for finding temporary work, including agencies for fruit-pickers.

## Horticultural and Viticultural Seasonal Work

Temporary and short-term work visas and permits with stringent limitations may be granted to seasonal fruit-pickers and grape harvesters.

# Family Categories

New Zealand citizens and permanent residents may sponsor other members of their family – husband, wife or *de facto* partner (straight or gay); dependent children; parents; adult children or siblings – to come and live with them in New Zealand (**Family Permanent Residence**). All these relatives may in any case qualify to visit temporarily, if not permanently (**Family Temporary Entry**).

To gain residence under the **Family Category (Partnership Policy)** your spouse or partner must be a New Zealand citizen or resident and be prepared to sponsor you. Together you must be able to prove that you have been in a relationship for at least 12 months. Such evidence may range from a marriage certificate or shared bank accounts, tenancy agreements and birth certificates of your children, photographs of you as a couple or 'evidence of you being committed to each other emotionally and exclusively, such as evidence of joint decision-making, an exclusive sexual relationship, and the sharing of household duties, parental responsibility, and spare time'. Although grillings *à la* 'Green Card' are rarely heard of, it doesn't do any harm to know what brand of deodorant your partner uses. Proof of good character, good health and good English are prerequisites, as for all migrants.

**Parents** of New Zealand residents may be sponsored by their child to get a residence permit or visa. The child must have been resident in New Zealand for at least three years and be able to meet a minimum income requirement ($29,897.92 (gross) per annum). Crucially, the 'centre of gravity' of your family must be in New Zealand. This is a complex equation, the essence of which is that most of your children must be resident in New Zealand, or more in New Zealand than in any one other country. (The Immigration New Zealand website lists examples, but even the immigration people seem to find the equation confusing: in some of the examples the figures do not even add up.) Grandparents and legal guardians may qualify in the place of deceased parents.

Under the **Family Category (Dependent Child)** policy, dependent children of New Zealand residents aged under 16 and in some circumstances 17–24 may get a visa or permit to live with their parents in the country. They must be declared on the parents' original residence application and the parents must be lawfully and permanently resident in New Zealand. If the parents are divorced or separated and only one parent is resident in New Zealand, things get complicated: custody and visitation rights of the other parent must not be breached by the child's New Zealand residence.

Brothers, sisters and adult children of New Zealand residents may be able to move to New Zealand under the **Family Category (Sibling/Adult Child)** policy. In order to qualify, they must not have any other immediate family members in the country where they live, must be sponsored by the New Zealand resident sibling or parent and must have an offer of employment.

## Business and Investor Categories

Investors, entrepreneurs and business people are welcomed with open arms to New Zealand, although there are hoops to jump through. There are three basic options to get a visa or permit: the Long-term Business Category, Entrepreneur Category or Active Investor Migrant Policy.

### Long-term Business Category

You can apply for a visa or permit under this category for an initial period of nine months, in which to establish a new business in New Zealand. You will need to demonstrate at the outset that your plans are genuine, that you have a good business plan, investment capital and sufficient funds to live on. You may be able to apply for permit extensions up to three years if you need more time to get the business established.

### Entrepreneur Category

Once your business has been successfully up and running for two years you may apply for permanent residence. You will need to provide full and extensive paperwork to demonstrate that the business is benefiting New Zealand, including the business's certificate of incorporation, accounts and tax records.

### Active Investor Migrant Policy

The Active Investor Migrant Policy, launched on 26 November 2007, aims to attract investor migrants with business experience, international connections and financial capital to New Zealand, to support the country's economic transformation and contribute to the development of innovative, productive and globally competitive firms in New Zealand. It is the millionaire's option for settling in New Zealand. The policy is divided into three categories:

- **Global Investor Category** – for migrants investing NZ$20 million in New Zealand, including at least NZ$5 million in active investment.
- **Professional Investor Category** – for migrants investing NZ$10 million in New Zealand, including at least NZ$2 million in active investment.
- **General (Active) Investor Category** – for migrants investing a minimum of NZ$2.5 million in New Zealand, who have an additional NZ$1 million for settlement funds.

Funds must be invested in an 'acceptable investment' – one that makes money for New Zealand (property development is excluded) – for four years after residence is granted, and investors are required to spend a certain number of days in New Zealand each year.

*Immigration Consultancy*

It is possible to use immigration consultants to help with getting visas and permits. A few well-known and reliable ones are **Immigration Unit (www. immigrationunit.com), New Zealand Association for Migration and Investment (NZAMI; www. nzami.co.nz)** and **Malcolm Pacific (www.malcolm pacific.com)**. *See* **References**, p.254. Many legal firms do immigration consultancy too. In many cases, consultants may not be needed; they are unregulated, and often the information you need for a visa application is readily available. Business migrants, however, may find it worthwhile to seek advice, and consultants also do suggest things you may not think of mentioning, to help tailor your application and ensure the best chance of success.

# Good Character and Health

In order to apply for an extended stay in New Zealand, you will need to provide evidence of good character and health, in the form of a police and a medical certificate. The police certificate must be obtained from the police of your home country and any country in which you have lived for five years or more. It is a statement of your criminal record (excluding driving offences). The procedures for getting this information vary from country to country.

## Police Certificate

In the UK, you are legally entitled to gain access to information about yourself under section 21 of the Data Protection Act 1998. You need to ask for 'Person Record: Prosecution/Criminal History'. Enquiries can be directed through your local police station to the National Identification Service, Room 1229, Metro Police Service, London SW1H 0BG. A fee is payable of approximately £10. (Please note: Inspector Knacker has been known to query applications by phone in the early hours NZ time, so forewarn your family, friends and flatmates that you are not the subject of an Interpol inquiry.)

For details of where and how to apply in other countries, visit the Immigration New Zealand website, **www.immigration.govt.nz**, or enquire at your nearest Immigration New Zealand office.

## Medical Certificate

To obtain a medical certificate, you will need to visit a registered medical practitioner. An approved list of panel doctors can be obtained from Immigration New Zealand, or if there is none in your country your own general practitioner should be able to complete the form. A fee may be payable. An X-ray certificate must also be completed by an approved examining radiologist, or, where there is none, any registered examining radiologist.

## Checklist of Supporting Paperwork Needed for Visa and Permit Applications

• an application form.

• the application fee (depends on where application is lodged, country of citizenship and type of application; around NZ$1,400 for skilled migrants.

• photographs (two recent passport-sized photographs with name and date the photograph was taken on the back).

• passport or full birth certificate showing names of parents as well as child (originals or legally certified photocopies).

• medical and X-ray certificates.

• a police certificate.

• evidence of relationship to spouse or *de facto* partner (*see* p.127), children or other family members (family categories).

• sponsorship form (family categories).

• job offer or proof of continuing New Zealand employment (skilled migrant and work to residence categories).

• proof of qualifications and occupational registration (skilled migrant and work to residence categories).

• proof of work experience (skilled migrant/work to residence categories).

• business plan and proof of investment funds (business and investor categories).

• proof of English-language ability (all categories).

# Citizenship

New Zealand residents may apply for New Zealand citizenship after five years' residence. They must prove their intention to reside in New Zealand, good character, good English and an understanding of the responsibilities and privileges of New Zealand citizenship.

If granted citizenship, you will be invited to attend a special ceremony where you are asked to swear an oath of allegiance to the country.

Grants of citizenship are administered by the **Department for Internal Affairs**, t 0800 22 51 51 (New Zealand only), t + 64 (0)4 474 8123 (from outside New Zealand); **www.dia.govt.nz**, **citizenship@dia.govt.nz**.

# Living in New Zealand

New Zealand has everything to recommend it in practical terms as a place to live. It is easy, and relatively inexpensive, to find a place to live, and, when you've found somewhere you like, the process of renting or buying is straightforward, with plenty of uncomplicated legal guarantees. It's no hassle setting up your water, gas, electricity and phone connections. If power is expensive, at least you have a range of choices in the world of telecommunications – from iPhones to broadband connections (in a world where 75 per cent of people have never even used a phone). Banks are lined up along the high streets waiting to look after your money (and currently offering very competitive interest rates – as much as 8.7% in some cases); they are efficient and highly competitive, with all the modern knobs on like Internet banking, ATMs and electronic transactions – to make it painless for you to spend your money in bland big box shopping centres or the rare groovy boutiques. You'll need a car to get around, but there's almost no traffic, and if you want to go further afield domestic flights will take you to most parts of the country. Unless you get into the P (pure amphetamine) scene or become part of a criminally challenged family you have little to fear from crime and are unlikely to get into a scrap with the police. If you do get in a fight, the excellent healthcare system is there to stick you back together again – or even to cure you of minor ailments – almost for free. Mothers and small children are well looked after by the medical establishment and the welfare service, which will subsidise you to go back to work. You can get a fantastic education, from pre-school to university level, most of it free until the age of 18, too. And you can even retire here on your UK state pension and leave your worldly goods and chattels to your heirs free of inheritance tax.

# Finding a Home

Most people moving to New Zealand end up buying a house, as property prices are considerably lower than in the UK and owning your own home here is almost a must – you won't have anything to talk about at barbecues if you don't. While a relatively small amount of equity from the sale of a property in the UK will go a long way in New Zealand, property prices have shot up in the last five to 10 years, excluding many native New Zealanders from buying a first home, and making the mortgage-free dream of expatriate Brits unrealisable.

## Rental

When you first arrive in New Zealand, however, you may want to rent a house while you decide where you want to live, get to know the area and get a feel for the property market. Since New Zealand has such a high level of home ownership, the stock of rental housing is less extensive than in many other countries, and rental costs are relatively high. It is always advisable to visit a property before agreeing to rent it. First appearances can be deceptive, so make sure you check the basics as well as checking out the general feel of the neighbourhood and factors such as proximity to transport, shops, schools and potential workplaces. Parts of New Zealand can be cold and damp in winter and most New Zealand houses are not well insulated or heated; houses that do not get a lot of direct sun may have problems with damp during the winter months.

Most rental properties are let unfurnished, apart from curtains and carpets, an oven and laundry tub. You may have to provide your own fridge, washing machine and heaters.

## Where to Look

One good place to start looking is the 'To Let' columns of the local newspapers; days vary by publication, but listings are continuously updated on newspaper websites. As in most places, you need to act fast: phone about potentially interesting properties as early as you can. Once you've seen the property, you may also need to make a snap decision if you like the look of it.

Many real estate agents also deal in rental properties, although most prefer to focus on the more lucrative property market. Commission charges, due once a rental contract is completed, should not exceed one week's rent. Letting centres exist too, which charge a fee for you to look at their listed properties – even if you don't find a property from the listings.

## Tenancy Agreements

Once you have found a satisfactory property to rent, you need to sign a **tenancy agreement form** with the landlord. This is a standard form, which your landlord should provide. The agreement should set out the conditions of the lease, in plain language that both sides can understand. Both the tenants and the landlord sign the agreement and keep a copy. The agreement is only legally binding, however, if its terms fall within tenancy law. A landlord cannot enforce what is outside the law, and the tenants cannot give away their legal rights. All tenancies are governed by the Residential Tenancies Act 1986, which provides considerable protection for tenants.

A tenancy agreement must include:

- **the names and addresses of the landlord and tenant, and the address of the property.**
- **the date the tenancy agreement is signed.**
- **the date the tenancy starts.**
- **addresses for service for both the landlord and the tenant (a permanent address, which might be a friend's, family member's or employer's).**

- whether the tenant is under the age of 18.
- the bond amount.
- the rent amount and how often it will be paid.
- the place or bank account where the rent is to be paid.
- any real estate or solicitor's fees paid.
- if the tenant is to pay for metered water.
- a list of chattels (light fittings, curtains, oven and so on) provided by the landlord.
- the type of tenancy (fixed-term or periodic; *see* below).
- the date a fixed-term tenancy will end.

Other conditions may be included too, such as an agreement not to sublet or a limit on the number of people living in the property.

Along with the agreement you will need to complete a property inspection report form, on which you and the landlord record any furniture and fittings provided, and the condition of the property and chattels. For example, if there is a burn mark on the carpet, this needs to be noted so that you will not be held responsible for it when the tenancy ends.

## Bonds

Most landlords require tenants to pay a bond that is generally equivalent to two or four weeks' rent. The landlord will provide you with a **bond lodgement form** that both you and the landlord are required to complete and sign. The landlord must deposit the form and your accompanying cheque for the bond with the Tenancy Services Centre within 23 working days of receiving it. A receipt will then be sent to both you and the landlord. The bond will be refunded to you when you leave the property, unless you have not paid rent or have caused damage. If there is damage to the property, some or all of your bond is used to pay for the repair. When you give notice to move out, the landlord will inspect the property to make sure you have not caused damage. To recover your bond, complete a bond refund form, signed by both you and the landlord, and send it to the Tenancy Services Centre. If you cannot reach agreement with the landlord over the return of the bond, contact Tenancy Services (*see* p.142).

## Rental Costs

Market rentals vary considerably around the country, and depending on the size of the property rented. In 2008 the average weekly rent was between NZ$169 and NZ$486 for properties ranging from a one-bedroom flat to a five-bedroom house. In Auckland, the most expensive region, average rents can be as high as NZ$800 a week or more for a four-bedroom house in the most sought-after districts of the city, and are well over NZ$400 for a similar property in most areas. Wellington rents are almost as high, while Christchurch rents tend to be somewhat lower. The lowest rents are in remote rural areas, small provincial towns and the southernmost tip of the mainland, Invercargill.

To find out the likely cost of rental in the area you are moving to, visit the Department of Building and Housing website and go to the market rent information page, **www.dbh.govt.nz/housing/tenancy/Market-Rent**. This gives a detailed and up-to-date guide of current average and median rental costs, by type of property and area, including the variation in rents in different districts of the major cities. The Department of Building and Housing helpfully describes market rent as what 'a willing landlord might reasonably expect to receive, and a willing tenant might reasonably expect to pay for the tenancy'. While you would expect this equation to settle it in most cases, the **Tenancy Tribunal** can intervene and ask landlords to reduce the rent if they are charging significantly more than is being charged for other similar properties in the area.

Before you set about looking for a rental property, bear in mind that you may have to put down a substantial amount of money up front. You usually need to pay a **fee** to the letting agent if you have used one, a **bond**, and **rent in advance**. You will also need to pay for getting phone, electricity and maybe gas connected. So if your rent is NZ$250 a week, you may have to pay as much as NZ$2,000 when you first move in (e.g. four weeks' rent as bond, two weeks' rent in advance, one week for the agent's commission, phone and power connections).

## Types of Tenancies and How to Terminate Them

The most common form of tenancy is a **periodic tenancy**. This is any tenancy that is not for a fixed time, and that continues until the landlord or the tenant ends it by giving notice, or the Tenancy Tribunal orders that the tenancy is over. Tenants wanting to leave must give 21 days' signed notice in writing and provide their tenancy address and leaving date. If notice is sent by mail, four working days must be added to the notice period. A landlord must give a tenant written notice of at least 90 days, or 42 days if the property is needed for family or employees, or has been sold. Once a landlord gives a tenant notice, the tenant can live in the property until the tenancy ends. Tenants can, however, move out sooner if they give 21 days' written notice to the landlord.

The alternative is a **fixed-term tenancy**, which finishes on a date recorded in the agreement; in this case neither the landlord nor the tenant can end the tenancy earlier. The tenancy automatically ends on the stated date, although you may be able to talk to the landlord about renewing it.

Some fixed-term tenancies are not covered by tenancy legislation – tenancies of less than 120 days and tenancies of five years or more. It is advisable to seek advice from Tenancy Services before signing any contract for these types of tenancies.

## Paying Rent

Rents are determined by market demand and can vary considerably depending on the desirability of the property (*see* 'Rental Costs', pp.134–5). If you think your rent is higher than it should be compared with similar properties, you can apply to the Tenancy Tribunal through Tenancy Services for a market rent assessment. If the tribunal orders a lower rent, the landlord must comply with this ruling and cannot increase the rent for six months. If you have a periodic tenancy, your landlord cannot increase the rent within six months of either the start of the tenancy or the latest rent increase. Rents for fixed-term tenancies, too, cannot be increased more frequently.

Rent is usually paid fortnightly in advance, but it is possible to make monthly payments if your landlord agrees. The landlord must give you a receipt for the rent you pay. If you use automatic bank payments or pay by cheque, your bank records act as receipts.

## Repairs

If something needs repairing, try to talk to the landlord first. If, however, something needs fixing urgently, for instance a leaking hot water cylinder or a blocked toilet, and you cannot contact the landlord, you may get the repair work done yourself and the landlord must refund you the repair cost.

If you ask the landlord to do necessary repairs and then nothing is done, send your landlord a letter requesting that the work be done within 10 working days. If the repairs are still not done, you can make an application to the Tenancy Tribunal. If the problem is serious, the landlord may be ordered to pay you compensation, or you may be able to end the tenancy.

On the other hand, if you damage a rental property or make it unfit to live in, the landlord can give you 10 working days to put things right. If the work is not done, the landlord may ask the Tenancy Tribunal to order you to do the required cleaning or repairs, or the tenancy may be ended.

## Insurance

While the landlord should insure the property itself, contents insurance is important for people who are renting accommodation as it can cover both household possessions and liability for accidental damage to a rental property.

## If It All Goes Wrong

Hopefully it won't, but disputes can and do occur. In the first instance, try to talk to your landlord about any problems. If this does not work, either party can make an application to the **Tenancy Tribunal** by filling in an application to the tribunal, and lodging it with the nearest office. These forms are available at all **Tenancy Services Centres**. An application fee of NZ$20 has to be paid for all applications. Once an application is lodged, Tenancy Services staff will seek to resolve the dispute through mediation. If an agreement is reached it is then usually written down as a mediated order signed by the mediator, landlord and tenant. This order is binding, and can be enforced as if it were a tribunal order.

If mediation fails to find a solution, the two parties can go in person to the Tenancy Tribunal, a court presided over by an adjudicator.

# Buying a Property

The level of home ownership in New Zealand is among the highest in the world, and New Zealanders are renowned for the time and effort they put into building, maintaining and renovating their properties and gardens. (The shed or garage is an essential feature of most properties.)

The New Zealand property market has been going through a sustained boom since 2000–2001; at the time of writing, however, the market has slightly cooled, and may well continue to suffer a knock-on effect from the jittery global economy. While property prices are still much lower than in the UK, they may be more than treble what they were 5–10 years ago. The market varies considerably by region, and even within a region prices can vary considerably from neighbourhood to neighbourhood. Auckland properties are the most expensive, especially in the most desirable city districts, but Wellington property prices have soared too and Dunedin has enjoyed its own mini-boom. Areas popular with foreigners – around Nelson, Napier and Queenstown, for example – have also had runaway property markets over the last few years. The least expensive properties tend to be in rural areas that are not popular tourist destinations, the southern tip of the mainland (Invercargill), and in the less glamorous provincial towns. The rainier, pastoral and remote west coasts of both islands are still quite cheap.

A range of properties is available. Rural '**lifestyle blocks**' – houses with several acres of land on which to keep a pony, a couple of sheep, a cow, a pig and some chickens, and grow your own fruit trees and vegetables – are particularly popular with people wishing to escape city life and make the most of what the country has most of: space. These large '**sections**' usually enjoy panoramic vistas but are within easy reach of an urban centre. The traditional New Zealand home was a suburban house on a quarter-acre section; the sections tend to be smaller now (and to be measured in square metres), but a **suburban home** with a garden large enough to get the lawnmower out every weekend is still where most New Zealanders live. **Apartment** living is beginning to catch on, mainly among students and Asian immigrants.

You won't find many houses more than 150 years old, but dotted around the country are some magnificent wooden **colonial homesteads**, and plenty of **1900s villas** have survived in the cities – many recently restored as their value is recognised. Some regions have their own styles too, such as Napier's Art

Deco buildings, erected en masse after an earthquake razed the city in the 1930s. Architecturally, a lot of recent housing leaves something to be desired. Most **new houses** are put up by developers, with more of an eye for profit than for design or aesthetics, or by owners, who are more likely to use a draughtsman to create the blueprint for their dream home than an architect – often with incongruous results.

The **materials** available since the country's colonial forebears ravaged the forests of native timber a hundred years ago are limited too. While older houses are wooden, there are few brick or stone buildings and most contemporary buildings are timber-framed with some kind of man-made cladding. Many houses are built without attention to their environment, either: they may not make the most of sunshine, may be badly insulated and rarely have central heating (most houses are heated by wood burners, supplemented by gas and electrical heaters; electric 'heat pumps' have caught on in the last few years). Most houses, however, are reasonably solid, and controls over building practice have been tightened, since a scandal over 'leaky homes', by the Building Act 2004 (*see* box 'Leaky Homes', p.140).

## Finding a Home

It is best not to rush into buying a home, even if you are keen to settle as soon as you can. Take time to look around the area you want to buy in and become familiar with the local market. Think realistically about what sort of property meets your needs. You may have rural fantasies, but how much driving do you want to have to do to reach work, schools, shops and other services? Try to look at as many potential properties as possible to get a good idea of what is on offer. And don't let yourself be rushed by real estate agents keen to make a sale and scenting the whiff of foreign money. Even if property values seem to be rising fast, you are better off taking the time to find the right house.

Special property features are run in the Wednesday and Saturday editions of most major newspapers, and a range of free publications providing illustrated property listings is also available from real estate companies. The Real Estate Institute provides national listings at **www.realenz.co.nz**. Properties for sale can also be viewed on the Trade Me website (New Zealand's equivalent of eBay), **www.trademe.co.nz/Trade-Me-Property**.

These are excellent places to start looking, but, once you've done your market research, contact as many real estate agents dealing with your chosen area as you can, as they may be able to show you properties that have not been advertised, or to let you know about new properties as soon as they come on the market.

Most houses are sold through agents who operate on sales commissions, which are agreed with the vendor before the property is offered for sale and are generally around 3–4 per cent of the sale price (much higher than in the UK). Agents can take you to see properties, but you may also be able to view houses

## Property Inspection Checklist

It may be worth engaging a professional building inspector to assess the state of a house before you buy it, but you can start by making your own inspection. Organise a time with the agent when you will not be hurried and check the following points:

• On the exterior, check the general condition of cladding, drainpipes and roof. In particular, look for damaged paintwork, rotten wood, rust, holes, cracks and crumbling mortar, and broken roof tiles.

• Check that cladding is at least 225mm above the ground (grasses or garden), or 150mm from floor level to paved surfaces.

• Under the house, check the piles. Look for makeshift repairs and test wooden piles for rot by prodding with a screwdriver.

• Test floors by jumping up and down to see if the floorboards are springy or squeaky. This, and cracks in the walls and windows, or doors that don't close properly, may indicate problems with the piles or settling.

• Does the house smell damp, or can you see any signs of damp such as stains on walls and ceilings, mould, bubbling or stained paint, bulges in the walls and rotting skirting boards?

• Check power points are working using a power-point tester (from hardware stores) and look for scorch marks.

• In kitchen and bathrooms, check for broken tiles, damp around sinks and showers, mould and missing sealant.

• Check that built-in appliances, such as the oven, are working.

• Turn on taps and check water pressure and strange noises in the plumbing. Check the age of the hot-water cylinder.

• Check for insulation under the floor or in the ceiling.

• Check the condition of fences, paving and driveways, and look over boundary fences for potential issues with neighbours such as overhanging trees or car-wrecking.

without an appointment at 'open homes', held at weekends and advertised in the local paper or real estate publications, when you can just drop in and have a look around.

## Rateable Valuations

Each year the local council provides owners with a 'rating valuation' – what they consider the property (land and buildings) is worth. These values are used to set 'rates', which property owners pay to cover water supply, road maintenance, rubbish collection and other public services. This valuation is a useful price guide, but properties may sell for more (or less), depending on market

## Leaky Homes

In a scandal that erupted in 2002, it emerged that some houses built in the 1990s and early 2000s suffer from leaky home syndrome – they let the water in. Those most at risk of leaking are those using 'monolithic cladding systems' – textured wall surfaces made out of plaster over polystyrene or fibre cement sheeting. They often have recessed windows, roofs with narrow or no eaves, more than one storey, design features such as solid balustrades or complex roof design and envelope shapes where roofs frequently intersect with walls on upper floors, and balconies that jut out from walls. These features do not allow for adequate deflection or drainage of water, and in addition many of these homes were built with untreated, kiln-dried framing timber, which is susceptible to rot if it gets wet. The result is that water can get under the cladding and into the frame, causing rot, damp and mould.

If you are looking at a house to buy and it has any of the design features mentioned above, get a proper inspection by an inspector, listed in the *Yellow Pages* under 'Building Inspections'. Members of the New Zealand Institute of Building Surveyors or BRANZ Accredited Advisors are recommended. Timber and building standards have been raised since the scandal, so more recent building should not be affected. See also **References**, pp.263–4.

demand. It is also possible to have the property professionally valued for a fee of around NZ$500, or to assess market values for yourself using the Quotable Value website, **www.qv.co.nz** (*see* p.142).

## The Buying and Selling Process

Although it is not a legal requirement, most homebuyers use a **lawyer** to assist with their purchase. A lawyer can protect your interests and guide you through the sale process. Legal services may include helping you to negotiate the purchase price with the sellers, carrying out a 'title search' to make sure there are no legal problems with the property, checking the contract, advising you of any tax implications, drawing up the documents to transfer ownership and arranging the settlement (conveyancing).

Properties may be sold in a variety of ways. The most common is for the seller to set an asking price and then negotiate on the nearest **offer**. In the recent overheated market, sellers of desirable properties have opted to sell by tender or auction instead. To **tender** for a property, you will be asked to make an offer before a certain date. There will be no price guideline, so you will have to work out the market value and guess what other bidders might be prepared to pay. Both this and the **auction** process are obviously intended to push the price as high as possible. An auction at least is more transparent. It may take place at the property itself, or at the real estate agency, where several properties may be auctioned at once. You can nominate someone else to bid for you, although you may need to be present to give last-minute instructions to the bidder if it seems to be a close call.

Whichever process is adopted, you will at some point make a formal **offer in writing**, on a standard form provided by your agent or lawyer. This document will include the price you are willing to pay and details such as which chattels you get with the house (for example curtains, light fittings and oven). The chattels are negotiable. There may be several counter-offers before an agreement is reached. Most first offers are **conditional** (depending on market conditions – if the market is hot, unconditional offers may be more likely to be accepted). Conditions may include approval of finance, an independent valuation, a title search, a building inspection, sale of another property, and a **Land Information Memorandum** (LIM – the local council provides information on issues that may affect the property, such as coastal erosion, road construction or conservation issues).

When an agreement to purchase is reached, you will be required to pay a **deposit** (usually 10 per cent) to the agent or your lawyer. The contract will also state the '**settlement date**' – the date when your lawyer pays the final purchase amount to the seller, the house becomes your legal property and you can move into it. If the sale does not go ahead once the conditions of your offer have been met, you may be penalised. You need to make sure that your house is insured from the settlement date.

## Borrowing Money

Most buyers will need to arrange a mortgage to buy a house, and banks and financial services organisations offer a wide range of mortgage options and combinations. Bank processing is efficient, and mortgage finance can be arranged within as little as 24 hours.

The rate of payment and value of your mortgage obviously depends on your financial circumstances. Mortgages are usually capped at 95 per cent of the property's sale price.

The mortgage market is highly competitive and it is worth shopping around for a good deal. The Real Estate Institute of New Zealand website, **www.realenz. co.nz**, provides an up-to-date survey of interest rates and an online mortgage calculator. Note that assets held overseas, such as equity from the sale of a house in the UK, will not be accepted by banks as a mortgage guarantee.

# Further Information about Renting, Buying or Building a Home

The **Department of Building and Housing** oversees all legislation relating to the building, renovation and conversion, and letting of properties. Its website, **www.dbh.govt.nz**, provides information about building regulations and controls, the laws governing tenancy and where to seek redress if problems arise with a building project or rental. Tenancy agreement forms, property inspection report forms, bond lodgement forms, bond refund forms, bond transfer forms and useful information such as a new tenant's checklist and sample standard letters for resolving differences between landlords and tenants ('10 working day notices to remedy a breach') can all be downloaded from **www.dbh.govt.nz/housing/tenancy/Forms**. The forms can also be purchased at stationery shops such as Whitcoulls and Warehouse Stationery. The website also lists current rental market values by region and type of housing. **Tenancy Services** can be contacted by phone on **t** 0800 836262 or from outside New Zealand on **t** + 64 (0)4 238 4695.

The **Housing New Zealand Corporation** provides subsidised rental accommodation to those on low incomes, known in New Zealand as state housing. Visit the website, **www.hnzc.co.nz** for more information, or call **t** 0800 739717. The **Land-online** website, **www.landonline.govt.nz**, is an online database of land title and survey information (user pay service).

For current house sale prices, visit the website of **Quotable Value** (the ratings valuation body) at **www.qv.co.nz**. This is not a free service, but for a small fee QV can provide you with price trends and recent sale values in a specific area, a demographic profile of the area and a full market valuation of any property you are interested in.

The **Real Estate Institute of New Zealand**, **t** 0800 732536, **www.reinz.co.nz**, also publishes up-to-date price surveys on national, regional, city and neighbourhood levels. It can provide individual reports on rates, sales history, property history and comparative valuations, all for a modest fee. Its sister site, **www.realenz.co.nz**, includes comprehensive national and regional property listings, and a survey of mortgage interest rates.

The **Consumer Build** website, **www.consumerbuild.org.nz**, a combined initiative by the Department of Building and Housing and the Consumers' Institute, has masses of useful information on how to protect your interests when buying, building or renovating a house. Information ranges from how to do your research when buying a house or section, to how to find architects, builders and other tradespeople, and the legal issues around building.

## Real Estate Agents

There are numerous companies operating around the country. Most are national, some operate only in certain regions. Although the sales pressure applied by agents may be intense, all companies are reputable and are regulated by their professional body (REINZ). Some of the better-known companies are listed below:

- **Bayleys, www.bayleys.co.nz**. Specialises in glossy marketing of 'absolute waterfront' and grandiose lifestyle properties to overseas buyers.

- **Cox Partners, www.coxpartners.co.nz.**
- **First National Real Estate, www.firstnational.co.nz.**
- **For Farms, www.forfarms.co.nz.**
- **For Homes, www.forhomes.co.nz.**
- **Harcourts, www.harcourts.co.nz.** An established national company.
- **Harveys, www.harveys.co.nz.**
- **Home Sell, www.homesell.co.nz.**
- **L. J. Hooker, www.ljhooker.co.nz.**
- **Open2View, www.open2view.com.**
- **Professionals, www.professionals.co.nz.** Central and lower North Island.
- **Property Brokers, www.property.brokers.co.nz.**
- **Ray White, www.raywhite.co.nz.**
- **Tremains, www.tremain.co.nz.**
- **Williams and Kettle, www.wilket.co.nz.**
- **Wrightson, www.wrightson.co.nz.**

There are also many local companies. Which company has the best listings depends on individual agents and their contacts in any area; the glossiest are not always the best. Private sales have ballooned, too, as property values have risen (inflating agents' commission). One alternative is to buy and sell through **Green Door, www.greendoor.co.nz**, which provides basic advice and marketing tools to sellers for a set fee. Other buyers simply paint a sign and put it up outside their door, or advertise on the Internet.

# Renovating or Converting a Home

If you buy an existing property and decide to renovate it, you will need to follow many of the same steps as for building your own home from scratch; *see* the following section overleaf. Design and management costs for major alterations can be high. With a new house the architect or designer is starting with a clean slate and the design and build process can be quite straightforward. But when you are doing alterations, the architect or designer has to take into account the style and materials used in the existing part of the house and try to match them. And when the work actually starts, there are sometimes a few surprises that appear when wall boards are removed. Sometimes the architect or designer has to return to the drawing board and start over again.

For all new buildings and renovations you will need to apply for building consents and in some cases resource consents, *see* p.155.

# Buying a Section and Building Your Own House

With the population of New Zealand constantly growing, and not enough houses to go around, there's masses of new building going on around the country. Most foreigners are unlikely to build their first home in New Zealand, but many New Zealanders do build their own home. In order to build there are several steps you will have to follow. The first is to find a '**section**' (or plot of land), most likely in a new 'subdivision', and probably with the help of a real estate agent. You will need to consider very carefully the suitability of the section for your needs, as well as the surrounding area. Then you will need to work out a budget, choose and brief a designer, a project manager, builder and other contractors, write a contract with the builder including guarantees and insurance, get building and resource consents, organise building inspections by the Building Consent Authority during and at the end of construction, and think about landscaping. It's a lengthy process, and not one to be embarked on lightly. New houses are erected hourly by developers, speculators and individuals who have chosen to create their very own 'dream home'. Sadly the dream can turn to nightmare without proper forethought, so here are some tips for what to think about if you decide to build your own home.

The obvious appeal of building your own home is that you can do it just as you like it. But costs may prevent you from living out all your fantasies, and you will need professional guidance to make it happen. Most Kiwi home-builders eschew the services of an architect, on the grounds of cost, with some dire functional and aesthetic consequences. A draughtsman can draw up a plan of your home to fit your chosen layout, but an architect can help you to make sure that the building will really work. The draughtsman option is cheaper in the short-term, but may cost you more in the end. See the **Consumer Build** website, **www. consumerbuild.org.nz** (*see* p.142) for lots of useful information.

## Choosing a Section

Sections are sold through real estate agents in the same way as houses. If you read your local newspaper you will be able to follow the planning of new 'sub-divisions' – areas of land designated for development and drawn up into sections. These are sometimes on the fringes of existing settlements, but might also be rural 'lifestyle blocks' where a landowner or farmer has decided to sell some land for development. It is essential to work out a realistic budget before you start, as a section may seem cheap compared to the cost of a pre-existing building, but will seem much less so once you have added on building costs.

When you check out a section, you may have a gut feeling about it, but try to think rationally too. Ask yourself questions such as how close are amenities, like schools, shops, hospitals and public transport? Think about the site aspect. Is it sunny? Is it windy? Does it have a view? What about privacy? You might need to visit at different times of the day, and in different weather conditions. Does there seem to be good drainage? Consider also the different times of year – how much sun will it get in winter when the sun is low? Decide what is important to you. Consider whether access is difficult, not only from the vantage point of your living needs, but from that of a building site, as it could have a big impact on building costs (as well as convenience when you move in). Assess if there's room for garaging or off-road parking.

Find out what services (water, sewerage, power, phone, gas) are connected to the site. Your local council can tell you what services are available from the road, but you'll have to check the subdivision plan for services on to the section. You may have to pay to bring services on site. Find out if you will be on public sewerage or a septic tank. Check with the neighbours whether there is good television and mobile phone reception.

Ask yourself the sort of questions you would raise if you were looking at a house. What do the neighbours seem like? Are their properties well-kept? Are there overhanging trees that could cause a nuisance? Could there be a noise problem from them or their pets? The location will affect the price you pay but if a section seems too cheap there's probably a good reason. Ask a valuer or real estate agent for a comparison with other sales in the area and, if it still seems cheap, do some further investigation.

Drive around the neighbourhood at different times of the night and day, and at the weekend. Watch for traffic and noise from community activities like sports. Get a feel for the area. If you are looking in a rural area, consider smells, and noise from animals or harvesting that goes on around the clock. Is there any vacant land nearby? Find out whether the council has any plans for it. Research the zoning classification and what can and can't be built under the district plan.

## Location, Location, Location and Building Costs

The location of your section can have a bearing on building costs. For example, your new section may have an amazing view, perched on a cliff overlooking the sea. But it will also be exposed to the wind, the risk of erosion or flooding, and the risk of corrosion to materials.

Houses exposed to high winds have to be designed appropriately, for example the building may need extra bracing. There is provision in the Building Act 2004 for the council to refuse to grant a building consent if the land is at risk of a natural hazard, such as erosion, flooding, subsidence or slippage, or if the building work itself is likely to accelerate the problem. If the council decides that there is a risk from a natural hazard but the building work won't worsen the problem, it may grant a building consent but must advise the Registrar-General of Land, who will note on the certificate of title that a building consent has been issued under section 72. So take special care to check the certificate of title for any section 72 endorsements on the title, which will alert you to the fact that the land is at risk of erosion, flooding or subsidence. Note, it may appear as a section 36 endorsement under the prior 1991 Building Act.

Insurance may also be a problem if the section has an erosion risk. The Earthquake Commission (EQC) insures against earthquake, natural landslip, volcanic eruption, hydrothermal activity, tsunami, and, in the case of residential land, a storm or flood; or fire caused by any of these. You are automatically covered by EQC insurance when you take out private insurance cover for your home or belongings and the EQC premium is built into the premium you pay your own insurance company. However, subsidence is not covered by the EQC. So if you are buying a section with a risk of erosion or subsidence you may need to get extra private insurance cover for risks not covered by the EQC.

If the house is near the sea it will need to have corrosion-resistant features in the roofing, joinery and structural connectors. It may also need more frequent washing and painting after you've moved in. Some of these problems can be offset by using adapted designs that suit the environment without being significantly more expensive. A good designer should be able to advise you on this. Their advice could influence your decision to buy the section or not.

Before you sign up to buy a section, it is very important to ask your architect or designer to check out the site for you. They can advise you if your ideas are work-able given the shape and size of the section.

If you are still keen on the section after your initial inspections, there is further information you should research before buying. You can do this yourself, or your designer, project manager or lawyer will do this work for you if it is part of their brief. You should:

- **Get a copy of the certificate of title.**

- **Check the certificate of title for covenants, easements and consent notices placed at the time of subdivision that might limit your use of the site.**

- **Check the district plan – this will tell you things like height or boundary restrictions, and will let you know what your neighbours are permitted to do.**

- **Also check the district plan to find out if you need any resource consents (*see* p.155) before you start building.**

- **Get a Land Information Memorandum (*see* p.141) from the council.**

- **Decide if an engineer's report is necessary before you buy (your designer can advise you on this).**

- **Find out what wind zone the site is located in. The council will provide this information or direct you to someone who can.**

- **Check the survey information.**

• Get a valuation to decide if the price is right; this may be needed for mortgage purposes.

• Make sure you have a satisfactory sale and purchase agreement.

# Designing Your House

You may choose to have your house designed by an architect, an architectural designer or an architectural draughtsman. Each has different skills, qualifications and expertise.

A home designed by an architect has the value-added factor. It will stand out as being individual and is likely to attract a higher resale price. Architects will usually want to manage the whole project for you, too, as they will have a keen interest in seeing their designs faithfully followed by the builder and sub-contractors. Other types of designers may not be able to offer the same level of project management skills.

The choice of designer will probably come down to how much money you want to spend. But it can be a mistake to stint on the design phase. Opting for a less experienced or qualified person may cost you more in the long run. If money is really tight, a skilled architect/designer should be able to explore ways to make your budget and ideas fit.

When you choose someone other than an architect, you need to be confident they understand the **Building Code** requirements and the need for good materials and construction methods to avoid problems like leaky building syndrome (*see* box, p.140).

## Types of Architect or Designer

### Architect

An architect is a person who has studied architecture at university, has gained an **architectural degree**, passed a professional examination and is registered with the **New Zealand Registered Architects Board (NZRAB)**. At present, only a person registered with the NZRAB can call him- or herself an architect and he or she must hold a practising certificate issued by the NZRAB to be able to practise. Under the Registered Architects Act 2005, only a person registered with the NZRAB is entitled to be called an architect. When you are hiring someone to design your house, ask what qualifications they hold.

There is some confusion about the difference between an architect and other house designers, so if you specifically want the training and expertise of an architect, you need to know that the person you employ has the right qualifications. A person with an architectural degree has learned about design, building science, lighting, acoustics, interior design, landscaping, indoor/outdoor design and managing the contract processes. They will be able to consider your ideas and come up with innovative solutions for you.

Most architects in New Zealand also belong to the **New Zealand Institute of Architects**, www.nzia.co.nz.

## Architectural Designer

An architectural designer will usually be cheaper than an architect, depending on their training and experience. They will probably have studied at a **tertiary institution** but may not have the training necessary for more complicated designs. They should be familiar with all the Building Code and local authority requirements (such as building and resource consents) and be able to design residential buildings.

The **Design Association of New Zealand (DANZ)**, www.danz.co.nz, is the professional association responsible for licensing design practitioners (this association represents designers from many fields, not just housing and building). Like architects, licensed designers have to pay an annual licensing fee and comply with a code of ethics. Architectural designers are represented by **Architectural Designers New Zealand (ADNZ)**, www.adnz.org.nz. ADNZ does not have a licensing role, but members have to achieve certain standards of education, training and professional practice.

## Architectural Draughtsperson

An architectural draughtsperson can draw up plans from your basic ideas. They will be cheaper than an architect or architectural designer but you may not get the same design flair. They usually have **technical institute training** and some may be members of ADNZ, while others may be members of DANZ.

# Fees

Paying architect's fees may seem like a lot of money, but in reality they are a small part of the total cost of a building project, and have to be considered in the light of the cost-effectiveness and overall value that the architect will add to your house. Expect to budget between six and 15 per cent of the total cost of the job, depending on its size and value and what services the architect provides. The three usual ways of charging are:

- **By the hour – but this could become very expensive for a big job.**

- **As a percentage of the total cost of building – this is the most popular method. It means the cost of the design service remains proportionate to the final cost of the house and you have a better idea of your total costs. The percentage can range from as little as 1.5 per cent for initial sketch plans up to about 15 per cent for full design and administration services. Fees vary among architects and according to the complexity of the project.**

- **Fixed fees calculated on an hourly rate.**

Ask for a detailed breakdown of the costs for each stage of the design process, from the initial design work through to the contract administration fee. This should roughly break down to:

- 15 per cent for initial sketches.
- 15 per cent for developed design.
- 40 per cent for final plans.
- 30 per cent for periodic observation while building is in progress, and contract administration.

Fees are usually negotiable. However, don't just look for the cheapest price – the fee should reflect the quality and value of the professional services being offered, and be fair to both parties. You can ask the New Zealand Institute of Architects (NZIA), **www.nzia.co.nz**, for the latest recommended fee scales. While the scale will give you an indication, there are a number of factors that will affect the fee:

- **The complexity of the project. You would expect to pay less for a basic three-bedroom house than for an innovative, multi-level design.**
- **The service being offered, i.e. whether the architect will manage the project right through to completion or just parts of it.**

Be aware also that you will be charged GST (sales tax) and other expenses such as extra printing, travel costs, and photography on top of the fee. Also, any applications for resource consent (*see* p.155) will be an additional cost. These extra costs should be agreed at the same time as the fee is negotiated.

You should expect to pay less for an architectural designer, and less again for an architectural draughtsperson. But this will depend on the expertise the particular designer brings to the job, the complexity of the design, and how much of the total project they manage.

## Engineers

An additional cost to factor in is where the services of an architectural engineer are required. An engineer's expertise is likely to be needed at two stages of a house-building project.

- **If there is concern about the stability or compactness of the earth, a geotechnical engineer will be called in, usually by the architect or designer, to do some testing. If there are problems, a special design of the foundations will be required, with input from an engineer.**
- **To design difficult details imposed by the design, or to make certain elements safer or more efficient.**

Engineers may also provide expertise where there are other features out of the norm, for example, where weather extremes are likely. The engineer would calculate methods of developing lateral restraint, providing adequate support, and anchorage against wind uplift and snow loading, as well as overall stability. Your architect or designer should let you know if an engineer is required and what the extra costs will be.

## Choosing an Architect or Designer

Once you have chosen your preferred type of designer, it is time to find the person. Personal recommendations are a good way to find someone, or else ask the relevant professional organisations for a list of their members.

Also browse the web – most architects and design firms showcase their designs online. Work out the design style that appeals to you.

Once you have a list, ask around to see if anyone you know has used them. Try to find out what they were like to work with. It is very important to find a person you can communicate your ideas to and feel that they are listening. Avoid designers who appear more interested in showcasing the latest design fad than designing to your needs.

Meet with each person on your shortlist. Most architects and designers offer a free first meeting. It may be useful to involve a builder at this stage. At this initial meeting a lot of information will be gathered to establish what is needed and how it might be achieved. You need to know in advance:

- **the size of your budget.**
- **what type of house you want, i.e. basic, middle or superior.**
- **what size of house you want.**
- **some of the design features you want to include, such as solar heating.**

At the initial meeting, ask:

- **what are their qualifications?**
- **are they a member of one of the professional organisations?**
- **do they have professional indemnity insurance?**
- **does the person or firm have the capability and resources to do the job?**
- **for examples of work they have already done.**
- **what range of services they provide – clarity about who is to do what.**
- **about fees. But don't expect a fee proposal (which breaks down the percentage of the fees paid at each stage of the project) at this point – it will be too soon for an accurate proposal.**
- **for references from other clients who might be willing to talk to you and share their experience of working with the architect or designer.**

Show the architect/designer your notes and rough sketches and get their initial reaction (but be open to suggestions). It's possible that you might all jump in the car and go look at the section.

Talk budget and ask if they think you are being realistic.

Consider getting a preliminary design done first for a set fee and have it costed by a quantity surveyor, usually for a separate fee.

If the architect or designer is too busy to take on the job, they should say so at that first meeting. They may be able suggest someone else. However, people are often prepared to wait months for the right person.

At the end of the meeting, ask the architect/designer to write down their understanding of what they think you want so you can confirm or change it. They should outline the services they can offer and find out what services you require.

Note that some architects/designers might want to contract in specialist designers, for example, to do the kitchen or bathroom, or lighting.

They will most likely use the services of a number of other people, for example surveyors and structural engineers, whom they would engage on your behalf. This should be sorted at the initial meeting.

### Professional Indemnity Insurance

Make sure the person you employ has professional indemnity (PI) insurance. A person offering professional services must take responsibility for the advice they give. If an architect or any other type of designer gives you bad advice (for example, by drawing designs that result in leaks) they are said to be 'negligent' in their duty to you.

PI insurance is for the immediate benefit of the architect/designer, not the client. But it is in your interests that the person you employ has it. If they don't have PI insurance and something goes wrong, and they can't pay for the repairs, you are likely to be out of pocket yourself. It is not compulsory for an architect/designer to have PI insurance, but it makes sense to use one who does have it.

### Materials and Features

A good architect/designer should know about all the materials, latest products and innovations in design. They are responsible for producing designs that meet the manufacturers' requirements for the materials. For example, you have advised your architect/designer of the type of roofing material you want used. It is likely that this roofing material comes with installation instructions which recommend the pitch at which the roof should be built. The architect/designer would have to design the roof to the recommended pitch otherwise the roofing material cannot be installed to the manufacturer's recommendations. They should also be able to advise you about environmental and energy features.

## Briefing your Architect or Designer

Once you have selected your architect/designer, and depending on how much ground was covered in the initial meeting, the next stage is a more thorough briefing. In this briefing:

- **Go over your ideas – the architect or designer should be able to tell you what will look good as well as be functional.**

- **Be flexible. If you are too fixed in your ideas, the architect/designer won't have any room to design and come up with exciting ideas you haven't considered – let the designer design!**

- Have a budget and be prepared to shuffle items within the budget – usually area and space, but savings can be made elsewhere, for example, using corrugated steel instead of slate on the roof.
- Sort out exactly which of the following services the architect/designer will be providing:
    - site selection.
    - design – initial sketches through to final plans.
    - budgets.
    - managing the building process, getting building consent, selecting the builder and various subcontractors and liaising with the council or building certifier over completion of the project.
    - interior design and selection of furnishings and appliances.
    - landscaping
- Have everything agreed in the contract and reviewed by your lawyer.

## The Full Service

Most architects prefer to be engaged for a full service. This means they manage the whole building process for you including selecting the builder and subcontractors, and monitoring construction. Observation on the building site is an important role carried out by architects and designers, and lack of supervision is often the reason things go wrong. Some architectural designers will also manage the project for you if this is part of their brief.

If you contract either just to do the plans, you could rehire them later at an hourly rate to advise on changes or solve unforeseen problems. But be aware that most architects are not comfortable with taking on only part of the process – they would rather see the whole job through from design to completion. This may include internal furnishings and fittings and colour schemes. They will want to see the contract documentation followed faithfully to prevent mistakes by the builder or subcontractors. This way they are on the spot to keep the project on track and anticipate problems. For example, if the builder uses a different grade of timber than specified, and it is not noticed until the house is nearly built, you could find that the affected area will need to be rebuilt.

## The Contract

You should get an agreement in writing regardless of the size of the job. Both NZIA and ADNZ have standard contracts, which are very detailed and likely to cover every possible situation that arises.

Whatever contract form is used, make sure you understand it and, if you don't, get your lawyer to check it. Make sure it includes clauses about what happens if any disputes arise. The contract must cover the full scope of the architect/designer's involvement in the project.

You will need a separate contract with your builder for the construction of your home.

## Information-gathering

Once engaged, the architect/designer will start gathering information on the building site (your section). This might include the certificate of title, drainage plans, and zoning and town planning information. They may take photographs and organise to have the site surveyed on your behalf for its contours and boundaries. They will also look at trees, water courses and soil type, if it could affect the building process. They may recommend you get an engineer's report. Have an agreement with the architect/designer about who is responsible for this information-gathering and any extra charges involved, for example, paying the engineer or quantity surveyor if any are engaged.

# Making Plans

There are normally three stages to the plans that the architect/designer will draw. (Depending on who you are talking to they might give different names to these stages, so they are all noted here.)

- **The initial sketch plans (or concept, preliminary or discussion drawings).**
- **The developed designs.**
- **The final documentation (tender, building consent, construction or working drawings and specifications).**

## Initial Sketch Plans

After you have briefed your architect/designer, they will go away and draw up some initial sketches or concept plans. These will give you an idea of how they see the house taking shape. They are likely to include a floor plan and a perspective drawing from various angles. They take into account site conditions, your budget, and any special town planning requirements.

This is the time when you:

- **Sort out what you like and what you want to change on the initial sketches.** Changing your mind later, when the detailed drawings have been done, or once construction has started, will be more costly.

- **Consider some of the technical limits that have arisen,** such as height restrictions or how the house might fit on the section.

- **See how it is all going to impact on your budget.** Your architect/designer should be able to guide you here.

- **Decide if you feel comfortable enough with your chosen person to go right through the whole process with them.** Don't feel bad about letting someone go. It's not unusual for people to brief more than one person to prepare the initial sketch plans before finding someone they are confident to proceed with.

• **Apply for a Project Information Memorandum (PIM) from the council.** A PIM will include confirmation that you can build the house subject to the necessary resource and building consents. This will normally be done by the architect/designer on your behalf if it's in their brief. Make sure you (or your architect, designer or project manager) apply for a PIM early.

## Developed Designs

Once you have a set of agreed concept plans, your architect/designer will draw up the developed designs, which include the changes you've asked for in the initial sketch plans.

If not already done, now is the time to find out whether you will need resource consent, for example, if the house is going to be built closer to the boundary than allowed on the district plan. At this stage, if the design is particularly cutting-edge, you might decide to get a second opinion for assurance that it is workable. One option is to pay another architect or building consultant to review it for you. You will also discuss the materials you will use – the exterior cladding, flooring, roofing, windows, doors and interior fittings and fixtures – with the architect/designer. Also talk about power points, cable jacks, exterior taps, light location, attic access, and so forth.

At this stage you may use a **quantity surveyor** to estimate the costs of the project before you put the job out for tender and get closer to an accurate budget. To find out about the work of a quantity surveyor, look at the **New Zealand Institute of Quantity Surveyors** website, **www.nziqs.co.nz**.

## Final Plans and Specifications

The final documentation (tender, construction, or working drawings and specifications) includes detailed drawings as well as specifications for every feature, such as claddings, ventilation, natural lighting, wall and roof bracing, and so on. The plans are used:

• **in the tendering process to get quotes from contractors, subcontractors and perhaps quantity surveyors.**

• **to gain building consents.**

• **by the builder and contractors contracted to build the house as the blueprint for the construction.**

When the costs come in, you may need to revise your plans and talk to your builder, architect/designer or quantity surveyor to see where savings can be made. If you have your building consent, changes to the plans may mean that you need to apply for an amendment to the building consent. At this stage you can go to the bank to finalise your finance if you haven't already done so. Good plans will save arguments during construction – if the plans aren't clear or full enough they can be misinterpreted by you or the builder, leading to disputes over what was or was not priced and which systems and products should be used. This could also create difficulties in getting a code compliance certificate.

## Interior Design

Many architects work with an interior designer or do the interior designing themselves. Or you may prefer to hire your own interior designer, or do it yourself, but it is important that everyone is comfortable working together. You can decide every detail, right down to taps, in the specifications for the final plans. Or the architect can set aside a fixed sum for some things, for example, hardware and light-fittings. This leaves you to choose the items yourself. If you choose the most expensive items, you will need to find extra money to pay for them.

## Getting Consents

There are two types of consents – you'll always need a building consent, and you'll often need a resource consent. Building consents are intended to ensure building work is carried out to satisfactory standards that comply with the Building Code, as defined by the 2004 Building Act. The code sets minimum standards for safety, durability, weatherproofing, fire resistance and energy efficiency. Resource consents relate to the environmental impact of any new building, as it fits into the regional, city or district council plans for management of the environment. They may affect issues such as building height or access. Make sure you also get a **PIM** (*see* p.154) at the earliest possible stage.

Consents must be applied for from the territorial authorities (councils) before you start any work, and the work must be signed off by a building inspector when it is finished. If you employ an architect or builder, he or she will oversee this process for you. The council keeps a record of all consents for the life of a building, so you can check the building history of a house.

Getting a **resource consent** is not usually part of the service provided in the architect's or designer's fee. But it is something they can do for you (for a fee). The need for a resource consent will become apparent at the initial sketch stage. The architect/designer should be familiar with the district plan and know, for example, how close to the boundary you can build, or whether there are any height restrictions. Any less obvious restrictions should be discovered when the plans are being looked at by the council staff when assessing them for building consent.

To get **building consent** the design documents must be drawn with sufficient information to show that the proposed house will meet the performance requirements of the **Building Code**. For example, the documentation must clearly show how the house will keep water out by specifying such things as ground clearances, balcony and deck details, claddings and joinery, flashing details and guttering, and so forth. You also need to provide details of proposed inspections by the designer or project manager. Each aspect of the Building Code requirements has to be covered in detail in the plans and specifications. If the documents are not full enough, the building consent authority can ask for more information, which will slow down the whole process. The building consent application forms must be filled in and lodged with your plans. A fee is payable (usually based on the value of the work). The building consent authority has 20 working days to process it.

Depending on the scope of your designer's brief and contract, they can take care of organizing the consent for you.

### Exceeding Minimum Standards

You should be able to rely on your designer's knowing all the Building Code requirements. The Building Code is designed so that houses built to the Code will be safe and healthy. It is best to aim for a house that will easily meet minimum requirements, taking into account modern construction methods and variations in materials and techniques. A house can be built so it is significantly more energy-efficient, safe and comfortable than the minimum standards required by the Building Code.

## Building Your House

Now that you've designed your house, you will need to think about the stages in a building project.

Once the plans are drawn up, the materials have been chosen and your finance is arranged, the next steps in the building process are likely to be:

- finding a builder (and subcontractors if you are managing the building project yourself).
- getting tenders and quotes.
- revising the budget, if necessary.
- making your selection of builder and subcontractors.
- signing the contracts.
- making sure the appropriate insurance has been organised.
- applying for building and resource consents if not already under way – the applications may already have been lodged by you or your architect or designer.

Once construction starts, your jobs will consist of:

- monitoring progress.
- making progress payments.
- approving variations to structure or materials.

- building inspections by the council inspectors.
- dealing with problems when things go wrong.

In the final stages of the project, the steps are:

- completion and final inspections for the code compliance certificate.
- retentions and remedial work.
- final payment.
- landscaping.

Often these steps happen together, or in a different order, depending on your circumstances.

Although you can ask your architect, designer or building foreman to do a lot, it is a good idea for you to take the final responsibility for all stages, such as making sure building consent has been issued, making sure that you understand all the documentation – have the architect or builder explain the plans and specifications to you and make sure you are happy with the design, as changes during construction are likely to be costly – talking to a lawyer about the contract, ensuring that the site is cleared and ready for the builder to start work, and making sure your builder has unhindered access to the site.

Once work is in progress, try to develop a good working relationship with your builder. If you have any concerns about the work, discuss them right away. Keep changes to a minimum and instruct your builder in writing about all variations to the specified work and ensure you get a written costing. Choose materials and finishes carefully and approve them before use. If you are responsible for choosing the appliances and any other materials or fittings and fixtures, make sure they are already bought when the builder reaches that stage. Keep to the payments schedule and pay promptly.

When the work is complete, report any urgent defects to your builder promptly and in writing. List any non-urgent defects for your builder to correct at an agreed time. Settle the final account promptly.

## Where to Look for a Builder

It may be part of your brief with your designer that they engage the builder and subcontractors. Usually an architect/designer works with a pool of builders (who in turn work with a pool of subcontractors). So the architect/designer will advise you who they usually work with.

If you are going to select the builder yourself, start looking around early. If you see a house you like, ask the owners who built it and if possible talk to them about any problems with construction and what the builder was like to work with. Ask for recommendations from friends and colleagues, your mortgage manager, the real estate agent and others in the house business. Word soon gets around about who is reliable and who you should avoid. Get a list of names and start a pre-selection list.

Other avenues are websites of builders and building companies, the *Yellow Pages* and the trade organisations, such as the **Certified Builders' Association of New Zealand** or **Registered Master Builders' Federation**.

## Pricing the Job

Before you invite tenders from builders, you may want to get some costings for the job to get an idea whether you can afford to go ahead. You can use a quantity surveyor to get an accurate costing before you put the job out to tender. Then when the tenders come in you have a good basis to evaluate them.

### Quantity Surveyors

A quantity surveyor (QS) is a person trained in construction methods and costs. They work closely with you and the architect/designer, engineer and builder to itemise the quantities of materials and labour needed to build the house, using the design drawings.

The quantity surveyor's estimate can give you a reasonable idea of the costs and it can be used by the builders when tendering their quotes. (Note that the builder should only be given the QS estimate of materials required, not the price.) Make sure that when you engage a quantity surveyor you know what sort of service they are providing. If you ask a general question, such as 'How much to build a garage?' you will get a best guess which may be way off target. But if you ask for a precise costing, you will get more accurate information.

A QS can also be used to calculate progress payments and to cost variations during construction. They can also advise on the type of contract or the meaning of any special clauses that should be included in the contract. You can buy part of a QS service, for example, you might only use them for progress payments. You would most likely use a QS if you are only getting one quote. Or if you are managing the project yourself. That way you have a benchmark to see if the quote is fair. You can also use a QS to estimate costs of alterations and renovations.

The **New Zealand Institute of Quantity Surveyors** represents QSs. A full member of NZIQS is entitled to use the initials MNZIQS (Member of the New Zealand Institute of Quantity Surveyors Inc).

### Inviting Tenders

It is a good idea to invite at least three builders to tender. Let each one know that you are getting others to tender. This is in fairness to them but also so they are more likely to give you a competitive quote. You should also let them know that you won't necessarily pick the cheapest tender but will be considering other criteria like reputation and qualifications.

When you send out the invitations to tender, you need to give the builders the detailed drawings and specifications outlining the extent of the work and the materials, the construction details, the location of the building site and position of the house on the site. Also give them the QS's estimates for materials if you have any.

Specify the type of building contract the work is to be under (full, labour only, or managed labour only). The more information you give, the more reliable the quotes. This will help to avoid disputes later when the job starts to reflect the actual costs, as opposed to guesswork on the part of the builder due to insufficient information.

Tender documents received from the builders should provide exact costings (including GST or sales tax) for all the materials and fittings, and for the labour of the builder and subcontractors, as long as you specify that you want this level of detail and you have provided the schedule of materials, and so on. Also ask for the builder's hourly rate (including GST) so that you know how much to expect if you ask for any additional work to be done. The builders you have asked to tender may be tendering on other jobs at the same time. If the builder gets other work they should tell you if they have to pull out of the tender, or ask if you are prepared to wait until they are available.

Even if you bypass the tender process and go straight to your favourite builder, always ask for a detailed quote in writing.

## Quotes and Estimates

There can be a big difference between an estimate and a quote. An estimate is only a best guess at what the job will cost and the builder is not bound by it. However, it is reasonable to expect it to be within 10–15 per cent of the final cost. A quote is an explicit promise based on detailed specifications and is the price you pay, barring matters outside the builder's reasonable control or increases in the cost of materials or labour (if the contract allows this), or other variations.

All estimates and quotes should be in writing, signed and dated. Never use one builder's quote as leverage to get a lower one from someone else. It is unfair to them, could compromise workmanship, and you should be looking at more than just price. You should be comparing tenders on other criteria, such as their levels of experience and reliability, which will also have a bearing on their price.

Be wary of low tender prices compared to others as it could mean the low tenderer has misunderstood the building project. Be careful of provisional sums in the quote – this is where the price is uncertain, for example the cost of some materials. Provisional sums are often underestimated, so if they appear in the quote ask the builder to confirm that the amount quoted will be adequate for the quality of goods you are expecting.

## Guaranteed Maximum Price

A guaranteed maximum price (GMP) is where the builder/contractor guarantees a maximum price in the contract. These sorts of contracts can work well as an incentive to the builder to finish on time and within the budget. You avoid the risk of uncontrolled extra costs and time. But you will pay a premium under these types of contracts because the risk of delays and extra costs will be factored into the price.

If any savings are made during construction, generally these savings will be shared between you and the builder. The ratio of sharing should be specified in the written contract. The incentive to make savings has the advantage of ensuring co-operation between you – you'll both be trying to avoid overrunning the GMP. The builder is also more likely to employ reliable subcontractors who will meet deadlines and work within budgets. Any variations you ask for will be outside the GMP and you will have to pay for them.

### Prime Cost Sums

Sometimes the architect/designer sets aside a fixed amount, known as prime cost (PC) sums, for certain items, for example the taps and door handles. This leaves you to choose them yourself. If you choose the most expensive items, you will need to find extra money over and above the specified PC sums to buy them.

### Reality Check

Once the tenders are in, you will be able to see how close they are to your original ideas of how much the project would cost. If the quotes are far higher than you budgeted, then you will have to revise your plans, take out a larger mortgage, or change some items to get closer to your budget. The architect/designer should have designed to your budget, so your first move would be to go back to them, or the quantity surveyor if you used one, and see if they can point out areas that have caused the costs to explode. Sometimes, if there has been a long delay between finalizing the plans and seeking tenders, the cost of materials and building costs may have significantly increased.

If you have already put in your application for the building consent, any major changes to the plans at this stage will mean you have to either put in a new application, including a new set of documents, or ask for an amendment. Building consent authorities can advise what you need to do, depending on how major the changes are and also what additional fees are payable.

## Building Contracts

You should have a written contract with your builder. The builder, as main contractor, will organise the contracts with the subcontractors. However, if you are managing the project yourself under a labour-only contract with the builder, you will have to arrange contracts with each of the contractors, for example, the plasterers, painters and plumbers. Contracts don't have to be written to be legally binding but, when all the terms and conditions are clearly spelt out and recorded in writing, it means there is less room for argument about who is responsible when something goes wrong. Some people rely on the written quote, or a list of tasks given to them by the builder, as the contract.

This is fine provided everything goes according to plan. But if something goes wrong, these bits of paper are unlikely to provide enough detail about the rights and responsibilities of the builder and yourself.

## Form of Contract

Many building companies and individual builders will have their own form of contract. There is also a New Zealand Standard form of contract that has been independently developed by Standards New Zealand: NZS 3902:2004 House Building Contract. Even if you decide to use another form of contract, it might be useful to compare it to the NZ Standard to make sure the one you are being offered is fair and reasonable. There are also a number of other standard contracts available from these organisations:

- **Certified Builders Association of NZ (CBANZ).**
- **Registered Master Builders Federation (RMBF).**
- **NZ Institute of Architects (NZIA).**

The CBANZ and RMBF contracts are only available to members, but you can buy a copy of the NZIA contract. It is likely that your builder is familiar with them or has a copy. Don't accept them at face value; you may want to negotiate changes to some of the clauses.

## Alterations to Contracts

To make changes to a contract, you can rule out by hand what you want to delete and write in the changes. You and the builder will both have to initial the changes. Be careful of what effect the changes might have on other clauses, as clauses in a contract are often interrelated. Finally, make sure that changing the contract won't affect any guarantees. If you have any doubts, seek legal advice.

# Insurance

Make sure you and the builder have the right insurance to cover risks on the building site and risks to other people and property.

If you are building under a full contract, the building contract should specify the types and amounts of insurance cover the main contractor holds.

The builder should have cover for:

- **accidental damage to the building (builder's all-risk policy or contract works insurance).**
- **accidental damage to adjoining property, and in some cases for personal injury (public liability).**

They may have cover for theft or damage to their tools, but that is their concern.

Subcontractors may be covered by the main contractor's policy. This is something the main contractor should sort out with the subcontractors, but for your own peace of mind it is good to find out who is covered for what. If the plumber causes a leak, for example when doing work in the upstairs bathroom, which damages the walls below, you need to know that the damage is covered under the main contractor's policy. If the plumber is working independently, find out if they have cover for this type of mishap.

If building under a labour-only contract it is usually your responsibility to arrange the insurance. You need to tell your own insurer when you are having alterations done to ensure you are covered for accidental damage to both your house and contents while work is under way. Make sure your contents insurance covers the new appliances and fittings being installed.

## Public Liability Insurance

All builders and contractors who are self-employed should have public liability insurance for protection against damage to third party property and personal injury to others caused by the contractor's negligence, for example, if a sheet of roofing iron falls off the roof and damages your car. The amount of cover should reflect the type of buildings the contractor is working on – if the electrician manages to burn down your brand new million-dollar home in the final stages of construction, you need to ensure he has public liability insurance up to that amount.

In the case of personal injury, this would generally be covered by the ACC (*see* p.190). But there may be an occasion when you have been injured because the contractor was grossly negligent and you think you should be entitled to exemplary damages. The contractor's public liability insurance should be sufficient to cover the costs and any damages awarded to you in a successful lawsuit.

## Contract Works Insurance

The builder should take out contract works insurance to provide cover for property that is in the course of construction, i.e. damage to his own work. However, in the case of alterations and renovations, it might have to cover all building works. In the case of a labour-only contract, it is usually your responsibility to arrange this insurance.

It generally covers subcontractors' damage to the site or project, damage to existing building and structures, theft, vandalism and arson, environmental damage from storms, floods, hail, snow, frost or earthquakes. It does not cover damage to the builder's plant and equipment – this would be covered under their own policy for theft or damage to materials and tools, and so on.

## Upon Completion

Arrange the final inspection by the Building Consent Authority and apply for a **code compliance certificate**. Make your own final inspection and liaise with the builder and council to resolve any outstanding issues.

# Home Utilities and Services

## Electricity and Gas

The power system in New Zealand is 240 volts, 50 cycles. Most home appliances are run on electricity, although in some areas gas is also an option for heating, hot water and cooking. Bottled gas (LPG, butane or propane) is widely used too for cookers and heaters.

The cost of electricity, supplied by private companies, is high and the supply is periodically threatened by drought (which lowers water levels in lakes used to generate hydroelectric power). After a spate of winter blackouts, the government has been pressuring suppliers to find new energy sources (building new power stations, exploiting coal reserves, expanding wind farms).

The four electricity retailers, Contact Energy, Genesis Energy, Energy Online and Meridian Energy, compete not only on price and service, but also on environmental sensitivity ('greenwash'), customer bonuses (AA membership and FlyBuys) and sponsorship of kiwis, babies and the terminally ill. While the smaller companies may undercut the prices of the larger ones, you may lose out on customer service.

For all companies, different pricing plans are available depending on your patterns of consumption. Customers are billed monthly. Bills can be paid by a cheque in the post, direct debit, telephone or Internet banking. To get connected, contact one of the companies with your details by phone or via the Internet.

The main gas and electricity suppliers are:

- **Contact Energy**, PO Box 624, Wellington, **t** 0800 809000, **t** (09) 359 6000 (mobile phone callers), **www.mycontact.co.nz**. Claims to be the largest wholesaler and retailer of natural gas in the country, and generates about 30 per cent of New Zealand's electricity. Contact has 10 power stations around the country including hydro, geothermal and gas turbine (using gas from the Maui gas field off the Taranaki coast). It supplies electricity to all areas, and gas to swaths of the North Island.

- **Energy Online Limited**, PO Box 8288, **t** 0800 086400, **www.energyonline. co.nz**. With branding that makes it look more like a hi-energy drink than a power company, Energy Online is the newest, smallest and claims to be the fastest-growing, electricity retailer, supplying chunks of the North Island. Its parent company is Genesis and it is New Zealand-owned.

- **Flame On Ltd**, **t** 0800 352636, **www.flameon.co.nz**. Gas supplier.

- **Genesis Energy**, **t** 0800 300400, **www.genesisenergy.co.nz**. State-owned Genesis claims to be New Zealand's largest energy retailer. It generates electricity at thermal, hydro, wind and biomass power stations. It says that it recognises the importance of renewable energy, at the same time as accepting the need to use non-renewable sources to maintain supply in dry years. It is involved in the development of the Kupe oil and Cardiff gas fields. Supplies both electricity and gas to most areas of the North Island.

- **Meridian Energy Ltd, t** 0800 496496, **www.meridianenergy.co.nz.** Claims to be the largest electricity generator in New Zealand, selling electricity to over 200,000 customers throughout the country. It says it is dedicated to generating electricity using renewable natural and physical resources – 'the lakes, rivers, wind and forests' – therefore putting less harmful gases into the air. New Zealand-owned Meridian supplies electricity to most areas.
- **Nova Gas Limited, t** 0800 668242, **www.novagas.co.nz.** Landfill-derived methane gas piped to your home anywhere in New Zealand.
- **On Gas, t** 0800 841212, **www.ongas.co.nz.** LPG (liquid petroleum gas) cylinders delivered to your home. Auckland, Wellington, Christchurch and other larger conurbations.

# Rates, Rubbish and Recycling

You will have to pay **rates** to your local and regional council once you move into your home. If you have bought a property, your details will automatically be passed on to the ratings department of the council when you sign the contract, and the council will calculate how much is owed for the remainder of the year. Payments are quarterly. Rates are assessed on the rateable value of your home (an assessment of how much the site – capital value – and the buildings on it – 'improvements' – are worth), reassessed annually; they will be higher if you live in a more expensive property. You can look up the rateable value of any property at the council offices.

Local (district or city) council rates vary hugely from council to council, and are often the subject of controversy. They pay for services such as roads, water and sewerage, rubbish disposal, town planning, building safety, animal control, fire stations, parks, libraries, swimming pools and sports grounds. Regional council rates, which are minimal, cover environmental matters affecting the broader region and the land transport network.

## Rubbish Disposal and Recycling

Kerbside rubbish collection and recycling is covered by your rates. The local council will be able to tell you how often and on what days your rubbish will be collected (usually once a week). There may be limits on how much rubbish you can put out for collection. You should also be able to recycle glass, plastic, cans and paper. Most councils run kerbside recycling schemes, otherwise you may have to take your recyclable waste to a recycling centre (usually located near shopping centres or schools). For excess rubbish, such as garden waste or old furniture, you may have to make a trip to the tip (or transfer station), for which you will have to pay a fee. Rural properties have to dispose of their own rubbish.

## Water and Sewerage

All urban and suburban and many semi-rural properties have water piped in and sewage piped out, while most rural properties collect their own water in tanks and get rid of their waste in septic tanks. Mains water is free up to a certain threshold, after which it is metered and you have to pay for it. It is one of the few public services in New Zealand that has not been privatised, and is provided by the local council.

In the rush to cover the country in concrete, semi-rural areas are gradually being encouraged to join the water and sewerage networks. Individual councils decide how to make this happen, often meeting with resistance: in some areas it has been made compulsory, in others the cost to ratepayers or individual householders has been extortionate. If you are on a storm water and septic tank system, it is up to you to service the tanks.

# Telephone and Fax

## Telephones

The main telephone companies in New Zealand are Telecom, TelstraClear and Vodafone (mobile phones only). Pricing plans are designed to confuse: former CEO of Telecom Theresa Gattung admitted as much in a statement which brought the company's share price tumbling down and her own career to an end. Most houses will have a telephone already installed; if not, you can buy one from an electronics retailer or telephone company. Your phone should be connected within two to three days of contacting a company.

The phone book for your area is supplied free and you can pick up new editions at the Post Office. Phone listings are also available on the Internet, at **www. whitepages.co.nz** (residential) and **www.yellowpages.co.nz** (business). Monthly bills are payable by cheque, Internet or phone banking or direct debit.

Details of the companies are:

- **Telecom NZ Ltd, t 123, www.telecom.co.nz.** A former public service mono-poly, and still the main landline operator. Offers a range of services on top of the basic phone connection, including call minder, caller display, call waiting and call diversion. Basic rental charges are around NZ$50 a month. Calls within your area are free, but toll calls are expensive. Cheap rates operate for long-distance and international calls in the evenings and early mornings, and at weekends. Alternative pricing plans and special deals are often available. Telecom is also one of the two **mobile phone** companies operating in New Zealand. Telecom mobile numbers have the prefix 027. Telecom and Vodafone (*see* below) offer a constantly changing and heavily marketed range of pricing plans from unlimited text messages to free calls at certain times. Pre-pay and pay-as-you-go options are sold. Pre-pay time can be bought on a card at dairies, bookshops, petrol stations and super-markets, with your EFTPOS (debit) card at an ATM machine or with a credit card. Check out the deals on offer at the time you get connected. There are countless mobile phone retailers in every town. Telecom also operates a dial-up Internet service provider and high-speed broadband service (*see* p.167).

• **TelstraClear Limited**, t 0508 888800 (freephone), **www.telstraclear.co.nz**. The alternative landline operator. Line rental charges are similar, but TelstraClear also offers a range of HomePlan pricing plans, with different rates for calls to mobiles, toll calls and at different times of day. It's mind-boggling, but if you can work out when you make the most calls and where to, you can save. Telecom and TelstraClear plans are remarkably similar, with just a few dollars between them. Also offers all the answering services galore, and operates a high-speed Internet service (*see* p.168).

• **Vodafone New Zealand Ltd**, t 0800 800021, t 777 (from a Vodafone mobile), **www.vodafone.co.nz**. The other mobile phone company. Vodafone mobile numbers have the prefix 021. A range of phones and price plans are on offer (*see* Telecom, above). Also offers Internet service, *see* p.168.

## Fax

All you need to send and receive faxes is a fax machine and a phone line.

# Internet and Television

## Internet

You can access the Internet from your home or business using dial-up or broadband services, wi-fi or in some areas satellite. ADSL broadband is now available in all but the most rural parts of the country. Until you get set up at home, cyber-cafés are ubiquitous. Mobile broadband is available in all major towns and cities, although the BlackBerry has not yet made it to New Zealand.

Broadband Internet penetration is slowly increasing in New Zealand, but it lags behind many OECD countries – 20th out of 30 – in uptake of the service. Around 16.5 out of 100 New Zealanders subscribe to a high-speed Internet service, compared to an average of 18.8 per 100 across the OECD and 29 per 100 in the top quartile of OECD countries (which includes Korea, Iceland, the Scandinavian countries, Canada and the Netherlands). At the last count, 800,000 New Zealand households were using broadband to check their emails, contribute to blogs, update their profiles on social networking sites, download movies and music, shop online, buy and sell on TradeMe (New Zealand's answer to eBay) and access all that marvellous and not-so-marvellous information on the Internet; and 675,000 households were still painfully watching their screen and waiting with dial-up services.

The reason broadband has been slow to take off in New Zealand is a stifling lack of competition. Telecom NZ still has a near-monopoly on broadband connections: it boasts a 77 per cent market share. As the main wholesaler of broadband access, it sets the terms for its competitors. It has taken repeated interventions from the Commerce Commission to persuade Telecom to offer more competitive terms to its rivals. While the cost of broadband subscriptions is relatively low (at starting prices of around NZ$25, or 1.5 per cent of per capita GDP – similar to other OECD countries), both download and upload speeds are slow (typically 256 kbps and 128 kbps respectively – compared to a standard speed of 5 mbps in more advanced broadband economies) unless you pay a significant premium. Most frustrating of all for those who have become accustomed to unlimited data transmission, most subscriptions include a bitcap (a limit on how much you can download every month); this varies depending how much you pay, but can go as low as 100 MB per month.

Most broadband Internet is delivered via ADSL. Wireless transmission is available from some providers in areas the cables haven't reached, but tends to cost more. One provider, Iconz, offers Internet access via satellite.

## Internet Service Providers

A bewildering range of monthly pricing plans and options is on offer – though when you plough through the small print there is often little difference between what the different companies are trying to tempt you with. Consumer NZ, **www.consumer.org.nz** (New Zealand's answer to *Which?*) publishes frequently updated reports (available online for a modest fee) on the best deals and service providers around. Many companies offer incentives to join them – most commonly a free modem and connection. 'Bundling' of services, though often under investigation by the Commerce Commission, is common. The Internet Service Providers' Association of New Zealand, **www.ispanz.co.nz**, has information and links to some of the country's more than 50 ISPs (other than the Telecom and TelstraClear duopoly). Some of the best-known are listed below.

### The Big Four

- **Telecom NZ, www.telecom.co.nz, t** 0800 00 30 40. For better or worse, the former state telecoms monopoly is still the market leader. Offers a range of deals for home phone, broadband, wireless broadband, dial-up, mobile phones and mobile broadband. Broadband plans start at $29.95 for a monthly maximum data allowance of 200 MB. The top-of-the range plan, at $149.95, has a cap of 50 GB.

- **TelstraClear**, **www.telstraclear.co.nz** (all services), **www.telstraclear.co.nz** (internet), **t** 0508 888800. Telecom's closest competitor. Offers a remarkably similar range of deals for home phone, broadband and dial-up services. Plans currently start at $26.95 for up to 1 GB of downloads.

- **CallPlus**, **www.callplus.co.nz**, **t** 0800 892 000. The third largest telecoms company, CallPlus offers technical support in Chinese and Korean. Its residential arm, **Slingshot**, **www.slingshot.co.nz**, offers competitive home phone, broadband and dial-up services. A starter deal costs $24.95 a month for up to 15 GB of downloads.

- **Ihug**, **www.ihug.co.nz**, **t** 0800 GETIHUG. Now owned by Vodafone, and greedily guzzling up smaller rivals. Offers home phone, mobile, broadband and dial-up, with deals for combinations of the four. Broadband combined with home phone starts at $30 per month for up to 1 GB.

## Some of the Rest

- **Actrix**, **www.actrix.co.nz**, **t** 0800 ACTRIX. Broadband and dial-up. Quite business-orientated.

- **Compass**, **www.compass.net.nz**, **t** 0800 240 840. Home phone, Internet and wi-fi.

- **Earthlight**, **www.earthlight.co.nz**, **t** (03) 479 0303. Dial-up, broadband and business services such as website hosting and web design.

- **Enternet Online**, **www.eol.co.nz**, **t** (07) 577 0066. Dial-up and wi-fi.

- **Eznet**, **www.eznet.co.nz**, **t** 0508 273 887. Unlimited dial-up.

- **FX Networks**, **www.fx.net.nz**, **t** 0800 65 65 38. High-speed, flat-rate bandwidth, mainly for business.

- **Iconz**, **www.iconz.co.nz**, **t** 0800 843 638. Broadband, dial-up, wireless and even satellite services, which extend as far as the Chatham Islands. Also offers website hosting and other business services.

- **IGrin**, **www.igrin.co.nz**, **t** 0800 244 746. Internet Group, Northland.

- **InSPire Net**, **www.inspire.net.nz**, **t** 0800 4THENET.

- **Intersol**, **www.intersol.co.nz**, **t** (09) 826 3908. Internet services for business in the Auckland region.

- **ISPNZ**, **www.ispnz.co.nz**, **t** (03) 203 9999. Broadband and website hosting for Southland.

- **Kinect**, **www.kinect.co.nz**, **t** 0800 87 87 82. Can supply you with power as well as phone and Internet.

- **KOL**, **www.kol.co.nz**, **t** 0800 438 565. Kiwi Online (no relation to America Online) offers home phone, dial-up, broadband and webmail services.

- **Maxnet**, **www.maxnet.co.nz**, **t** 0800 629 638.

- **Orcon, www.orcon.net.nz, t** 0508 564 687. Fast-growing provider, offering home phone, dial-up, broadband and Internet for business.
- **The Packing Shed, www.ps.gen.nz, t** 0800 323 002. Franklin-based.
- **Paradise Net, www.paradise.net.nz, t** 0800 467 272.
- **Plain Communications, www.plain.co.nz, t** 0800 999 669. Website hosting as well as dial-up and broadband.
- **PlaNet, www.pl.net, t** 0800 PLANET. Pre-pay dial-up and broadband.
- **Snap, snap.net.nz, www.netaccess.co.nz, t** 0800 500 638. Home phone, broadband, dial-up and 'Naked DSL' (it's not pornographic).
- **South Net Ltd, www.southnet.co.nz, t** 0800 476 884. Internet services for Southlanders.
- **Woosh, www.woosh.com, t** 0800 4 WOOSH. Specialises in wireless broadband and phone. Also wired broadband.

## Television

Terrestrial TV is free – you just have to endure the interminable commercial breaks, even on TVNZ (the public service broadcaster). The other option is **Sky** (popular for its live rugby), either digital or UHF. The usual sorts of packages are available. You just need a dish, then you pay an installation fee and a monthly fee for your package (**www.skytv.co.nz, t** 0800 800759, and branches in towns).

# Postal Services

**New Zealand Post, t** 0800 501501, **www.nzpost.co.nz**, is reminiscent of the Royal Mail in its heyday: friendly, efficient and fast. Every town has its post shop and the NZ Post Paper Plus bookshops, and some dairies (corner shops) provide a postal service too. As well as standard postal services, post shops offer *poste restante*, fax, bill payment, foreign currency exchange, money transfer and other services.

Mail delivery around New Zealand is speedy and reliable. There are three types of delivery on offer: **standard post** (delivered in two to three days maximum – less if it's not travelling far), **fast post** (next-day delivery – simply put two standard stamps on any letter) and **registered post** (guaranteed delivery). Parcels can also be sent from post shops by **packet post** (small packets), **parcel post** (large parcels) or **Courier Post** (next-day delivery, with 'track and trace' facilities). Special Courier Post 'trackpacks' are on sale at post shops. There are also three types of delivery available overseas: **international express** ('fast and secure courier delivery worldwide' – with track and trace from pick-up to delivery overseas and compensation up to NZ$2,000); **international airmail** (delivery to the

UK in 4–10 days); and **international economy** (delivery to the UK in around three weeks, costing around 15 per cent less than airmail).

Several other companies offer courier services around the country and overseas. They may be slightly cheaper than Courier Post, but are likely to be less convenient unless you are running a business (you may have to drop parcels off at depots in out-of-the-way industrial zones). Some companies to try are:

- **Courier Post, t** 0800 268 7437, **www.courierpost.co.nz.**
- **Fastway Couriers, t** (06) 843 3143, **www.fastway.co.nz.**
- **New Zealand Couriers, t** 0800 800841, **www.nzcouriers.co.nz.**
- **Post Haste Couriers, t** 0800 106 828, **www.posthaste.co.nz.**

In the era of e-mail, NZ Post still offers *poste restante* – a place for you to receive parcels and letters if you don't have an address on arrival in the country. Once you are settled, you can have your mail delivered to a post office box, which may be more secure than having it left in a kerbside mail box, especially if you are away from home often. (Many businesses use a PO box.) Even if you live way out in the sticks you can still get a daily mail delivery from the Rural Post as long as you register your name with NZ Post, and when you move you can get your mail redirected to your new address. You can also send and receive faxes using NZ Post's Faxlink.

NZ Post's **financial services** include payment for all household bills including banking and insurance, gas and electricity, telephone, rates and car registration. Alternatively you can register with NZ Post for **eBill**, which enables you to both receive and pay your bills over the Internet. You can also buy and sell foreign currency and Travelex travellers' cheques at NZ Post, and send and receive money from overseas via Western Union Money Transfer. **Kiwibank**, a New Zealand-owned bank, operates from post shops, too. It promises low fees as well as all the usual bank services: home loans, term deposits, credit cards, savings and cheque accounts (*see* 'Money and Banking', below).

# Money and Banking

The current **exchange rate** at time of publication is: £1 = NZ$2.48; US$1 = NZ$1.27. To check current rates, look on **www.xe.com/ucc** or bank websites such as **www.bnz.co.nz**.

## Banks

It is easy to open a bank account in New Zealand. You do not need to be a resident or provide references, but you must show evidence of a permanent address (a post office box is acceptable, but not a hotel or motel), identification (passport or driver's licence) and a small deposit (around NZ$200). The bank should be able to get your account up and running in 10 days or less.

Banks are normally open Monday to Friday 9–4.30pm, with ATMs operating 24 hours a day. To find a bank branch in your area, look under 'Banks' in the *Yellow Pages*. The big banks are:

- **ANZ, www.anz.com.**
- **ASB, www.asb.co.nz.**
- **Bank of New Zealand (BNZ), www.bnz.co.nz.**
- **Kiwibank, www.kiwibank.co.nz.** The state-owned bank that operates out of post offices.
- **National Bank, www.nationalbank.co.nz.**
- **TSB, www.tsb.co.nz.**
- **Westpac, www.westpactrust.co.nz.**

All banks offer similar services, although they compete fiercely over interest and mortgage rates. In addition to cheque and savings accounts and foreign exchange services, New Zealand banks offer personal loans, home loans, insurance, investment, credit cards, and property and business finance.

It may come as a bit of a shock to British bankers that most banks charge a fee for every transaction made, including ATM withdrawals, cheques and **EFTPOS** (Electronic Funds Transfer at Point of Sale – debit card) transactions. Charges can be as high as NZ$1.50 for cheques or when dealing with a teller in person.

Banks may offer special terms for some accounts, which might include a certain number of free electronic transactions per month. All major banks offer **online banking**. Cheques are not widely used, and, when accepted, are only valid with ID such as a driver's licence or passport. New Zealand banks do not routinely issue debit cards, and will not issue you with a credit card unless you are a resident. If you earn income in New Zealand, the bank will need your IRD number (*see* 'Taxation', p.172).

**Foreign exchange** services are efficient, although you may need to allow a considerable time lag for the processing of overseas cheques (up to six weeks). One option is to open a foreign currency account into which you can pay foreign currency cheques or transfer your savings, exchanging the cash for New Zealand dollars at an opportune moment. To transfer money from a UK account you will need to make arrangements with your British bank before departure, and then issue all instructions to your bank in writing. Fees for international transfers tend to be high (around £20 per transfer).

Debit cards issued by British banks can be used directly for electronic payments and cash withdrawals in New Zealand, although there is a surcharge for ATM withdrawals (check with your bank in the UK before departure, as these charges can be exorbitant; they do not usually apply to credit cards).

# Taxation

Inland Revenue, known as the **Inland Revenue Department (IRD)**, **www.ird. govt.nz**, is the government department that collects taxes. You will need to contact the IRD to obtain an **IRD number** before you start a job or open a bank account. The New Zealand **tax year** is from 1 April to 31 March.

For Inland Revenue phone numbers in your area, consult the *Blue Pages* (Government listings) in your phone book. For independent tax advice, look in the *Yellow Pages* under 'Taxation Consultants'.

If you are **employed**, your tax will be deducted from salary or wages by your employer as you earn your income, under the pay-as-you-earn (PAYE) system. Your bank will deduct tax on any interest earned too.

If you are **self-employed** or for any other reason have not paid tax on your income as it was earned, you will be required to file a tax return at the end of the year to work out your tax liability. After the first tax return you will be expected to pay provisional tax in instalments through the year, based on the previous year's income. Inland Revenue will be happy to assist by providing you with an **IR3 form**. If you **operate a business as a sole trader, limited liability company or other business entity**, you have to account for your own tax progressively during the year. This is referred to as provisional tax. It is payable in three instalments during the year, based on what you expect your tax bill to be. Provisional tax paid is then deducted from your tax bill at the end of the year. If you go into business you will need to contact the IRD to establish what tax rules apply. Current tax rates for individuals, sole traders and partners in partnership are 19.5 per cent for all earnings up to NZ$38,000, then 33 per cent on earnings between NZ$38,001 and NZ$60,000, and 39 per cent for earnings over NZ$60,001. There is a flat 33 per cent tax rate for companies.

New Zealand residents are liable for income tax on their **worldwide income**. If you are a New Zealand tax resident you will need to pay income tax on all income you receive from New Zealand and overseas. New Zealand has a **double taxation agreement** with the UK, so you will not have to pay tax twice (i.e. in both countries).

You are a **New Zealand resident for tax purposes** if you are in New Zealand for more than 183 days (just over half a year) in any 12-month period. You are considered to be a resident from the day you arrive in New Zealand. The 183 days need not be consecutive. You will also be a New Zealand resident for tax purposes if you have an 'enduring relationship' with New Zealand. This is assessed on the basis of such things as whether you are in New Zealand for continuous periods from time to time; whether you own, lease or have access to property in New Zealand; your social ties (for example if your immediate family is in New Zealand or your children are being educated in the country); your employment (if you work in New Zealand); your economic ties (bank accounts, credit cards, investments or life insurance); your personal property (if you own or keep possessions here); whether you receive welfare benefits, pensions or other payments; and whether you intend to live in New Zealand.

**Goods and services tax (GST)** is charged on almost all goods and services in New Zealand, at a rate of 12.5 per cent of the price of goods or services. You will also pay **Resident Withholding Tax (RWT)** on interest you earn from bank accounts or other investments. Your bank will deduct RWT when it credits interest to your account.

On the positive side, you may qualify for 'Working for Families' assistance, financial help from the IRD for low- to middle-income families with children under 18; it is not a welfare benefit, but a recognition of the costs of raising a family (*see* p.191). You may be able to receive Family Assistance if you are a New Zealand resident and have been in the country for at least 12 months.

There is no **capital gains** or **inheritance tax** in New Zealand, but you will remain liable to pay these taxes in the UK for five full tax years after you move to New Zealand.

# Shopping

New Zealand has gone the American way of consumerism. Most retailing is done in big supermarkets and megastores, with a few new-generation boutiques springing up in city centres. The range of goods available is not huge (whatever came in on the last ship from China is likely to be on offer in all the main shops) and you will soon become sceptical of the endless rounds of discounts offered by the large chains. New Zealand-made goods tend to be of a higher quality than the Chinese imports, but also more expensive. Products shipped from as far away as Europe or even the USA are regarded as luxury items; they tend to be expensive at the outset in NZ dollars, and become more so as they accumulate air – or sea – miles.

## Food Shops

If all you want is a litre of milk, a newspaper and a bar of soap, your needs will be met by the local 'dairy' – the New Zealand name for a corner shop. **Four Square** is a well-known chain, but many dairies are independently owned and run. You won't find much fresh produce here, and prices for the convenience of popping into your local shop may be up to twice as much as in one of the supermarkets.

**New World** is New Zealand's very own supermarket chain, and as good as they come. Although individual stores vary, they tend to stock high-quality meat, fish, fruit, vegetables and freshly baked breads as well as all the essentials from tea and coffee to toilet paper. **Food Town** or **Woolworths** compete with New

World, while **Pak'n'Save** and **Countdown** compete fiercely in the cheap food market (but are not necessarily always cheaper). There are plenty of regional variations on the formula too: Wellington is the proud home of **Moore Wilson**'s, a wholesaler open for retail too, which is particularly good for all the fresh stuff. Wellington and Auckland are home to large Asian supermarkets too (Wellington's biggest is called, originally enough, **A-mart**), selling masses of Chinese, Japanese, Korean, Thai and Indonesian foodstuffs that are fiendishly difficult to identify. **The Warehouse**, affectionately known as the Red Box, piles it high and sells it cheap; it has been fighting a long battle to be allowed to enter the food market.

You may be able to avoid the big supermarkets if you want to. If you live rurally, befriend the owner of the nearest field with cows or sheep in it, and come slaughter you may well have the chance to buy a whole animal (butchered) to put in your freezer; alternatively raise your own – many New Zealanders do (*see* 'Butchers – Homekill Services' in your *Yellow Pages*). If this is all too down-home-on-the-farm for you, most towns still have a traditional butcher. Sadly much of the meat on sale is nowhere near the 'export quality' lamb you can buy in the UK; organic poultry and meat is unheard of, and sausages nasty. Again, rural dwellers will find fruit and vegetables are often sold at roadside stands or directly by the growers – both better and cheaper than at the supermarkets, although you may not get such a range and you won't find the out-of-season imported produce such as American grapes or Australian oranges and lemons.

Traditional bakers are having a resurgence, led largely by Italophiles baking focaccia and fabulous German bakeries. Old-style New Zealand bakers do a good range of sweet breads, buns, tarts and old-fashioned delicacies such as the lamington (a sponge square dipped in raspberry jam and coconut shavings). If you want to find all the high-class fresh stuff in one place, including small-scale cheese-producers, try to find one of the many weekly farmers' markets. Many towns have their own 'health-food' shop, too.

## Wine

Perhaps surprisingly, given New Zealand's new-found wine connoisseurship, there are few wine boutiques or small-scale wine specialists. For large volumes of booze, there are a number of liquor chains with such sensitive names as Liquorland, Liquor King, Liquor Plus, the Liquor Store, Super Liquor, Cut Price Liquor, The Mill Liquorsave or, for variety, Swig – drive-in stores where you can pile crates of beer, wine or hard liquor into the boot of your car. If you live in a wine-producing region, most of the wineries offer cellar sales if you have time for a leisurely drive around the vineyards, but the best selections of wine are available at the better supermarkets (New World and Woolworths have good wine buyers). Here you will find not only a selection of New Zealand wines often at good discounts, but the cheaper Aussie wines and some French, Italian and

Spanish wines – often better value and better drinking than some of the local produce. You must be over 18 and able to prove it to buy alcohol or consume it in a public place.

# Household Goods

There's no shortage of places to buy essential household goods, although you'll soon become familiar with the lack of variety epitomised by the pile 'em high, sell 'em cheap approach of the big chains. These stores advertise heavily on television, with discount sales on every possible occasion or even when there is none, so it won't take you long to know their names – and to have their infuriating jingles going around in your head. **The Warehouse** ('making the affordable desirable') is New Zealand's very own. If you can face the glare of fluorescent lights, the schmaltzy piped music and the anarchy in the aisles you can pick up bargains from shoes to electronic goods – but don't expect them to last. **Briscoe's** ('you should have known better') is a couple of notches more upmarket for household goods from China to Manchester; its basic prices are high, so that it can make more sales by discounting, and it stocks some good quality stuff. **Harvey Norman** ('go Harvey, go Harvey, go Harvey, go') sells the sort of large, comfortable, ugly furniture that has long been the thing in New Zealand. **Farmer's**, a New Zealand institution akin to Marks & Spencer, sells everything from socks to sofas; it is another chain that suffers from endemic sale-itis. **Farmlands** is its rural equivalent (no relation), selling everything from gumboots to cattle feed.

If you plan to do up your own home, you'll be spoilt for choice. **Mitre 10** ('maitre dix') is one of the best-known hardware chains, with branches all over the shop (you won't find a friendly, independent local hardware store to help you choose the right-sized nail in New Zealand). **HTL Hardware** is another place to shop for door-handles and locks. For building supplies, there are any number of big-box chains – **Placemakers, Carters, Benchmark, ITM, Smith** and so on (with regional variations), as well as more specialist suppliers of individual components from plasterboard to plumbing. You'll be equally spoilt for choice in the paint and decorating supplies department: **Colourplus, Dulux, Guthrie Bowron** ('it's all in the name'), **Levene** and **Resene** are just a few of the giants jostling for your business in this area. There are plenty of places to hire machinery, too, in line with the Kiwi DIY ethos.

There's heavy competition in the home appliances and home entertainment markets, from chains such as **Noel Leeming, Duckworth's** and **Dick Smith** as well as some of the stores mentioned above. They will all dump flyers in your mailbox by the hundreds, so you'll never be short of liners for the cat litter box, or a job for teenage offspring delivering them. Prices for all hi-tech goods tend to be low, due to the relative strength of the New Zealand dollar and the proximity of Asia, where most of the goods are made, but do fluctuate with the exchange rate. Home cinema is hugely popular in the country where more sophisticated forms of entertainment are not readily available to all – despite the fact that most video rental is controlled by a couple of giants (**Video Ezy** and **United Video**), which do not stock much other than the latest mainstream blockbusters. The catalogue of **Arovideo** online, which is based in Wellington but will courier videos or DVDs around the country, provides a welcome antidote to the usual range of action movies and supernatural thrillers. There are now several commercial online DVD rental sites too (**www.moviestars.co.nz**, **www.dvdunlimited.co.nz**, **www.dvdvideo.co.nz** and so on).

## High-street Fashion and Boutiques

At the top end of the fashion market, there are some excellent New Zealand designers (**Zambesi**, **Trelise Cooper**, **Karen Walker**, **Marilyn Sainty**, **Nom D**, **Workshop** and **World**, to name just a few of the best-known), who sell through their own flagship stores in Auckland, Wellington, Christchurch or Dunedin, and through boutiques in the provincial towns. At the lower end of the market, high-street chains dominate (**Glassons** is ubiquitous – the Topshop of the South Pacific– alongside **Hallensteins** for men). 'Op shops' (*see* right) are everywhere, although increasingly eschewed for cheap Chinese-made teenage fashions. Wellington boasts its own department store, **Kirkcaldie and Stains**, with full snob value as well as a range of imported clothes. In the larger towns you will also find the work of small-scale designer/makers.

For children's clothes there are several chains, with **Pumpkin Patch** leading the way in style and quality. **Hannahs** is the place for good solid children's shoes (the Clark's of the south). It can be hard to find good shoes in New Zealand, with little middle ground between expensive imports and **No.1 Shoe Warehouse**, where the shoes are so cheap it doesn't matter if they only last a week.

## Books and Stationery

Once again, chains dominate. **Warehouse Stationery**, **Whitcoulls** and **Paper Plus** have basic stationery pretty much covered.

**Dymocks** is the best of the bookselling chains. Wellington, the most intellectual of the cities, has numerous independent booksellers and there are a few in smaller towns too. Good bookshops can usually order books that they do not stock, but you may have to turn to Amazon for some books that are not distributed in New Zealand. Whitcoulls and the NZ Post-owned Paper Plus both offer a broad, more downmarket range of books and magazines, with good bargains from time to time.

Newsagents do not exist in the same way that they do in the UK, as many people get their newspaper delivered by subscription – otherwise you can buy newspapers and magazines at dairies and supermarkets.

## Other Essential Shops

The pharmaceutical trade is big business in New Zealand, with drug companies allowed to advertise on TV. Pharmacies are everywhere, some with more of an emphasis on homeopathic and natural healthcare, others with a sideline in cosmetics. One or more will stay open late in any town. Dry-cleaners are not hard to come by, either. Some may be willing to pick up and drop off your cleaning. Launderettes are not so common in a land where most houses have a separate laundry area.

## Second-hand Shops and Street Markets

Churches and charities run countless 'op shops' where you can pick up old clothes for a pittance if you're prepared to rummage. Second-hand furniture shops are common, and some towns have their own auction rooms where you may be able to pick up anything from a dining-room table and chairs to a box of old LPs. Another option for old furniture is the weekly classified papers, specific to each area, or increasingly **TradeMe** (**www.trademe.co.nz**), New Zealand's answer to eBay. For obvious reasons, there aren't so many antique shops, although one or two entrepreneurs ship in old stuff from Europe by the containerload. Towns such as Wellington and Christchurch do, however, boast some serious fine art and antiques dealers.

Trawling street markets is a popular Sunday morning pastime in much of New Zealand, although the calibre of junk you find will depend on where you are. The Polynesian markets of South Auckland are famous for printed textiles from the Pacific islands and Maori fashion. Schools, rotary clubs and Scout groups often hold book sales or galas at which they flog general bric-a-brac. And if you really can't think of anywhere else to spend your money – or don't have very much – there's always the two-dollar shop, crammed with toxic Chinese plastic.

# Transport

## Public Transport

New Zealand is car country (and truck, tractor and trailer country, too); public transport is limited. Flights between the main towns are frequent and relatively affordable, while buses run infrequently (but more cheaply) between major towns too. Passenger trains are practically non-existent outside towns, other than one or two commuter services and a couple of tourist routes. Urban bus services are quite reliable, but most people still choose to have a car even in town.

The North and South Islands are connected by ferry.

## Domestic Flights

The main domestic flight operator is Air New Zealand (**www.airnz.co.nz**), which offers some good bargains. It operates nearly 500 flights a day between 25 destinations from Kaitaia in the north to Invercargill in the south. You can fly direct to most places from Auckland or Wellington, and to many from Christchurch, but will have to change to travel between smaller places.

Discount fares start at around NZ$50, but you can find yourself paying up to five times as much at busy times. The usual criteria apply in the price lottery: the earlier you book, the more likely you are to get cheap tickets, unless you can chance it and get a last-minute deal or standby; busy times for business people are the most expensive times to fly; weekends are cheaper. **Tickets** can be booked online, at the airports or at travel agents in most towns.

## Coach

Coach travel is an economical way to get around the country, although surprisingly little used by most New Zealanders over student age. The main operators are **InterCity lines, www.intercitycoach.co.nz**, and **Newmans, www. newmanscoach.co.nz**. In association with each other they travel between most towns most days, with more frequent services between the big cities and popular destinations (120 services a day to 600 towns and cities across the country, from major cities to small rural towns, across vast plains and over mountain passes, from beaches to high plateaux). Marketed largely as a tourist service, coaches also go to national parks and the start of tramping routes. Special routes include Coast to Coast from Christchurch to Greymouth and Hokitika over Arthur's Pass, from Queenstown to the start of the Routeburn track, Te Anau and Milford Sound.

Special discount fares can start as low as NZ$10 from Auckland to Wellington but may be as much as NZ$100 for longer-distance routes. A range of flexi-passes and regional coach **passes** is available if you plan to travel extensively by bus. Coaches are modern and air-conditioned. **Tickets** can be booked online or at agents in most towns.

Other operators may run local coach services. To find out about these services, ask at information centres in your area.

## Train

Long-distance passenger train services have been practically non-existent in New Zealand since the privatisation of the railways in the 1980s. Those that do operate are run principally as tourist routes. **Tranz Scenic, t** 0800 TRAINS or 0800 872467, **www.tranzscenic.co.nz**, operates four routes: the Overlander, which travels from Auckland to Wellington and back daily via the central plateau; Capital Connection, a frequent Monday–Friday commuter service between Palmerston North and Wellington; the TranzCoastal, between Picton and Christchurch along the Kaikoura coast ('through 22 tunnels and over 175 bridges'); and the TranzAlpine, coast to coast between Christchurch and Greymouth over the Southern Alps ('16 tunnels and five viaducts').

As well as the pricey one-way or return **tickets**, you can purchase rail **passes** (NZ$300 for one week, NZ$500 for a month).

## Urban and Commuter Bus and Train

All the cities have their own locally operated bus services, with connections out of the city to the hinterland, and Auckland and Wellington also have commuter rail services. Despite pushes to get people on to public transport, however, the car remains the preferred method of transport, especially in sprawling Auckland – the only place with a serious traffic congestion problem. (Proposals for new motorways and bypasses are always under discussion, but repeatedly shelved, partly in recognition of the fact that the more roads there are, the more people will take to their cars.)

### Auckland

Auckland's commuter rail network is operated by **Veolia Transport** (the same people who collect your rubbish in some London boroughs). There are three lines, western to Waitakere, eastern and southern to Pukekohe (via Orakei and Ellerslie respectively). Trains do not run on Sundays.

**Stagecoach Auckland** operates the majority of urban bus services. Buses run daily from around 6am to 11.30pm, more frequently at rush hours and more infrequently at weekends. There are a few late-night buses on Friday and Saturday nights. Board buses at the front and get off at the back.

For both buses and trains you can purchase single **tickets** or a variety of one-day, weekly or monthly (zoned) travel **passes**. You can buy your bus ticket as you board the bus, while train tickets must be purchased in advance. Passes must be bought ahead of time from information kiosks or ticket agents (mainly in dairies and bookshops). The **Auckland Discovery Pass** is a new integrated pass that allows you to travel around most of the region on buses, trains and ferries on a single ticket; it comes as both a day pass and a monthly pass. Children, old people and students travel for less.

Other services to the more far-flung suburbs and islands are operated by Bayes Coachlines, Birkenhead Transport, Fullers, Hanhams, Howick and Eastern, Pine Harbour Ferry, Ritchies, Urban Express and Waiheke Island Buses.

- **Maxx Transport, t (09) 366 6400, www.maxx.co.nz**. The central information centre for Auckland transport, based at the Britomart Information Kiosk. Fares, timetables and other useful tips.

- **Veolia Transport, t (09) 969 7777, www.connexauckland.co.nz.**

- **Stagecoach Auckland, t** 0800 STAGECOACH or **t** (09) 442 0555, **www.stagecoach.co.nz.** Bus routes and times.

## Wellington

Wellington's commuter rail services are operated by **TranzMetro, t** 0800 STAGECOACH, **www.tranzmetro.co.nz**, which runs up the west coast as far as the seaside suburb of Paraparaumu, to Johnsonville, Melling, the Hutt Valley and Wairarapa. As well as one-way and return **tickets** you can get monthly passes or a range of special excursion and 'rover' tickets.

**Stagecoach** is the main bus operator for Wellington's urban services. For routes, times and fares look on the Internet, **www.stagecoach.co.nz**, or call the Metlink Service Centre, **t** 0800 801 700. A few services run after midnight on Fridays and Saturdays. A variety of daily and monthly **passes** are on offer, or you can get a block of 10 **tickets** for a 20 per cent reduction on the normal fare.

Mana Coach Services, Newlands, Cityline Hutt Valley, Community Coach Services, Tranzit Coachlines, Wairarapa Coach Lines and Thompson Passenger Service also offer public transport in the Wellington region.

## Christchurch, Hamilton and Dunedin

For Christchurch public transport information see **www.metroinfo.org.nz**, which includes details of routes, times, fares and special discounts available with a 'metrocard', or call **t** (03) 66 88 55.

In Hamilton, check **www.ew.govt.nz** and follow the links, or call **t** 0800 4287 5463 for buses around the Waikato region.

For Dunedin bus services, visit **www.orc.govt.nz** and follow the links.

## Ferry

As well as the ferry services that connect Auckland's islands, the principal ferry service is the one that connects the North and South Islands – from Wellington harbour to Picton in the Marlborough Sounds. It is a beautiful but surprisingly long crossing. Two companies compete on the crossing. The **Interislander**, **www.interislander.co.nz, t** 0800 802 802, crosses the Cook Strait up to six times a day with its two standard car ferries (crossing time around three hours) and the high-speed Lynx car ferry (135 minutes, but prone to cancellation on the notoriously rough Strait). It offers three price categories for the crossing, from the cheapest (non-changeable, non-refundable), around NZ$200 each way for a family of four in a car, to a fully flexible ticket, around NZ$300. Special deals may be cheaper. The alternative is the **Bluebridge ferry**, a classic roll-on, roll-off car ferry operated by Strait Shipping, **www.bluebridge.co.nz, t** 0800 844 844, which makes the Wellington–Picton crossing up to four times each way each day in just over three hours at a flat rate of around NZ$250 each way for a car, two adults and two children.

**Bookings** for either ferry service can be made online, by phone or at travel agencies and information centres around the country.

# Private Transport

If you're not in one of the bigger cities, you'll need a car to get around. When you first arrive you may need to rent one. You can arrange in advance to pick up a car at the airport from one of the big international car-hire companies (Avis, Budget, Hertz and so on), but you will get a better price if you look in the *Yellow Pages* under 'Rental Vehicles' and shop around. Often local companies offer the best deals. Prices start around NZ$35 a day, but you should be able to negotiate a better price for a longer rental.

Contact details for the main companies are:

- **Avis, t** 0800 655 111; **www.avis.co.nz.**
- **Budget, t** 0800 283 438; **www.budget.co.nz.**
- **Europcar, t** 0800 800 115; **www.europcar.co.nz.**
- **Hertz, t** 0800 654 321; **www.hertz.co.nz.**
- **Thrifty, t** 0800 73 70 70; **www.thrifty.co.nz.**

## Importing Your Car

You might consider importing your own car, which you can do free of customs charge if you have owned and used the car for at least a year prior to departure and do not sell it within two years of arrival. If you have owned and used the car for less than a year, you will have to pay GST (general sales tax) of 12.5 per cent on its value (the price you paid for it, minus up to 35 per cent depreciation; see **www.customs.govt.nz** for exact calculation of value). Obviously you will have to calculate if the shipping and insurance costs make it worthwhile.

## Buying a Car

Most cars in New Zealand, both new and second-hand, are Japanese or Korean (Nissan, Toyota, Subaru, Mazda, Hyundai, Lexus, Daihatsu and so on), Australian (Holden) or American (Ford). European cars are expensive, and perceived as glamorous. Most New Zealand cars are automatic, not manual, drive.

If you decide to buy a car in New Zealand, you're in the hands of the dealers. Second-hand car dealers have the same reputation here as anywhere else in the world. Although attempts are made to ensure that odometers have not been clocked and so on, there are no guarantees and it is up to you as the buyer to check out the vehicle before you buy it.

The majority of used cars sold by dealers in New Zealand are new imports – used cars imported in bulk from Japan for resale. Look in the *Yellow Pages* under

'Car and Truck Dealers' for dealers in both new and used cars. Official dealers may be slightly more reputable, but any dealer with the initials LMVD after the name is a licensed motor vehicle dealer, and subscribes to a code of ethics. These firms are bound to display the model name, year of manufacture, number of previous owners, warranty category and full price; by law they must also offer buyers a warranty for a set period (depending on the car's age).

If you are a risk-taker, you could try going to a car auction, or make a private purchase through the classified pages of your local newspaper or car trader magazine. In any case, you can arrange with the **Automobile Association (AA)** to make a full inspection for around NZ$100. Most dealers will be happy to arrange finance deals.

Once you have bought a car, you will have to make sure it has an up-to-date **warrant of fitness (WOF)** every six months (most garages can do this) and **registration**, which you can do at the post office (it costs around NZ$100 per year). You are also legally required to **insure** the vehicle against third party damage. Check the *Yellow Pages* for insurers and shop around. Premiums for car insurance is nowhere near as high in New Zealand as in the UK.

### Car Insurance Companies

- **AA, t** 0800 500221; **www.aainsurance.co.nz**.
- **AMI, t** 0800 100200; **www.ami.co.nz**.
- **AMP, , t** 0800 267467; **www.amp.co.nz**.
- **AXA, t** 0800 106652; **www.axa.co.nz**.
- **State, t** 0800 802424; **www.state.co.nz**.

## Driving in New Zealand

All drivers need a **driver's licence**, which you must always have on you when driving. You can be fined if you do not have your licence with you if stopped by the police. You can drive on a British or other foreign licence for up to a year, after which you will need to apply for a New Zealand driver's licence and pass an eyesight examination, as well as a driving theory and practical test; contact the **Land Transport Safety Authority (LTSA)** to obtain a New Zealand licence.

New Zealanders drive on the **left-hand side** of the road, which makes it easy for British drivers. **Speed limits** are 50km/h in towns, 100 km/h on the open road and 70km/h when indicated; LSZ means you can drive at 100km/h in good conditions but must slow down to 50km/h when conditions are bad.

While most rules of the road will be familiar, the **Give Way** rule is designed to trip up (or kill) newcomers: you must always give way to traffic crossing or approaching from your right (like the French *priorité à droite*); if you are turning left at the lights, and an oncoming car is turning right, the other car goes first. There are a lot of boy racers and macho drivers around, who like to drive too fast on roads that are often narrow – there are frequent news reports about road fatalities. They also consider it sissy to indicate or look in the rear-view mirror – be prepared for the car in front of you to stop in the middle of the road, then pull off and finally indicate when it's way too late.

It is illegal to **drink and drive** and the police are very vigilant about drink drivers and speeding, with substantial fines for both. **Seat belts** are compulsory in front and rear seats, and children under five must be restrained in an approved child seat (except in a taxi, when the child is allowed to travel in the back seat restrained by an ordinary seat belt). **Safety helmets** are compulsory for cyclists and motorcyclists, including children being carried on bicycles. There is a spot fine of NZ$55 for riding a bicycle without a helmet that conforms to safety standards. For the full rules, obtain a copy of the *New Zealand Road Code* from the LTSA, bookshops and stationery shops.

**Parking** is not usually difficult outside Auckland, but most towns have a metered parking system and will fine you if you overstay your limit. It is against the rules to park facing the wrong way on the street, on a yellow line or within six metres of an intersection or pedestrian crossing.

**Petrol** in New Zealand is expensive due to high levels of fuel tax. Prices have gone up and up with the soaring price of crude oil; at the time of writing you will have to pay NZ$1.75 for a litre of **unleaded** petrol. **Diesel** is cheaper, but you will have to pay a higher car registration fee for a diesel car. Some cars have been converted to run on **liquid petroleum gas (LPG)**, which is cleaner and cheaper.

### Useful Numbers

- **AA, t** 0800 500333, **www.aa.co.nz.**
- **Land Transport Safety Authority, t** 0800 108 809, **www.ltsa.govt.nz.**

# Crime and the Police

Dial **t** 111 for any emergency including police.

Media reports give the impression that New Zealand is in the grip of a frenzy of drug-fuelled violence but, despite the odd headline-grabbing spree, crime here is nothing to be alarmed about. Recorded crime has fallen steadily since the late 1990s: just over a thousand criminal offences were recorded per 1,000 people in 2007, down from 1,224 in 1997. Unfortunately this decrease in criminality did not apply across all genres of crime: 127 violent crimes per 10,000 people were recorded in 2007, a significant increase on the 105 per 10,000 of 1997; 81 per cent of these violent crimes were, however, resolved. Sexual crime rates have remained steady over the past 10 years at around 8 per 10,000 people. Drugs and antisocial offences have tailed off slightly, from 146 per 10,000 people in 1997 to 136 in 2007, with a 93 per cent rate of resolution. Dishonesty has fallen markedly, from 770 to 559 offences per 10,000 people –

## P, Ice, Ecstasy and Other Amphetamine-type Stimulants

*More generally, increased offending around amphetamine-type stimulants and incidents of gang-related violence are nationwide problems.*
Briefing to the incoming Police Minister, 2002

*Methamphetamine, a scourge on society.*
Police Commissioner Rob Robinson, 2004

New Zealand crime's only real growth area is 'non-cannabis drug offences' – the manufacture, possession, use and sale of amphetamine-type stimulants such as speed, pure, P, burn, goey, crank, meth, crystal, ice and Ya Ba. Methamphetamine is an extremely addictive, powerful stimulant. It produces wakefulness, hyperactivity and a euphoric effect. The crystal form of methamphetamine, called 'ice' due to its appearance, is the most pure. This highly addictive form of methamphetamine has more pronounced effects on the central nervous system and is becoming increasingly common.

As these drugs are being more readily available, serious violence and domestic violence have become associated with methamphetamine use. Since a peak in 2003, however, when recording crimes involving methamphetamine reached 3,978, drug-fuelled crime has diminished. During 2004, 190 clandestine laboratories ('clan labs') were closed down.

Contrary to stereotype, many P-users are educated, affluent young white men from Auckland, who use their mobile phones to conduct deals by text message, typically spend about NZ$350 each time they buy drugs, and binge for up to 48 hours every fortnight. Amphetamine drug-users have high levels of full-time employment, come from a range of occupational backgrounds including professionals, earn mid-level incomes and have relatively high levels of educational achievement; large numbers are European and disproportionately more live in urban settings, in the upper half of the North Island and in Auckland.

New groups of methamphetamine users are consistent with the diffusion of methamphetamine use from the 'originator' sub-cultures, such as the dance party community and motorcycle gangs, to broader society which includes lower socio-economic groups and Maori and Pacific peoples. Reports of increased drug-dealing by methamphetamine-users and a greater cross-section of people selling the drug are consistent with the spread of methamphetamine to wider sections of society. The sale of smaller weights of methamphetamine at lower prices, and reported sales of methamphetamine

although at 22 per cent these are much less likely to be resolved. Property damage has inexplicably soared over the last couple of years, from around 100 to 123 offences per 10,000 – an increase of over 20 per cent – but property abuse, conversely, has fallen. Murder rates have remained steady at 0.1 per 10,000 – although that is an average of around 50 murders a year in a population of just over 4 million; if it's any reassurance, most are resolved. The big triumph for the from cannabis drug houses, suggest marketing strategies aimed at lower socio-economic groups, teenagers and traditional cannabis-users. All of this might make amphetamine sound like a harmless (if illegal) party drug. But nearly half the users have mental health problems and amphetamines exacerbate these. Many say the drug makes them angry. Frequent users of methamphetamine who report pre-existing mental health problems including tendencies to self-harm find that use increases their levels of 'anxiety', 'mood swings', 'short temper', 'paranoia', 'depression' and the level of suicide. And increasingly methamphetamine is being linked to violent crime. Almost one in 10 people arrested has used an amphetamine-based drug just before offending, and 21 per cent have used the drug in the month prior to arrest. Arrestees report that the use of these drug types is a factor in their criminal offending. About a quarter of the arrestees who recently used amphetamines considered their use of these drugs to have played a major part in the activities they were subsequently arrested for. Serious violence and domestic violence are frequently associated with methamphetamine. One-fifth of frequent users have problems controlling their methamphetamine use.

Add to this picture the patterns of production and trade: frequent methamphetamine users are often involved in other illegal activities such as drug-dealing and drug manufacture. One-third of the frequent methamphetamine-users has sold methamphetamine and about one in five has manufactured it or exchanged it for stolen property – although amphetamine-sellers report selling only to 'close friends and family members'. The proceeds of the illicit drug trade are likely to be concentrated among a relatively small number of local organised criminal gangs who have been instrumental in the introduction of methamphetamine manufacture to New Zealand. Informants indicate high levels of involvement by organised criminal groups in the import, manufacture and sale of methamphetamine in New Zealand. Apart from importation, where 'Asian triads' are identified as a leading group, three local and established gangs (the 'Mongrel Mob', 'Black Power' and the 'Tribesmen') are identified as the groups most often involved in the trade in New Zealand. The 'Hell's Angels' and 'Headhunters' were also commonly mentioned. Successful busts often involve Asian students bringing the ingredients into the country. The estimates of the dollar value of the illicit markets for amphetamine and ecstasy suggest that the combined value of these markets is approximately NZ$168.3 million, approaching the dollar value of the entire market for cannabis in New Zealand.

police is that rates of burglary have fallen around 30 per cent in the last 10 years, from 207 to 147 crimes per 10,000; unfortunately this category of crime is rarely resolved. Theft, burglary and 'car conversion' still account for 60 per cent of recorded crime, while violent crime accounts for less than 10 per cent. Around 45 per cent of all crimes are resolved. The Auckland City and Counties Manukau districts (South Auckland) traditionally record a significant proportion of the country's recorded crime, followed closely by Eastern (Hawke's Bay, Gisborne and the East Cape).

The police budget of more than NZ$1 billion a year is at its highest level ever, with police numbers at 10,300 also the highest ever. The Labour Government may be liberal, but no one could say it's not fighting crime.

Burglary is a high-profile crime, perhaps because many New Zealanders have had some contact with it – either having had their homes burgled or knowing of someone else who has had their home burgled. In a 1996 National Survey of Crime Victims, one-third of the respondents felt there was a crime problem in their neighbourhoods, with more than three-quarters of these identifying burglary as the major cause for concern. In fact, theft accounts for 50 per cent of all so-called 'dishonesty offences', while only a quarter of those recorded in 2000 were house burglaries. Since the late 1990s, police have targeted resources towards reducing the incidence and effects of burglary and car theft, but the resolution rate for burglaries remains very low, with only 16 per cent of burglars being identified and dealt with. Theft, burglary, car conversion, fraud and the receiving of stolen goods have all, however, decreased since the mid 1990s. And while the media have tended to play up fears of 'home invasion' – burglary mixed with violence – it is not in fact very common. People expect to feel safe and secure in their own homes and statistically the likelihood of a physical encounter with an intruder is low.

Two of the media's favourite bugbears are the proliferation of 'P' labs, where the pure amphetamine drug known as P is produced, and cases of sometimes homicidal violence against children, nearly always within families. While the horror of a case back in 2004 in which a P-addled stepfather was convicted of murdering his stepdaughter is not diminished by the passing years, it remains the exception that grabbed the headlines.

Although violent crime has traditionally aroused the most public concern and comment, it constitutes only around 10 per cent of all recorded offences. While the media attention given to violent crime may be out of proportion in terms of its contribution to overall crime levels, the effect of violent crime on the victims and the general public's perception of community safety contributes to its high profile. Serious assaults, minor assaults and intimidation or threats account for about 88 per cent of all violent crime, but serious assaults have decreased since the mid-1990s. More than half of all serious assaults involve men attacking women; the police practice of arresting perpetrators of family violence, developed since the late 1980s, is likely to have had an effect on the number of recorded assaults by men on women – which is to say that most of these assaults take place within the home.

New Zealand police provide services 24 hours a day, 365 days a year, operating from more than 400 community-based police stations by land, sea and air. Police respond to more than one million 111 calls each year, and are involved in crime prevention as well as responding to crime.

# Health and Emergencies

Dial **t** 111 for emergencies (police, fire or medical).

## The Public Health System

New Zealand has a good public health system, which provides comprehensive lifelong medical care to everyone. All essential healthcare is provided free, although there may be charges for some routine services such as visits to local doctors and dentists. UK citizens are entitled to the same treatment as New Zealanders under a reciprocal agreement between the two countries. Anyone who gains New Zealand residence is similarly entitled to treatment.

Your first point of contact with the health system will probably be your general practitioner or family doctor. Local GPs are listed in the front of the phone book under 'registered medical practitioners and medical centres'. Registering with a GP is free and easy: all you need to do is to provide the doctor's receptionist with your address, phone number and the names and ages of your family, plus any medical records in English and details of any health problems. You can choose which GP to register with. Most doctors' surgeries are open from 8am to 6pm, with some practices extending their hours to evenings and Saturday mornings. In an after-hours emergency GPs will either make a home visit or tell you who to contact. Routine services such as immunisation and cervical screening are often conducted by a practice nurse.

Visits to the doctor cost around NZ$50 a visit, unless you qualify for a government subsidy. Children under six can see the doctor for free, and children up to the age of 17 are partially subsidised. If you are on a low income you may qualify for a **Community Services Card**, which entitles adults to a NZ$15 subsidy and children to a NZ$20 subsidy for GP visits (**t** 0800 999 999 for information). Similar subsidies are available with a **High Use Health Card** for people with conditions requiring frequent medical care (**t** 0800 252464 for information).

If you need specialist medical care, your GP will give you a referral. The public specialist health system is free, but waiting lists can be long (depending on your condition and the area). If you prefer a private specialist (who will probably be able to see you sooner), you or your insurer will be required to pay all fees.

New Zealand has 80 public **hospitals**, including some with special facilities for the old and disabled. With minor exceptions, such as cosmetic surgery, hospital treatment is free. Nobody can be refused emergency treatment because they cannot pay, but if you are not a New Zealand resident you may have to pay for some services. Again, waiting times for essential surgery vary; if your case is urgent, you will be put on an urgent waiting list. Ambulances are provided by non-profit, community-based services, which may make a part charge to help with running costs.

Hospitals, specialist clinics, midwives, residential care centres and after-hours pharmacists are listed in the front section of phone books under 'hospitals and other health service providers'. Other practitioners, such as osteopaths, dentists and opticians, are listed in their respective sections in the *Yellow Pages*. Although it is best to register with a GP or practice, you can find walk-in clinics in many towns – often employing young British and other non-New Zealand doctors.

## Maternity Care

Maternity services are free. This includes all care needed during pregnancy and childbirth, from the diagnosis of pregnancy to pre- and post-natal care for mother and baby. You can choose to have your baby at home, though most babies are born in hospital. Hospital stays usually last two to five days. Most women are cared for throughout their pregnancy and at the birth by an independent midwife, though some women choose a local maternity hospital or a GP who provides maternity care (the last increasingly rare). If women need specialist care they can choose to be referred to a free hospital clinic or to a private specialist. If your family doctor or midwife refers you to a specialist within the public system, their services will be provided free of charge. Those who choose a private specialist for maternity care have to pay all fees. For maternity care, find GPs and midwives in the phone book under 'Registered Medical Practitioners'. GPs and midwives also commonly provide family planning services after the birth of a child. At other times these may be provided by Family Planning Association clinics as well as your family doctor. These services are subsidised, and free to anyone aged under 22.

## Child Health

Many health services for children are free. These include immunisation against serious diseases, basic dental care, hearing and eyesight checks and visits to the doctor.

The **Plunket Society**, **t** 0800 933922, **www.plunket.org.nz**, provides free care for mothers and babies. This includes child health and development checks, and parenting advice if desired. You will be referred by your midwife or GP to a Plunket nurse, who will visit you at home or arrange for you to see her at a clinic. Plunket also rents car seats for babies and small children, compulsory by law for safety, and may provide a forum to meet other parents.

## Prescriptions

GPs do not dispense medicines directly, but provide you with a written prescription, which you can present at a pharmacy of your choice. Repeat prescriptions can only be obtained from the pharmacy that issued your initial prescription. Adults pay between NZ$3 and NZ$15 per prescription item for up to 20 items a year. If you use more than 20 items a year, you may be eligible to get the rest free with a prescription subsidy card. Prescription medicine for children under six is free. Some medicines are subsidised, which means the government pays part of the cost. If there is a manufacturer's premium, this is charged in all cases, even when the prescription is free. Non-subsidised items are available at full cost.

Pharmacists are trained to give advice on medicines and on some minor health problems. They can also sell non-prescription medicines. Emergency pharmacies, open until around 11pm, are listed under 'Urgent Pharmacies' in the 'Hospitals' section at the front of your phone book.

## Mental Health

Emergency mental healthcare is provided by public hospitals. Some community-based services are available, especially for alcohol and drug abuse. Most other care, such as counselling services, are not subsidised, although your GP may be able to refer you to a suitable counsellor.

# Private Healthcare

Many New Zealanders elect to take out private health insurance, as it may provide access to private hospitals for the immediate treatment of non-urgent conditions. The network of private hospitals and clinics provides a range of services that include recuperative care, elective procedures and general surgical procedures through to specialist procedures such as heart surgery. There are also private radiology clinics and laboratories for blood tests. Several insurance companies offer a range of health policies, from basic care to fully comprehensive cover. As with all insurance, read the small print and be prepared for exclusions (for example chronic conditions). Policy premiums vary widely, so shop around. **Southern Cross, t** 0800 800 181, **www.southerncross.co.nz**, is one of the best-known health insurers. For others look in the *Yellow Pages* under 'Insurance – Medical', and *see* also **References**, pp.266–7.

# Dentists

Routine dental checks are provided free for all children through school clinics. Free dental treatment is also available on request. Many families prefer to undertake dental work through a private dentist. A government dental benefits scheme aims to cover the cost of private dental care for teenagers up to the age of 18, but involvement in the scheme is voluntary and many dentists choose not to participate. There are also restrictions on the type of dental care available. To obtain this free service you must register with a dentist who subscribes to the scheme. Except for the treatment of the under-18s, dental care is not subsidised. Dentists' charges vary widely, but might be NZ$50–90 for a routine check-up. The cost of emergency dental care is subsidised for people on low incomes. Some public hospitals also have dental departments that provide low-cost services to outpatients. To find a dentist, look in the *Yellow Pages*.

Water is fluoridated in most parts of New Zealand, although fluoridation continues to arouse controversy.

## Accident Compensation Corporation

All residents are covered by government-run accident insurance, managed by the Accident Compensation Corporation (ACC). It covers a full range of personal injuries, from injuries suffered at work to sporting or domestic injuries. In New Zealand, you cannot sue anyone for compensatory damages if you are insured. Instead, the ACC helps pay for your care, starting with free hospital treatment. Other types of treatment provided by registered healthcare professionals are subsidised by the ACC. If you cannot return to work, the ACC will also help with income compensation and other benefits. Visit **www.acc.govt.nz**.

# Social Services and Welfare Benefits

New Zealand's immigration criteria are designed to ensure you do not become a welfare beneficiary once you have moved to the country (for most categories of visa or permit you are required to demonstrate that your income will exceed a certain threshold, that you have highly employable skills, or at the least that someone else is able and willing to sponsor you). You are unlikely to be eligible for the 'main benefits' – unemployment and sickness. It is possible, however, that your circumstances may change once you are a New Zealand resident, or that you may be eligible for some extra help from the New Zealand taxpayer if, for example, you are part of a working family.

Most welfare benefits are administered by **Work and Income New Zealand (WINZ)**, while some are the responsibility of the **Inland Revenue Department (IRD)**. WINZ offers help finding work, income support where needed, and support to people in work but on low incomes. It has service centres nationwide, with regional offices in 11 regions and a national office in Wellington. Look in the blue government listings pages at the front of the phone book for details of local centres. Some of the benefits it administers include unemployment, sickness, invalidity, widows, domestic purposes (sole parents) and orphans benefits. It also administers superannuation payments for retired people, student loans and allowances, and the community services card (for access to subsidised healthcare). You will only be eligible for NZ superannuation if you have lived in New Zealand for more than 10 years before you are 65.

- **WINZ, t** 0800 559009, **t** 0800 774004, **www.workandincome.govt.nz.**
Working for families, *see* below.
- **Inland Revenue Department, www.ird.govt.nz.**

# 'Working for Families'

The benefits most likely to affect newcomers to New Zealand come under the umbrella of 'Working for Families', a government initiative to make life easier for families in which one or both parents work, but who nonetheless struggle to make ends meet. Almost all families with children earning less than NZ$70,000 are eligible for some help, and many earning up to NZ$100,000; even very large families making more than this may qualify for some extra support. A further tax credit is available of up to $60 a week for families with up to three children, and $15 a week for each additional child, as long as the parents between them work 30 hours a week (20 hours for sole parents). A **Childcare Subsidy** or **OSCAR Subsidy** of up to $3.40 per hour per child is available to families earning less than NZ$1,800 per week, to help pay for the costs of childcare for pre-schoolers and after-school care for schoolchildren, respectively. Working parents are eligible for up to 50 hours' subsidised childcare a week, while all parents can get a nine-hour subsidy. As well as help with the costs of childcare, families on low incomes may qualify for family support or 'in-work' payments and a contribution to the cost of accommodation. Some assistance currently takes the form of tax credits. Bewilderingly, family assistance is administered by the Inland Revenue, but accommodation supplements and childcare subsidies by WINZ (**www. workingforfamilies.govt.nz**).

# Parental Leave

New Zealand has recently extended its parental leave allowances. Mothers-to-be are entitled to up to 10 days' special leave during pregnancy for visits to midwives, doctors or specialists. Paid **maternity leave** is available for up to 14 weeks for employees who have worked a certain number of hours in the previous six months. Leave may be commenced up to six weeks before the date of the birth, if the employer agrees. **Partner's/paternity leave** is available for up to two weeks if the partner has worked a certain number of hours in the previous 12 months, or up to one week if he has only been working for six months. Either parent is eligible for up to 52 weeks' unpaid leave in the first year after the birth of a child (the leave can be shared between the parents).

Employees who are eligible for parental leave may also be entitled to a taxpayer-funded payment for up to 14 weeks of the parental leave they take. The payment can be taken by one parent, or shared between two eligible partners. The payment for parental leave replaces an employee's wages or salary up to a maximum amount of NZ$391.28 per week. Employees and self-employed parents are entitled to either their gross weekly rate of pay or $391.28, whichever is lower. If self-employed parents make a loss or earn less than the equivalent of 10 hours' pay at the highest rate of minimum wage, they will receive the minimum rate of $112.50. You are eligible for the payment if you have been employed by the same employer for the previous six or 12 months and worked an average of at least 10 hours per week, including at least one hour every week or 40 hours per month, for that employer during that period. You should apply for parental leave in writing at least three months before your baby is due, and you are required to give three weeks' notice of your intention either to return or not return to work.

- **Employment Relations Service** (Department of Labour), **t** 0800 800863, **www.ers.dol.govt.nz**. Information on paid parental leave.

# Retirement and Pensions

New Zealanders retire at age 65, to a quiet life of fishing and boating or touring the country in a caravan. Many give up big farms or move out of town to live by the beach; some abandon the suburbs for rural lifestyle blocks, while others abandon market gardens and orchards for the convenience of a suburban section. In fact, there's a ceaseless flow of retired people between country and city, seaside and hilltop – and then back again looking for something to do. Favourite retirement spots include the Kapiti Coast, Hawke's Ba, Nelson and Russell. Those who can afford it get out of the country, making extended trips to Tuscany and London to make up for all the years they've spent working and going on camping holidays in New Zealand.

For Britons thinking of retiring to New Zealand there are two obstacles. First, it is difficult to get a long-term or permanent visa once you're over 56 unless you plan to set up a business or invest substantial amounts of money in some other enterprise, or most of your family is already living in New Zealand. Second, you need to consider whether you can get a pension. If you have a good private or employment pension scheme, where you take it up should be your own business. In order to qualify for New Zealand superannuation (state pension), however, you need to have been a permanent resident in the country for at least 10 years. If you rely on a British state pension, you should be able to take it with you, but there are some vital caveats.

## Getting Your UK State Pension in New Zealand

A UK state pension is normally payable in New Zealand, but **you will not get annual increases in the benefit** once you have ceased to be normally resident in the UK. This means that your pension will stay at the same rate as when you left the UK, or when you first qualified for the pension if you were already living in New Zealand at the time. After 20 years, even with minimal inflation, you could be seriously less well off than when you first retired, and than if you had stayed in the UK where the pension is index-linked.

There is a special agreement with New Zealand, which allows periods of residence there to count towards your pension in the UK, as long as you are actually living in the UK. This agreement may also allow you to qualify for New Zealand superannuation when you reach pension age in New Zealand by allowing you to treat your residence in the UK as residence in New Zealand. If you qualify for New Zealand benefit, the amount of your UK state pension will be deducted from the New Zealand benefit which would otherwise be payable to you.

HM Revenue & Customs can provide retirement pension forecasts for people who are outside the UK or are about to go outside the UK (if the person is not within four months of UK retirement pension age), which will tell you how much state retirement pension you can expect to get based on the UK National Insurance you have already paid. It will not include any insurance contributions you may have paid in a country with which the UK has a social security agreement, such as New Zealand, which may entitle you to additional payments.

If you have paid National Insurance contributions in the UK, the Inland Revenue will usually send you a claim form about four months before you reach UK state pension age. This form asks you about any insurance and residence you may have in other countries. You will usually be paid straight into your bank or building society account in the UK or your bank account abroad, if you have one. Or, if you wish, you can choose to have your pension paid by payable orders sent straight to you by post. Whichever you choose, payment is made every four or 13 weeks in arrears. UK widow's benefits or bereavement benefits are also normally payable in New Zealand. For full details see the Department of Work and Pensions Social Security Agreement between the United Kingdom and New Zealand, available on the DWP website.

- **Department of Work and Pensions (UK), www.thepensionservice.gov.uk.**
- **HM Revenue & Customs (UK), www.hmrc.gov.uk.**
- **Work and Income New Zealand, www.workandincome.govt.nz.** Information on New Zealand superannuation.

# Dying Abroad

If you decide to die in New Zealand, you can at least plan for it by drawing up a will. Any lawyer can do this for you (for a fee) or you can do it for a nominal fee through the **Public Trust, t** 0800 371471, **www.publictrust.co.nz**, a government entity established to help people sort out their legal affairs without paying the prohibitive fees of commercial lawyers. Public Trust can also help you to draw up an enduring power of attorney, set up family and education trusts, or carry out the financial planning to buy a house and so on. If you have a UK will, this will be valid even if you are resident in New Zealand. The normal practice, however, is to make your will in the country in which you have the balance of your assets, or where you are domiciled. The advantage of dying in New Zealand, if you have been a tax resident there for more than three years, is that your heirs will not be liable to pay any inheritance tax.

Public Trust can help you with funeral finances and planning too. Otherwise your doctor or hospital will tell you what you need to do in the case of death, and funeral undertakers will deal with arrangements for funeral and burial or cremation (look in the *Yellow Pages* under 'Funeral Directors'). Don't even think about trying to ship your body home for burial – it's more complicated, and a lot more expensive, than importing your pet dog or cat. If you have a sentimental attachment to the home country, let someone take your ashes in an urn for scattering.

# Education

New Zealand has a good public education system, from pre-school to university level. The Labour government of Helen Clark has keenly promoted access to early childhood education for all, to get children off to a good start when they start at a primary school – most of which are excellent. The weakest point of the state system is secondary education, where the quality of schools varies widely and many have reputations for a rough and tough culture that is antithetical to learning. It is at this stage that some middle class or aspirational parents choose to send their children to one of New Zealand's private schools, where they will benefit from an arguably better education mixed with a certain amount of snob value. At tertiary level, it's back in the melting pot for all, with a choice of eight good universities and 22 polytechnics.

Check out **www.teamup.govt.nz**, a government-sponsored website with information about education at all levels.

## Early Childhood Education

New Zealand has a wide range of early childhood services. Many are run by private operators, community church groups and voluntary agencies. The government funds the cost of children aged three and four to attend early childhood education (ECE) for up to 20 hours a week. This is for up to six hours a day at any teacher-led ECE service (kindergartens, centre-based and home-based) and some kohanga reo. Some centres may still charge over and above the government subsidy level. Early childhood education is not compulsory.

**Kindergartens** ('kindies') provide early childhood education for children aged 3–5. Some have waiting lists. You can put your child's name down when he or she turns two. Children attend either morning or afternoon sessions, up to five times a week. Sessions are informal and focus on developing social skills and learning through play. Although kindergartens have trained teachers, parents are expected to help out with class supervision, fundraising and committee work. A donation is generally asked for.

Other **education and day-care centres** offer all-day or half-day care, usually over longer hours than kindergartens. Care is charged on a daily or weekly fee, with an hourly fee for casual care. Centres may take under-two-year-olds, over-twos, or both. They include specialist centres such as Montessori.

**Playcentres** are run as parent co-operatives, with parents closely involved in running the centres and working with children during session times. There may be between one and 10 sessions a week, with individual children attending up to the age of five. Parents, who run the sessions on a roster, can undertake training to supervise playcentre sessions.

**Home-based or family day-care**, provided in a caregiver's home, provides supervised care for small groups of children. Fees are charged by the hour and times are flexible. Agencies such as Porse provide some guarantees.

**Nannies** can also be found through agencies or independently. Certification is not required.

**Playgroups** are community-run play programmes for children, similar to but less structured than playcentres. Parents are required to supervise their children during sessions. **Pacific Island Early Childhood Centres and Groups** are usually based within community churches or schools. **Kohanga reo** ('language nests') have been established to provide Maori children with full immersion in the Maori language (te reo) in a play-based learning environment.

# Secondary Education: Compulsory Schooling

Schooling is compulsory for all children from their sixth until their 16th birthday, although most start soon after their fifth; in fact the tradition is for New Zealand children to start school on the day after their fifth birthday. Schooling is free at state schools until the age of 19. Parents are expected to meet minor costs such as school books, stationery and uniforms.

The school day usually begins at 9am and finishes around 3pm, with a short break in the morning and a long lunch break. Students are classified in year levels, starting with year 1 and moving up a class each year until year 13. Years 1 to 3 (ages 6–9) are called primers, years 4 to 6 (ages 10–12) standards. Years 7 and 8 (ages 13–14; intermediate), just to confuse things, are known as forms 1 and 2, and years 9 to 13 (ages 15–19; secondary) as forms 3 to 7. Class sizes are set by the schools in accordance with Ministry of Education guidelines.

Children must be enrolled at a **primary school** by their sixth birthday, but may start any time after they are five. Oversubscribed schools have waiting lists, so it is a good idea to enrol your child before his or her fifth birthday. Children in years

7 and 8 may have the option of moving on to **intermediate school** in some urban areas, while other primary schools continue right through to secondary age. Children attend **secondary school** – also known as high school, college or grammar – from year 9 to year 13. Here, students will still be grouped in classes but attend lessons in different subjects with different teachers. In some rural areas, primary, intermediate and secondary are all rolled into one **area school**.

The **school year** begins in late January or early February, after a six-week Christmas and New Year summer holiday, and ends in early- to mid-December. It is divided into four terms with two- to three-week breaks between them: term 1, end of January to early April; term 2, late April to end of June; term 3, mid-July to late September; term 4, mid-October to mid-December. Secondary school holidays are slightly longer than those of primary schools.

## State, Integrated and Private or Independent Schools

Most New Zealand children attend **state schools**, fully funded by the government. Every child has the right to enrol at the state school nearest to their home. Primary and intermediate schools are mostly co-educational; secondary schools may be single sex or mixed. If the school is oversubscribed, it can set a geographical 'home zone'. Children within this zone are automatically able to enrol for it, but children beyond the limits of the zone can only enrol in special circumstances – such as having siblings at the school, or needing access to specialist subjects taught only at that school. In some cases, schools operate a ballot for places.

To find out about schools, you can get reports from the Education Review Office, or read them on the Internet at **www.ero.govt.nz**. The ERO also publishes two useful guides: 'Choosing a School for a Five Year Old' and 'Choosing a Secondary School'. The Ministry of Education website (**www.minedu.govt.nz**) has a full directory of schools, which you can search by area and type. You can arrange to visit schools and meet the principal and staff before enrolment. It is worth trying to enrol your child early to get a place at the school of your choice.

**Integrated schools** mostly have a religious base (for example Roman Catholic schools, very popular for their more disciplined approach) or follow a secular philosophy (such as Montessori and Steiner schools). They used to operate as private institutions, but have now been integrated into the state system (hence the name), receive government funding and follow the state curriculum. A number of private or independent schools also exist. They are not government funded, and parents are required to pay fees, which may be substantial (each school sets its own fees).

**Private** or **independent schools** are governed by their own independent boards, but must meet government standards and are subject to the same ERO audits as state schools. Many middle-class parents believe that they offer better schooling.

**Boarding schools** exist mainly at secondary school level. There are 78 state and integrated boarding schools, and 24 private ones in the one country. New Zealand not being as egalitarian as it would like people to think, some of the private schools have a definite snob appeal and may well give little Jack and little Emily access to a valuable old boys' or old girls' network in later life (as well as, arguably, a better education). A few of the most high-profile names bandied about include Christ's College, Wanganui Collegiate School and Samuel Marsden Collegiate School. You do, however, pay for the privilege, and state schools are nothing like as bad as some of the British ones – in fact many have excellent reputations.

## Curriculum and Qualifications

The New Zealand curriculum is built around the acquisition of essential academic and practical skills. It identifies seven academic or 'essential learning' areas – language(s), mathematics, science, technology, social sciences, the arts, health and physical well-being – as well as eight practical or 'essential skills' – communication, numeracy, information, problem-solving, self-management, social and co-operative, physical and work and study skills. Primary schools offer a core curriculum of maths, art, health, English language, physical education and technology. Secondary schools offer a wide range of subjects from accounting, agriculture and art to textile design and typing – as well as the more traditional core subjects (maths, sciences, arts, languages and so on).

A controversial 'standards-based' qualification known as the **National Certificate of Educational Achievement** has recently replaced traditional exam-based awards. For the NCEA, credits are awarded for meeting 'achievement standards' in each subject area, broken down into skills and knowledge within the subject (for example speaking, reading, writing and research are all components of English). NCEA Level 1, awarded at the end of year 11, is roughly equivalent to GCSE. NCEA Level 2 is awarded at the end of year 12, and NCEA Level 3 at the end of year 13.

University bursaries and scholarship examinations are taken at the end of year 13, and dictate entrance to university and cash allowances for further study.

# Tertiary Education

## Universities

New Zealand has eight universities, all of which offer general undergraduate and graduate degrees in arts, sciences and commerce, as well as specialist degrees in particular disciplines. Undergraduate degrees such as a BA (Bachelor of Arts) or BSc (Bachelor of Science) take 3–4 years to complete. Vocational or professional training may take longer.

Each university publishes an annual calendar detailing the courses scheduled during the academic year, fees and entry requirements. These are held in public library reference sections or can be bought from booksellers.
Universities have a set level of competency for English.

- **University of Auckland, t** 0800 616263, **www.auckland.ac.nz**. Architecture, planning, engineering, medicine, optometry, fine arts, law.
- **Auckland University of Technology, www.aut.ac.nz**. Health studies, tourism, engineering, communications, hotel management.
- **University of Canterbury** (Christchurch), **t** 0800 827248, **www.canterbury.ac.nz**. Engineering, forestry, fine arts, journalism.
- **Lincoln University** (near Christchurch), **t** 0800 106010, **www.lincoln.ac.nz**. Agriculture and horticulture, natural resource management.
- **Massey University** (Palmerston North, Wellington, Auckland and extramural), **t** 0800 627739, **www.massey.ac.nz**. Agriculture and horticulture, aviation studies, business studies, design, food technology, social sciences, veterinary sciences.
- **University of Otago** (Dunedin), **t** 0800 808098, **www.otago.ac.nz**. Dentistry, law, medicine, physical education, pharmacy, surveying, theology.
- **Victoria University** (Wellington), **t** 0800 842864, **www.vuw.ac.nz**. Architecture, design, public administration, social work, law.
- **University of Waikato** (Hamilton), **t** 0800 924528, **www.waikato.ac.nz**. Law, Maori studies.

## Polytechnics, Colleges of Education and Private Training Establishments

In addition to the universities, New Zealand has 22 **polytechnics**, which offer a range of academic, vocational and professional courses. As well as three- and four-year degree courses, the polytechnics offer short full-time and part-time courses, scheduled throughout the year. Each polytechnic publishes an annual prospectus detailing the courses scheduled during the academic year, and fees and entry requirements. Short courses may be advertised in the local press too.

There are four **colleges of education**, or teacher training colleges, located in Auckland, Wellington, Christchurch and Dunedin. Waikato and Massey universities also offer teacher training.

There are also several thousand private training establishments in New Zealand, offering a wide range of courses (most are specialised in certain subjects). More than 800 of these are registered with the **New Zealand Qualifications Authority (NZQA)**. About a quarter are Maori-owned and -operated. Apart from the NZQA-registered institutions there is no independent quality control.

## Entry Requirements for Tertiary Education

There are certain academic requirements for entry to tertiary education in New Zealand. University entrance depends on the number of NCEA credits gained (a minimum of 42 credits at Level 3, 14 in maths at Level 1 and 8 in English at Level 2). Admittance to some courses is competitive, in which case only students with strong academic records are enrolled.

To study at a polytechnic or college of education, certain standards must be obtained at NCEA Level 2. For students from overseas and over-21-year-olds, requirements are more flexible, but you will still be required to demonstrate a certain level of ability and education. For entry requirements for overseas students set by individual institutions, see the particular university, polytechnic and college of education websites.

## Student Fees and Loans

The government funds state tertiary institutions and meets some of the costs of providing tuition. Currently, students contribute about 25 per cent of the cost of a course, which varies depending on the type of course taken. The first year of a full-time arts degree may cost about NZ$3,000, while the fees for the final year's training as a doctor or dentist might be as much as NZ$10,000. These very high levels of contribution for professional studies are largely held to blame for the mass exodus of qualified medics from the country (and the drive to recruit them from overseas); many students go overseas as soon as they have graduated, to start earning enough to pay off their student loans.

Government-funded **loans** are available to all students who are permanent New Zealand residents or citizens, to meet the costs of studying. The student loan is made up of three parts – compulsory fees, course-related costs and/or living costs. Student loans have to be paid back. As long as students are studying full-time, the loans are interest-free. Once students have completed their studies, repayments are made through the Inland Revenue department. Some **scholarships** from public and private sources are available (for details ask at individual universities when applying).

# Where to Find Out More

### General

- **Ministry of Education, www.minedu.govt.nz**. Everything from changes in the curriculum and qualifications to funding and details of individual educational establishments.
- **Early Childhood Development**, **www.ecd.govt.nz**. Advice on early childhood services.

- **Education Review Office, www.ero.govt.nz.** Individual school and pre-school inspection reports and general information about choosing schools and educational standards.
- **National Certificate of Educational Achievement, t** 0800 623243, **www.ncea.govt.nz.** Information about the new national qualifications for secondary school students.
- **New Zealand Qualifications Authority, www.nzqa.net/ncea.** Information on NCEA and university entrance requirements.
- **Studylink, t** 0800 88 99 00, **www.studylink.govt.nz.** All you need to know about student loans, from how to apply to how much you can borrow.
- **Work and Income New Zealand, t** 0800 559009, **www.winz.govt.nz.** Student allowances.

## Early Childhood Education

- **New Zealand Kindergartens Incorporated, www.nzkindergarten.org.nz.**
- **New Zealand Playcentre Federation, t** 0800 692737, **www.playcentre.org.nz.**

## Schools

- **Independent Schools of New Zealand, www.independentschools.org.nz.** Profiles of 43 top independent schools, with links to the websites of these and other private schools.
- **New Zealand Boarding Schools' Association, www.boarding.org.nz.**

## Polytechnics and Colleges of Education

- **Association of Colleges of Education in New Zealand, www.acenz.ac.nz.** Details of the teacher training colleges.
- **Association of Polytechnics in New Zealand, www.apnz.ac.nz.** General information on polytechnic education, with contact details of and links to individual polytechnics.
- **Open Polytechnic of New Zealand, www.topnz.ac.nz.** New Zealand's answer to the Open University.

# Taking Your Pet

You'd have to be barking to take your pet to New Zealand, but people do it. You will need to plan well ahead, both to arrange transport and to meet the Ministry of Agriculture and Forestry's very stringent standards (New Zealand is determined to keep pests and disease out of the country). If you're determined to bring Fido or Tabby with you, here's how.

A **permit to import** must be obtained before importation. Applications should be made to Import Management, Ministry of Agriculture and Forestry, PO Box 2526, Wellington, t + 64 (0)4 498 9624, **www.biosecurity.govt.nz**. The importer must supply the following information: name and address of importer; breed, sex, age and microchip identification of the animal. The permit to import and all the required documentation (veterinary certificates detailing animal health) must accompany the animal to New Zealand. All costs of selection, testing, treatment, transport, quarantine and veterinary supervision must be borne by the importer. The importer must make all arrangements for transport and obtain necessary transit authorisation from any third countries on the transport route. Eligibility for importation under this import health standard is confined to dogs and cats. Dogs of the following breeds (including crosses of these breeds) are not eligible for importation: American Pit Bull Terrier, Dogo Argentino, Japanese Tosa, and Brazilian Fila.

The animal must have been resident in the exporting country for the six months prior to export or since birth, and must be free of quarantine restrictions. Animals must not be more than 42 days pregnant at the date of shipment. Animals must be more than 16 weeks old at departure. Each animal must be identified with a microchip and the identification details must be shown on the accompanying certification. The identity of the animal must be confirmed by reading the microchip each time a treatment or test is performed, and at the time of export certification. The required health tests and treatments are stated in Veterinary Certificate A. All serological tests must be conducted at a government laboratory or a laboratory approved by the Government Veterinary Service of New Zealand.

If transported by air, the animal must be carried in an approved container that meets the International Air Transport Association (IATA) standards. The container must be nose- and paw-proof – only have ventilation openings of such size that it is impossible for the animal to protrude its nose or paws outside the container. The container must be new, or thoroughly cleaned prior to use. The container must be free of dirt and ticks. If consigned by sea, the master of the vessel must certify that the imported animal was confined on board and had no contact with animals not of a tested equivalent health status at each port of call. Consignment by sea requires prior approval of the transport method and route by the Director Animal Biosecurity, NZMAF.

The use of straw or hay as bedding is not permitted. Only sterilised peat, soft board or other inert approved products may be used. The door of the transport container must be sealed with a government approved seal before the container is loaded into the aircraft or vessel in the country of origin. The number or mark on the seal is to be recorded in Veterinary Certificate B. The construction of the container and the placement of the seal must be such that the container cannot be readily opened without breaking the seal. If the container is opened during shipment it shall be re-sealed and a certificate detailing the circumstances provided by an official veterinarian, port authority or captain of the aircraft. Instructions to this effect should be attached to the outside of the transport container. The container may only be trans-shipped (change of aircraft or vessel) in countries or territories that are rabies-free or where rabies is well controlled (as recognised by NZMAF). Trans-shipment will require the specific authorisation of the government veterinary authority of the country in which trans-shipment occurs.

The New Zealand Quarantine Service of the region in which the port of arrival is situated must be notified at least 72 hours before the expected time of arrival of any animal, giving the flight or ship number and arrival time. An inspector under the Biosecurity Act 1993 will examine the consignment on arrival in New Zealand. Providing the documentation is in order, the seal of the container is intact, and no ticks are found on the animal, in the bedding or container, a biosecurity clearance will be issued. If the documentation and seal are not in order the animal will be held by NZMAF and the details of the non-compliance referred to Import Management NZMAF, for direction. If ticks are found, they will be removed and the animal taken to an approved transitional facility. The animal will be treated for ticks and kept in the facility for a minimum of 48 hours to ensure any undetected ticks are killed. A biosecurity clearance will be issued when the inspector is satisfied that the animal, bedding and container are tick-free.

On arrival, the New Zealand address at which the animal will be domiciled should be verified as being that which is specified in section III of the Zoosanitary Certificate. An inspector may visit the premises to examine the imported animal at any reasonable time. Any illness in the imported animal should be reported to a private veterinary practitioner, who has an obligation to report any suspicion of exotic disease to NZMAF. All dogs should be registered with the local government authority within 14 days of arrival in New Zealand.

Dogs and cats must be tested for a range of conditions before departure, including canine heartworm, *Brucella canis*, leptospirosis, canine ehrlichosis, *Babesia gibsoni*, hookworm and other intestinal parasites, and where relevant treated before embarkation.

# Working in New Zealand

07

# Business Etiquette

Formality is not a New Zealand trait – and this goes for business dealings too, which are characterised by their informality. Directness is the epitome of New Zealand relationships (of all sorts). Most companies are small, with between five and 10 employees, and the owners and managers of such companies generally adopt a friendly approach to the people they employ: workers and bosses call each other by their first names and the 'good bloke' ethos prevails; friendliness, looking out for 'the guys' and sharing a joke are all part of the job. For manual labourers, the working week will almost certainly be rounded off by a few beers on Friday afternoon, while among the more sedentary occupations a glass of chardonnay or merlot is equally *de rigueur* – woe betide teetotallers. In all areas of business, a frank and open demeanour, cordial courtesy and a firm handshake will stand you in good stead. With few major corporations in the country, the corporate ethos is not widespread, although larger companies do tend to be slightly more hierarchical.

## The Basics

A straightforward, friendly, polite manner will be suitable in almost all situations. While manners might be less formally polished in New Zealand than in the old world, New Zealanders are impeccably well mannered, never failing to make introductions and treating each other with admirable forthrightness. Reliability and punctuality are as important here as anywhere, and you have fewer excuses for being late in most of New Zealand than in London, Paris or New York – unless there's been a flood or earthquake. (Auckland might be the exception, with its dire traffic problems.)

When you arrive at a business meeting, a meeting with clients or a job interview, a good, firm, no-nonsense handshake is the best way to get things going. Some people will shake hands at the end of a meeting, too. Follow your instincts: there is no really rigid code of conduct on this front. You can't really go wrong if you do go for a strong shake at every encounter, but you're unlikely to cause offence or discomfort if you skip it on the second meeting.

New Zealand business people are on to it in terms of slick marketing and presentation. Business cards are very widely – universally – used, and tend to be niftily designed and printed. Even the smallest companies will have commissioned their own logo and put considerable time and money into selecting colours, fonts and layout. It is essential to include all forms of contact on your card: phone, mobile phone, e-mail, business address and PO box number (if applicable) – and an after-hours phone number, as anyone who is serious about business in New Zealand makes sure they can be contacted night and day, weekdays and weekends. You won't get anywhere without a mobile phone, and you will be expected to keep it on at all times.

On the other hand, in a country that regularly comes top of the league in international anti-corruption rankings, corporate gifts are frowned upon. A small gift at Christmas, such as a bottle of wine, won't go amiss, but more extravagant gifts will be perceived as akin to bribery. Equally, you might go for a lunch, dinner or drinks with your business contacts, but lavish corporate entertaining is not the norm. There are variations across industries, though: film, fashion, media, tourism and of course wine-making go in for more entertaining than some other industries.

## Setting up a Business Meeting

Business people arriving from larger economies will be surprised at how easy it all is. All you need to do is find out the name of the person you need to meet and call them up. Few people, even senior CEOs, are likely to make themselves inaccessible provided you can come up with a good reason to want to see them. In general, people are keen to be helpful and pass you on to the right person. The biggest surprise may be how quickly you can set up a meeting: people may offer you an appointment the same week you call, or apologise if they can't see you until the following week. Once you have established a business relationship, you may be called on for a meeting on the same day. Personal contacts are not as important to get you to an initial meeting as they might be in a larger, more competitive environment. One word of caution, though: once you get involved in an industry, everyone knows everyone.

## Dress Codes

Dress codes depend on where you are, geographically, and what line of business you are in. The most consistent style of dress for business is smart casual or 'business separates' – a smart jacket, trousers, shirt and tie for men; for women, much the same, minus the tie; trousers are as acceptable for women in all walks of life as skirts or dresses. Auckland business people tend to be the most snappy, fashion-conscious dressers, putting Prada before propriety. Wellingtonians tend to wear black whenever they can (you can't go wrong in the capital with a black suit). Christchurch is in all ways more conservative (a tweed jacket or blazer wouldn't be surprising down south). The provinces tend to be more provincial in style, fashion-conscious and less formal; in rural communities gumboots and polar fleeces are as likely to be worn to the bank as in the fields. Only city lawyers, bankers and some high-ranking public servants wear the classic suit and tie. Some companies – such as real-estate firms and retailers – insist on a uniform for their staff. You'll soon get a feel for the level of formality expected for your type of business.

# The Labour Market

Thanks to a sustained period of economic growth, the New Zealand labour market has experienced rising employment, increased labour force participation rates (the percentage of working-age people who work) and falling unemployment since 2001. In the year to March 2008, the New Zealand labour market maintained its strong position. The demand for labour remained high, resulting in a 'tightening' of the labour market, with growth in employment, the highest ever level of participation and flat unemployment; in early 2008 the official unemployment level was 3.5 per cent – a record low. A total of 2,086,200 people are currently employed; out of a working-age population of 3,184,000 people, 68.1 per cent are in the labour force. The latest statistics also show that more women are now working, and in full-time jobs, than ever before.

From the point of view of the New Zealand economy, and anyone looking for a job, this is all good news, even though employers may moan that they just can't

## The Future of Work

A Department of Labour report on the future of work predicts that an ageing population and growing international migration will change the shape of New Zealand's workforce over coming years. On the ageing population, international research suggests that after around 2020 the number of young people entering the workforce will be considerably fewer than the number of people retiring, leading to a decline in the workforce. At the same time, the proportion of the workforce aged over 45 will increase significantly. This older workforce will have higher average levels of work experience and, potentially, higher productivity, but retraining may be necessary for these workers to keep up with changing skill demands. As fewer young people join the workforce, recruiting may become more difficult and employers may create more flexible working arrangements to retain older employees.

On growing international migration, labour is increasingly mobile internationally. The number of people migrating to and from New Zealand each year is higher than ever before, which makes it easier to gain skilled people from overseas, but also for New Zealanders to leave. An increasing proportion of the New Zealand workforce is likely to be made up of migrants from non-English-speaking countries, particularly Asian countries – all of which is going to affect people's work prospects and the strategies employers will put in place and have a bearing on the sorts of jobs New Zealand does well. Global labour flow is an issue that gets many New Zealanders hot under the collar – often irrationally. Opponents of greater migration flows argue that skilled migrants are taking jobs from hard-working New Zealanders, that unskilled migrants are a drain on the economy, with taxpayers funding their health, welfare and education, and that departing New Zealanders take the benefit of publicly funded find the staff these days. As the working-age population is not growing fast enough naturally to meet demand, the labour force depends on migrants to boost its numbers. The labour force demand has pushed wages up, although not as much as might be feared by employers or hoped for by employees. Perhaps surprisingly, public sector pay is considerably higher on average than pay in the private sector: average hourly earnings in the public sector are $28.45, whereas in the private sector they are just $19.94 – nearly a third less. Unemployment is lowest among Pakeha, at 2.6 per cent, and highest among Maori and Pacific Islanders, while households are increasingly polarised between 'work-rich' and 'work-poor'.

Regionally, the lowest unemployment is in Southland and the highest in Northland. Forecasts for the New Zealand economy are as uncertain, at the time of writing, as they are for the rest of the world. Isolated as it is geographically, New Zealand is liable to suffer knock-on effects of any global recession.

At times of global turmoil, however, it does tend to attract more immigrants, which boosts the economy. In this tight labour market, the country is keen to

education somewhere else. However, more liberal optimists believe that, if the right balance is found, the brain drain can instead be a brain exchange that enables New Zealand to tap into needed skills and to build valuable links into the global economy. The truth, boringly, is probably a bit of both.

On the upside, new migrants to New Zealand are younger and more highly skilled, on average, than the rest of the New Zealand population. At its peak in the mid-1990s, immigration added nearly 50 per cent to the annual total of university and tertiary graduates in New Zealand each year. Outward migration may take pressure off the New Zealand labour market at times of high unemployment. New Zealand can benefit substantially when New Zealanders work or study overseas and then return to New Zealand with experience and ideas, or build business relationships with New Zealand networks.

Yet the increasing freedom of people to travel the world for employment – the globalisation of labour – also contains threats for New Zealand. Particular challenges include the longer-term risk to the economy of skills shortages, as labour markets for particular types of skills become increasingly globalised. New Zealand faces ongoing challenges to ensure that it is able to attract and retain highly skilled individuals. Another challenge is the effects on obtaining and using skills. New Zealanders who leave the country use their training elsewhere; offsetting this, many migrants bring education and skills obtained at no cost to New Zealand. And a third challenge is ensuring good outcomes for migrants in the labour market. The potential benefits of migration are conditional on whether new immigrants and returning New Zealanders settle and find employment successfully. The New Zealand labour force includes a higher proportion of migrants than most countries in the OECD (the Organisation for Economic Cooperation and Development).

welcome new immigrants who have the experience, skills and qualifications that can fill the gaps in the New Zealand labour force. According to the New Zealand Immigration Service, many industries within New Zealand say that one of the most significant factors holding them back from achieving growth is the lack of qualified staff.

The NZIS publishes a regularly updated list of those occupations short of qualified, skilled, experienced practitioners. The **Long-term Skill Shortage List** lists occupations that New Zealand is actively seeking to recruit for the foreseeable future (*see* **Red Tape**, 'Work Visas and Permits', p.122 for details). Health professionals are always in demand, from anaesthetists to general practitioners, midwives, nurses, radiographers and surgeons, as are teachers from early childhood instructors to university lecturers. All sorts of IT professionals feature prominently on the list too. More surprisingly, perhaps, there is a shortage of builders, carpenter joiners, electricians, plumbers and fitter welders. Engineers, motor mechanics and even film animators and chefs are in short supply, according to the list. If you ply any of these trades you will easily gain enough points to get a work visa in the Skilled Migrant Category (*see* p.121), and should have no problem finding a job.

In addition, the **Immediate Skill Shortage List** (*see* p.123) lists current regional vacancies for qualified, experienced, skilled workers in myriad other occupations – ranging from turkey farm manager to dental hygienist. As long as the strong demand for labour continues, if you can do a job that is on this list, it will help you to find work and get the relevant work visa or permit. Although the immigration criteria are more stringent for this category, if you can secure a job offer before you apply for your visa you have every chance of getting it.

Obviously, you are far less likely to get into New Zealand if it looks as if you are going to take unskilled work away from other New Zealanders. Most visa and permit categories require you to have found work before you arrive, but if you get into the country with enough points for the Job Search scheme, or get residence through the Family Stream, you may be able to defer looking for a job until you get here. (Agencies in the UK may be able to find you a job from there, especially as a teacher or medical professional.)

Once in New Zealand with the right paperwork, similar job opportunities are open to you as are open to New Zealanders, although you may need sponsorship from an employer to prove that you are the best person for the job, rather than a native New Zealander (*see* **Red Tape**, 'Visas and Permits'). You will have been discouraged at the outset from moving to New Zealand in search of casual, unskilled work. Although the public sector is as much of an open market as the private sector, you are more likely to find work in the private sector, at least initially; the Maori language and culture requirements of many public service jobs advertised, not to mention the implicit patriotism, are a major disincentive to foreigners.

# Job Ideas

Most fields of work are open to non-New Zealanders in New Zealand. The best way to get a work visa or permit, and ultimately permanent residence (permission to stay for good), may be through your occupation: check the Long-term Skill Shortage List (*see* left and p.122) for details of the types of skilled workers New Zealand badly needs and is keen to recruit from overseas. (Ironically, many New Zealand medics end up overseas after qualifying, in an attempt to pay off their university fees, while hordes of British doctors and nurses end up in New Zealand, in search of better working conditions and a higher quality of life.)

You may also be able to find work in some or all regions of New Zealand in a range of other occupations listed on the Immediate Skill Shortage List (*see* left and p.123) that will make it easy for you to get a visa or permit to stay. Don't despair if you're not a doctor or a teacher: there are employers looking for specialists in every walk of life, from marine laminators to perfect binders, plastics die setters to radio frequency technicians, skydive tandem masters to sommeliers, trackwork riders to yacht riggers, jockeys to shepherds, furniture polishers to plasterers (fibrous and solid). If you have any sorts of useful skills, experience or qualifications, New Zealand is a land of opportunity. New Zealand is a practical country, and needs practical people.

There are other options for the more freewheeling – as long as you can get a visa or permit by some other means (such as family connections or working holidays). Newcomers to New Zealand are often drawn in their work to what attracted them to the country in the first place: its uncluttered landscape and coastline, mountains and rivers. One favourite port of call for the call of the wild is the Department of Conservation, which looks after the national parks and always needs people to maintain walking tracks and huts or to help conserve the native flora and fauna (*see also* 'Volunteering', pp.236–8).

Less wild but more lucrative is the tourist industry, with jobs on the ski and snowboard slopes (instructors and technicians), swim and surf beaches (lifeguards and instructors), white-water rafting rivers and bungee-jumps – not to mention on bus tours around the country (guides). Working holidaymakers may find work in other tourism-related areas such as bar-tending, waiting tables at restaurants and wineries, frothing cappuccinos in cafés (although the role of 'barista' is taken very seriously here), or less glamorous jobs such as hotel and motel chambermaids and cleaners. Inexperienced young people may not be able to cherry-pick their jobs, but they may find seasonal work picking fruit or harvesting grapes. The wine industry is fun, but competitive: don't expect to get a serious wine-making job without qualifications, experience and knowledge of viticulture; even then it may well be only for the six weeks of harvest.

A popular business venture for immigrants, who can sometimes see the country's potential more clearly than native New Zealanders, is to set up an eco or 'luxury' tourist venture – restoring an old house and converting it into a homestay, or building a country cottage complex hung with the best of New Zealand art and let out (to other foreigners) at an exorbitant fee. If you're in the millionaire league, you could start up a golf course complete with luxury lodge, or buy your own vineyard and build a deluxe winery on it. If you're more ecologically minded, New Zealand is a good place to get involved with organic horticulture, permaculture or biodynamics – often in combination with green tourism.

The kinds of jobs that foreigners are least likely to find are in the arts and media, where a combination of New Zealand's small market and New Zealand cultural nationalism may make it hard for an outsider to get an in. This is less likely to apply at the highest levels, where cultural practitioners of repute will be welcomed. And New Zealand's burgeoning mega-bucks film industry (*Lord of the Rings*; *King Kong*; *The Lion, the Witch and the Wardrobe*) has provided plenty of outlets for talent in all aspects of production and post-production, as well as for actors like Tom Cruise (*Last of the Samurai*) – even if more characteristically New Zealand films (*Whale Rider*) have relied as far as possible on local talent. There aren't many openings in marketing or real estate sales, either, as these are the jobs New Zealanders most aspire to.

# Being Employed (Private or Public)

## How to Find a Job

In spite of New Zealand's low unemployment rate, the job market is still competitive; the process of finding a job here can be as arduous as anywhere. If you fall into one of the sought-after occupational categories, it is well worth trying to find work before you embark for the new world (indeed, you may have to in order to get a work visa or permit). There are several agencies in the UK who can help you to do this.

If you land in New Zealand with a phalanx of talents but no job, the usual methods apply: scour the job adverts in the newspapers and on job websites – knowing all the time that any advertised job will attract many applicants, and that your dream job might be out there somewhere, unadvertised; send your CV speculatively to organisations you would like to work for, and who might realistically be able to use your skills; network like mad by making as many personal contacts as you can and entertaining them with your fabulous personality, while discreetly reminding them from time to time that you need a job. And if none of the above gets you anywhere, there are always employment agencies.

All the daily papers carry a Situations Vacant section advertising job vacancies. The most extensive listings can be found in the Auckland-based *New Zealand Herald* (**www.nzherald.co.nz**), the Wellington-based *Dominion Post* (**www.stuff.**

## Case Study: IT Is not an Easy Ticket

Tim Murchland moved to New Zealand in August 2002, with his wife, Marianne, and three children – a year after he and Marianne first decided to make the move. It took that long to sort out all the red tape – getting permanent residence and legal permission from his first wife to take their son Aidan overseas – and, crucially, to sell their house in the UK. The family settled in Wellington, close to Marianne's parents in Lower Hutt, and selected a suburb that was zoned for Wellington College, one of the better state secondary schools in the city. With the equity from their UK home they were able to buy a decent-sized house outright. Tim has now decided to go the whole hog, and is applying for citizenship.

Surprisingly – given that the New Zealand Immigration Service lists a whole host of IT specialisms on its Long-term Skills Shortage List (*see* p.122) – the main stumbling block for IT professional Tim was finding a job. Despite having worked his whole career in IT, and holding a senior position as the software development manager of a large team in a music organisation before moving to New Zealand, it took him nearly six months to find a job. Tim had been in touch with a specialist recruitment agency from England, but set out for the new world with no work lined up. The IT market was 'pretty flat', he says, and the agency, Absolute IT, was unable to offer any real help until Tim was over here and in a position to start work at once.

Two years and a couple of jobs later, Tim feels that he has made a name for himself and would be confident about finding another job – but it was not an easy start to his new life. It was hard to break into the market, he says, adding that personal contacts and New Zealand experience seem to count for a lot. His first job here was at the Ministry for Economic Development – a position in public service that was open to him as a foreigner, although not all are (he applied for one job at Internal Affairs, but was barred until he got citizenship). The MED gave him a foothold into Infinity Solutions, a medium-sized IT consultancy, where he is now a project manager overseeing a team of five, currently working at the Ministry of Social Development. 'From an IT point of view it's very interesting,' says Tim, who is glad to have given up some of the responsibility he had at his job in London, where he was managing 80 people after the Performing Rights Society and the Mechanical Copyright Protection Society merged.

There is nothing Tim misses from home. In fact the only hiccup now is that, after three years overseas, his son Aidan will have to pay foreign tuition fees at a British university – and his NCEA qualifications are not highly enough rated by the British system to gain him entry.

co.nz) or Christchurch-based *The Press* (**www.stuff.co.nz**). Jobs are advertised nationally in these papers. For regional jobs, look in the regional papers.

Wednesday and Saturday editions of the national papers carry the most extensive job vacancy sections; days vary for the regional papers.

For specialised professional jobs, vacancies are listed in most professional journals, or on the websites of the New Zealand Registration Boards of those professions (*see* 'Occupational Registration', pp.124–5). Teaching jobs at primary and secondary schools are advertised in the *Education Gazette* (**www. edgazette.govt.nz**), published by the Ministry of Education. Another place to look for school-teaching positions is **www.teachnz.govt.nz**, **t** 0800 832246, which provides full information on how to apply for teaching positions from overseas, including details of necessary qualifications and relocation grants (*see* 'Teaching', pp.220–23). Positions at universities and polytechnics are advertised in the major papers listed above, and on the websites of individual teaching institutions. All public sector jobs are advertised on the government website, **www.jobs.govt.nz**, and most of these are open to all applicants.

Many jobs are offered through private recruitment agencies, at every level from labourers to managers. You may be able to apply for a job before you move to New Zealand through an agency, which in some cases may be able to help you get your qualifications assessed by the New Zealand Qualifications Authority and process your visa or permit application too. Specialist agents operate in the UK to find work for midwives, nurses and medical practitioners in New Zealand. Well-known international agencies operate in New Zealand as well. As a rule, companies recruiting manual workers are known as **labour hire**, those dealing with lower-level staff call themselves **employment agencies**, while executive, professional and management positions are handled by companies calling themselves **personnel consultants**. For hirers, agents and consultants operating in your area, look in the *Yellow Pages*. Some agencies with good web listings are listed below. As a last resort, the state social security agency, Work and Income (WINZ), provides free job-seeking services for unemployed residents.

In New Zealand as much as anywhere, word of mouth and personal contacts are one of the best ways of finding work. If you work in a less structured occupation – such as media or the arts – talk to everybody you meet about what you can and want to do. Again, as in most of the Anglo-Saxon world, some well-researched letters and phone calls to potential employers may find you work that has not been advertised. Professional directories are one place to start identifying organisations you might want to work for, or **www.ubd.co.nz** offers a comprehensive directory of New Zealand businesses. The best approach is to send your CV with a covering letter that shows your understanding of the company you are approaching and what you can offer it, and follow it up with a phone call a couple of days later. Try to find out the names of specific individuals within a firm before you approach them.

# Job-seeking on the Internet

## Government Employment

- **Careers Services Rapuara, t** 0800 222733; **www.careers.co.nz.** Government careers services, with information on training, job application and employment opportunities.

- **Employment Relations Service, t** 0800 800863; **www.ers.govt.nz.** Information on the rights and obligations of both employers and employees.

- **Human Rights Commission, t** 0800 449 6877; **www.hrc.govt.nz.** Independent agency responsible for investigating complaints about human rights.

- **New Kiwis; www.newkiwis.co.nz.** Finds appropriate work for resident migrants by matching your details to employment opportunities.

- **New Zealand Government Jobs Online; www.jobs.govt.nz.** Public-sector employment vacancies.

- **Occupational Health and Safety; www.osh.govt.nz.** Responsible for identifying hazards, accidents and injuries in the workplace.

- **Skill New Zealand; www.etsa.govt.nz.** Comprehensive guide to vocational training courses and apprenticeships across all industries.

- **Work and Income, t** 0800 559009; **www.winz.govt.nz.** Information about finding work or getting income support.

## Job Agencies

- **www.alljobs.co.nz.** Specific regional and national jobs.

- **www.eeotrust.org.nz.** Equal Employment Opportunities Trust, an employer group that seeks to ensure equal opportunities for migrants.

- **www.jobcafe.co.nz.** Matches your experience to jobs on a funky, easy-to-use website.

- **www.jobs-on-line.co.nz.** Job listings online.

- **www.jobstuff.co.nz.** Web edition of national newspaper job adverts.

- **www.jobuniverse.co.nz.** New Zealand and overseas database of jobs.

- **www.monster.co.nz.** Career advice, interview tips and listings.

- **www.nzherald.co.nz/employment.** Online job ads from the *New Zealand Herald* newspaper.

- **www.netcheck.co.nz.** General job listings; specializing in IT, management and upper-level professional jobs.

- **www.nzjobs.co.nz.** Database of jobs in many fields.

- **www.seek.co.nz.** General employment website with online listings and company profiles; one of the best.

• **www.workingin-newzealand.com**. Links to agencies dealing with specific occupational areas; organises Opportunities New Zealand expos in the UK.

# The Application Process

While the job application process is broadly similar in New Zealand to anywhere else in the Anglo-Saxon world, it is not generally as drawn out. Maybe the population size means employers do not have to fight through the mountains of CVs on their doorstep that they do in the UK, but decisions seem to be made in days not weeks.

Similar rules apply to CV-writing in New Zealand as in the UK: keep it short and sweet, and highlight relevant experience and qualifications. It may be useful to attach a résumé emphasizing the most pertinent points of your CV, or you may wish to write these into your covering letter. Make sure you include contact details, residence status (e.g. work visa), qualifications, computer skills, professional and trade skills, work experience and achievements, and the names of referees. Standards of formality will depend on the type of job you are applying for (*see* 'Business Etiquette', pp.204–205), but a neat, well-presented document without spelling mistakes, typos or other kinds of misinformation will always help your case. It can be a bad idea to be too funky, unless you have a pretty good idea that funkiness is appropriate to the job.

The code of conduct at a job interview is governed by similar principles. There's no point turning up for an apple-picking job with a tie on, but if you're trying to get a job at a law firm, wear a suit. Again, certain universals apply – a friendly, polite demeanour and a firm handshake can't do you any harm, whatever the job. You may be invited to conduct an interview by phone.

The recruitment process for some public sector jobs may involve sitting tests. For any job requiring specific formal qualifications (such as medical jobs), you will be asked to provide evidence of these and their NZ equivalence early on in the process.

# Qualifications and Registration

The **New Zealand Qualifications Authority (NZQA)**, **www.nzqa.govt.nz**, evaluates professional and academic qualifications to determine how they compare with New Zealand qualifications and whether they meet New Zealand standards. It is advisable to contact the NZQA before leaving for New Zealand, and make sure you bring original or certified copies of all certificates, diplomas, degrees and professional qualifications with you to show employers.

As well as having your qualifications assessed, certain professionals and tradespeople, from doctors to plumbers, may need to register to practise. Contact the relevant **registration board** for your type of work (*see* box, 'Occupational Registration', pp.124–5). You may be required to demonstrate continuing experience and competency on top of your original qualification, as well as having to pay an annual fee to the board.

# Contracts and Terms of Employment

## Employment Agreements

All employers are legally obliged to offer their workers a written employment agreement, written in plain language. There are some provisions that must by law be included in agreements, and there are also a number of minimum conditions that must be met regardless of whether they are included in agreements. The agreement must include: minimum wage, the same rate for men and women in the same jobs, four weeks' paid annual leave after 12 months in the job, 11 public holidays per year, an entitlement to five days' sick leave and three days' bereavement leave after six months' employment, and up to 12 months' parental leave (mostly unpaid) after six months' employment. It is illegal to discriminate on grounds of race, colour, national or ethnic origin, sex or sexual orientation, marital or family status, employment status, age, religious belief or political opinion, or disability (Human Rights Act 1993).

Employment law also provides a framework for negotiating additional entitlements. The agreement may include conditions relating to duties and responsibilities, the term of the agreement, pay rates and basis for pay, other payments, the pay day, method of pay, pay review, hours of work, holidays and other leave, training, health and safety, consultation, company policies and codes of conduct, restraint of trade, ending the agreement (resignation, retirement and dismissal), redundancy and contract renewal. All employment agreements must by law be negotiated in 'good faith'.

## Fixed-term Employment

Most employment agreements are permanent, but sometimes employers and employees agree that employment will be for a set period of time (for six months) or until a certain event occurs (until a particular project ends) or until work is completed (until the fruit is picked). A fixed-term employment agreement can be ended when the agreement says it will end.

However, the agreement must have a fixed term for genuine reasons. An employer may not employ a person on a fixed-term agreement where the job is in reality a permanent one and the employer wants to avoid having to go through a fair disciplinary or dismissal procedure if there are problems.

## Resignation

Employees may resign at any time, provided they give reasonable notice. If the employee gives the required notice, the employer must pay the employee to the end of the notice period, unless the employee is justifiably dismissed during that period. The employment relationship continues until that date. The employee may be required to work for the full notice period or may be asked to stop coming to work before this date. In either case, the employee should be paid to the end of the notice. If an employee leaves work without giving notice, the employer is not required to pay for time beyond the employee's last actual working day. The employer must pay all holiday pay owing to the employee in the pay packet for the employee's final period of employment.

## Retirement

In law, there is no set age to retire from work, and employers cannot require employees to retire just because of their age. New Zealand's National Superannuation Scheme entitles all workers to a state pension at the age of 65. See 'Retirement and Pensions', pp.192–4.

## Dismissal

There must be a good reason for a dismissal and the dismissal must be carried out fairly. Employees have the right to be told what the problem is and that dismissal or other disciplinary action is a possibility. Employees must then be given a genuine opportunity to tell their side of the story before the employer decides what to do. The employer should investigate any allegations of misconduct thoroughly and without prejudice. Unless there has been misconduct so serious that it warrants instant dismissal, the employee should be given clear standards to aim for and a genuine opportunity to improve.

The sort of conduct that warrants instant dismissal may be set out in the employment agreement.

## Forced Resignation or Constructive Dismissal

If an employer puts pressure (directly or indirectly) on an employee to resign, or makes the situation at work intolerable for the employee, it may be a forced resignation or constructive dismissal.

## Redundancy

This happens when a position filled by an employee is no longer needed, or the employer has made a genuine decision to discontinue employment  for commercial reasons. Generally, there is no automatic entitlement to redundancy compensation unless employers and employees and/or their union have agreed to it. This can be done before or after a redundancy is planned. It is also up to the parties to decide what any redundancy compensation should be.

# Unions

Employees can choose whether or not to join a trade union. Jobs cannot be withheld on the basis of membership or non-membership of a union. Employees who choose to belong to a union are covered by the union's collective agreement on pay and working conditions. Employees who choose not to belong to a union must negotiate an individual employment agreement. Conditions for a new employee depend on whether a collective agreement covers the employee's work.

If there is no collective agreement, then an individual employment agreement is negotiated. The employer must make a written offer and give the employee the opportunity to get advice about it.

If there is a collective agreement, the employee has several options. If the employee belongs to the union, the conditions of employment are those in the collective agreement. The employer and employee can still negotiate additional conditions. If the employee is not a union member, the employee has an individual employment agreement. This comprises the conditions in the collective agreement plus any extra conditions negotiated with the employer. The employee has 30 days to decide whether or not to join the union.

Trade unions have not held much power in New Zealand since the infamous wharfies' strikes of the early 1990s, which were busted by the government of the time in a manner reminiscent of Margaret Thatcher and the miners in Britain. That said, the National Maritime Union of New Zealand was out on strike four times in 2007...

## Wages

Average annual salaries for full-time workers were NZ$41,392 in 2007 (less for women), but there is a wide range of incomes across different occupations, industries and levels of experience. For up-to-date information on salary ranges, market demand, training requirements and typical working conditions for different types of work, visit the Kiwi Careers website, **www.careers.co.nz**.

Employers are legally obliged to offer you at least the **minimum wage** – currently NZ$11.25 per hour, or $450 for a 40-hour week, for adults over 18, NZ$9 an hour for 16–17-year-olds (80 per cent of the adult rate). There are exemptions to the minimum wage for disabled people, by agreement, if the employer can demonstrate that they are doing less than the full job.

## Hours and Overtime

The standard New Zealand working week is 40 hours, although there is no statutory limitation on working longer hours and no automatic entitlement to overtime pay. Overtime may, however, be negotiated with employers. Employers may, voluntarily, agree to pay 'penal rates' to workers who work on weekends. This will be stated in the employment agreement.

## Annual and Public Holidays

Employees are currently entitled to a minimum of four weeks' annual holiday after a year's employment. In addition, employees are entitled to a paid day off on each of the 11 annual public holidays, if they fall on a day on which they would normally work. If Waitangi Day (6 February) or ANZAC Day (25 April) fall at the weekend, employees who do not normally work at the weekend are not entitled to payment for the day. All the other holidays are 'Mondayised', except Easter Friday. If Christmas, Boxing Day, New Year's Day and the day after fall on weekends, the following Mondays and Tuesdays are holidays, but employees are only entitled to a maximum of four paid days' holiday over the festive period.

An employment agreement may specify, however, that an employee may be required to work on public holidays, in which case the employee is entitled to at least time and a half for the day's work and an alternative holiday on full pay (a day in lieu). These last, recent provisions have been seen as too onerous by many employers and led them to close on public holidays, while many restaurants, bars and cafés have chosen to pass on the cost to customers in the form of a surcharge.

## Sick Leave

For most employees there is a minimum provision of five days' paid sick leave a year after the first six months of employment and an additional five days' paid sick leave after each subsequent 12-month period. It may be possible to antici-pate some sick days, by special arrangement with the employer. Unused sick days can be carried over, up to a maximum of 20 days. Employees can be asked to produce a medical certificate of sickness after three days' leave. Sick leave is not pro-rated.

## Bereavement Leave

For most employees there is a minimum entitlement to bereavement leave after the first six months of continuous employment. On the death of an imme-diate family member, you can take up to three days' paid leave. 'Immediate family members' are the employee's spouse, parent, child, sibling, grandparent, grandchild or the spouse's parent. Where there is a multiple bereavement, the employee is entitled to three days' bereavement leave in respect of each death. (For example, if all four of your grandparents are in a car that drives over a cliff, you are entitled to up to 12 days' bereavement leave.)

## Parental Leave

The Parental Leave and Employment Protection Act 1987 provides for unpaid leave from work for birth mothers, their partner/spouses and adoptive parents on either the birth of a child or the adoption of a child under six, and payment for up to 14 weeks of this leave. While this Act provides minimum standards, employers and employees can negotiate enhanced provisions. If you are considering applying for parental leave, you must choose between the two sets of provisions – those in legislation or those provided in your employment agreement. It is illegal to either dismiss or discriminate against an employee on the grounds of pregnancy or for taking parental leave under the Act.

There are four kinds of parental leave, with entitlements depending on whether you have worked for one employer for the previous six or 12 months. The pregnant mother-to-be is entitled to up to 10 days' special leave for visits to the doctor or midwife and ante-natal classes. The mother is entitled to 14 weeks' maternity leave, of which up to six may be taken before the birth. Fathers may take up to two weeks' paternity leave. Either parent may take up to 52 weeks' extended leave. All leave must be taken in the first year after the birth or adoption. Each partner must take any period of extended leave in a continuous period. The leave can be taken at the same time or separately to suit the needs of the parents and the child. Mothers, or in the case of adoption of a child under six either parent, are entitled to a taxpayer-funded payment for up to 14 weeks of the parental leave they take, to a maximum of $391.28 per week.

## Accident Insurance

Workplace injury is covered by the government's accident insurance scheme, which is managed by the Accident Compensation Corporation (ACC). In order to reduce the incidence of workplace injuries, the ACC runs incentive programmes which provide employers with discounts on their premiums if certain safety targets are met. Employers are responsible for paying ACC contributions for their employees, but self-employed people must pay their own contributions. *See also* 'Health and Emergencies', p.190.

## Tax

As a New Zealand resident you will be required to pay tax on all the income you receive. To do this you will need to apply to the Inland Revenue Department for an **IRD number** as soon as you open a bank account or start work. If you are employed, your employer will make pay-as-you-earn (PAYE) tax deductions. If you are self-employed, you will need to complete a tax return at the end of the tax year (31 March). You may be required to pay Provisional Tax in anticipation of your final end-of-year tax declaration. If you have any non-employed income, from rental properties, interest on savings, investments or other sources, you will be required to complete a tax return too. *See also* 'Taxation', pp.172–3.

## When Things Go Wrong

If problems arise in an employment relationship, either party can get advice from the Department of Labour's **Employment Relations Service, t** 0800 800863, or visit the ERS website, **www.ers.govt.nz**, which provides up-to-date information on all aspects of employer/employee relations.

If an employee believes that he or she has been unfairly dismissed, made redundant, forced to resign or pressured into retirement, sexually or racially harassed or discriminated against, or intimidated for his or her union membership, he or she may take legal action against his or her employer in the form of a personal grievance. The Employment Relations Service encourages employers and employees to seek resolution through good faith and mediation. If these prove ineffectual, however, an application can be made to the Employment Relations Authority to investigate the problem. A last resort is the Employment Court – a full judicial authority.

# Teaching

New Zealand is chronically short of teachers, and offers incentives to qualified teachers from English-speaking countries with similar educational systems, such as the UK, Ireland, Australia, Canada and South Africa, to relocate. Secondary teachers – of maths, physics, chemistry and technology – are in particular demand. Primary teachers are much in demand in Auckland, which has a fast-growing population. Government initiatives to boost staffing levels in primary schools mean that more teachers will be needed at this level throughout the country soon. Three years' teaching experience is a minimum requirement, but there is strong demand for qualified early childhood teachers too, since the government introduced 20 hours of free pre-school education per week for all 3–5-year-olds in 2007. There is, however, no British equivalent of the three-year New Zealand Early Childhood Education diploma. Teachers of children with special needs are also sought after, as are teachers of English to speakers of other languages. The main demand for teachers at all levels from ECE to secondary is in Auckland.

Schools in New Zealand employ their own staff, for which they advertise in the New Zealand *Education Gazette* (**www.edgazette.govt.nz**). Vacancy listings are searchable, are continually updated, and include school and location profile information. You can subscribe free of charge to be notified of new listings meeting your criteria. Most vacancies are advertised between September and January, for the new school year, which starts at the end of January. Several agents offer employment services to schools and to teachers looking for a job here. Overseas teachers seeking teaching positions may apply directly to schools as well as listing themselves with teacher recruitment agents (see 'Immigration and Employment Services for Teachers', p.223).

If you are applying from overseas directly to schools in response to advertised positions you should fax or email your application to the school well before the closing date on the advertisement. Your application should include a covering letter, specific to the advertised position; plus a curriculum vitae which includes details of your qualifications including subjects and course content, and of your teaching service, detailing length of service, type of schools, whether service was full-time or part-time, positions and responsibilities held, your curriculum specialities, co-curricular activities, experience and interest in sporting or cultural activities, plus your personal qualities. Also give references and referee names and contacts. It is suggested that you contact the school before you prepare your application to ensure that you include all the information that might be required.

New Zealand's two official languages are English and Maori. Teachers must be extremely competent in written and spoken communication in English for general teaching purposes. This is reinforced by registration requirements. Work or residence permits are required for all immigrant teachers. Overseas qualifications must be verified and checked for comparability with qualifications in New Zealand for registration and salary purposes. Verification is carried out by the **New Zealand Qualifications Authority (NZQA), www.nzqa.govt.nz**, and usually takes up to six weeks; fast tracking is available for an extra fee.

All teachers at primary and secondary level in New Zealand must be registered with the **Teachers Council**. To register as a teacher, if your qualifications were obtained in an overseas country you must provide a certified copy of the NZQA assessment report to the Teachers Council. Applicants must supply certified copies of certificates and statements of services covering all teaching experience. This process involves producing evidence of teacher education in the form of a degree or diploma. An NZQA equivalency statement is also required to ensure that teachers receive the correct salary. When you start teaching you will be paid as a beginning teacher until the NZQA statement is received.

If you are successful in your application for a position in New Zealand you should send a copy of the NZQA assessment report to your principal before you take up your position. This will be needed to assess your salary level. If you have already been offered a teaching position in New Zealand when you apply to NZQA to have your qualifications verified, you should attach a letter from the appointing school to your application giving the details of the job offer. You can download the application form from **www.nzqa.govt.nz**.

Once you have been granted registration you will need a work permit or visa from the New Zealand Immigration Service before you can accept a teaching position. For secondary teachers this is easy as, currently, a secondary teacher only has to produce evidence of registration and a letter of a job offer in order to get a work permit.

Some overseas trained teachers arrive without completing the process necessary for them to receive their correct entitlements. It is advisable to complete all the paperwork before you leave home, and bring several certified copies of all documents with you. Ideally before you leave home you should get the NZQA assessment report on your qualifications, complete teacher registration (**www. teacherscouncil.govt.nz**) and get a work visa or permit. You might, for example, be asked to provide a transcript of the teacher training course you completed if the course content has changed over time – much easier to do from just down the road than from the other side of the world. You must also provide evidence of previous experience on original letterhead from your employing school. The letter must state whether your position was full-time or part-time, and it must include start and finish dates and details of time you actually spent teaching. The allowable time credit – which determines your salary – depends on the exact number of days you worked.

The education system in New Zealand, at all levels, has many differences from and lots of similarities to the British system. To compare systems and the way education is delivered in 18 other countries, go to **www.inca.org.nz** (INCA stands for **International Curriculum Assessment Database**, maintained by the National Foundation for Education Research). To compare similarities and differences in the New Zealand curriculum go to **www.minedu.govt.nz** and look at the curriculum learning areas.

Primary and secondary teachers in New Zealand have pay parity but their unions, the **PPTA** (Post Primary Teachers Association) and **NZEI** (New Zealand Educational Institute), negotiate separately with the government and at different times. Both organisations have websites where you can check the latest salary information. Kindergarten teachers have parity with primary teachers. Salaries currently range from around NZ$26,000–$60,000.

The **International Relocation Grant** is an incentive to attract overseas-trained teachers to teaching positions in New Zealand. If you are an overseas-trained teacher relocating to New Zealand you may be eligible for a grant. Grants are NZ$1,500 where your term of employment is for at least six weeks but less than two school terms; NZ$3,000 where your term of employment is for two school terms or more. This grant must be applied for through your principal within eight weeks of commencing employment. To see if you meet all of the eligibility requirements of this grant, go to **www.minedu.govt.nz/goto/resourcingforms**.

Apart from the five largest cities – Auckland, Hamilton, Wellington, Christchurch and Dunedin – New Zealand has provincial cities like Nelson, Palmerston North, Napier, Hastings and Whangarei, but there are hundreds of towns throughout the rest of New Zealand which are predominantly rural in character, and all have schools and need teachers. There are specific rural areas of New Zealand where teachers are particularly sought, so if your vision of life in

New Zealand is pastoral you may be able to find work in a village school. These include Northland, the East Cape and Coromandel, King Country and the South Island's west coast.

## Immigration and Employment Services for Teachers

Of course you can apply to schools directly and do all the paperwork yourself, but a teacher recruitment agency may simplify the process for you. The New Zealand Ministry of Education has four preferred overseas teacher recruitment agencies, which offer their services free to teachers and can help you with the education system, immigration requirements, entitlements, pay and other professional information:

- **Education Personnel; www.edperson.co.nz**. Long-term or permanent education vacancies in Wellington and the rest of New Zealand, especially for technology and design, graphics, information technology, maths, chemistry or physics teachers. Also Wellington relief teachers.

- **Multi Serve Education Trust; www.multiserve.co.nz/recruitment**. Can take care of documentation checks and registration requirements for teaching in New Zealand. Looking for full-time primary teachers in Auckland and secondary teachers who specialise in science, maths, English, technology/IT or physical education. Also Auckland relief teachers.

- **Oasis Education Ltd; www.oasis-edu.co.nz**. Provides New Zealand schools with full-time staff and Auckland schools with relief teachers.

- **Select Education; www.selecteducation.com**. Part-time, long-term or full-time work at schools, early childhood centres and kindergartens. Can help with assessment of qualifications, teacher registration in New Zealand, immigration, police checks, travel and accommodation for teachers coming to New Zealand. Christchurch and Auckland offices.

# Freelancing, Part-time and Casual Work

## Part-time and Casual Work

Most work in New Zealand is in full-time employment, but there are opportunities for 'non-standard' work, too – part-time, 'casual' (on a fixed-term contract) or self-employed. Most people who work part-time do so out of choice – to better balance work with life, whether this means spending more time with their family, devoting more time to a second career as a surfer or photographer, or just having more time to hang out. Part-time work may be found in just about any sort of occupation, but is nearly always less well paid than full-time work. A lot of part-time jobs are in 'hospitality' (tending bars or waiting tables) and 'retail' (selling shoes or stacking supermarket shelves). Other options to explore might include relief work for teachers or shifts for nurses at hospitals.

Luckily, New Zealand has not fallen prey to the short-term contract culture in quite the way that Britain has, as employment law stipulates that fixed-term contracts can only be issued with good reason (such as until a specific project is finished). There is, however, plenty of casual work around, particularly of the seasonal variety: you could happily spend a New Zealand summer and autumn moving from fruit-picking to grape-harvesting job around the country; horticultural offshoots might include processing and packing vegetables. Identify the seasons, what's grown where, and follow the crops. Casual work for orchardists and viticulturists is usually advertised in local newspapers.

## Self-employment and Freelancing

New Zealand is as good a place to be self-employed as anywhere. Even if you don't plan to start your own business (see 'Starting Your Own Business', pp.226–36), you can still set yourself up as a **sole trader** in your area of expertise (assuming you have one). New Zealanders are increasingly opting for the freelance way of life, tempted by the flexibility and promise of financial gain it appears to offer. As anywhere, however, the difficulty with freelancing in New Zealand is to maintain a steady flow of work, and therefore a regular income, on a pendulum that can swing dramatically from underwork to overwork. For newcomers to the country, an additional obstacle is that freelance work tends to be generated by contacts and word of mouth; it may be a struggle to find work initially – unless you arrive with a book of contacts.

Popular freelance occupations include the building trades, retail and hospitality (suitable for part-time working) and all manner of work in the creative industries. You may be best off applying for advertised jobs or seeking employment through other more conventional routes first. Once you get to know a few people, you may be in a good position to go self-employed. If you can get a job as a plumber, electrician or carpenter on a big building development, you will be well placed to hear about future building work. When you've got your first job in a bar, café or restaurant, you'll soon hear where you could get more work when you're ready to move on. After a week or two at one supermarket checkout, you'll find out if the rates of pay are better at another one.

Similar principles apply to creative work – unless you plan to set up your own pottery studio or fine-art practice, or intend to retire to a remote rural retreat and write a 21st-century New Zealand version of *The Cherry Orchard*. Most people working in the visual arts, design and crafts are self-employed, often working freelance for several companies. A lot of this work is short-term and contract-based, which means you need to be adaptable and prepared to work in many different jobs. You may well have to combine your creative work with

other employment. Writers and editors are as likely to be occasional contribu-
tors to newspapers and magazines as employed in-house, and may earn their
crust doing copywriting for advertisers or technical writing. Again, this work is
not likely to be advertised, so networking and persistence are essential.

A useful resource for all creative practitioners from the culinary arts to the
wearable arts as well as dance, design, digital culture, the moving image (film
and TV), music, photography, visual arts and writing is **The Big Idea**, 'an online
community of New Zealand's creative industries'. Committed to helping
creative people find work and income, the site provides access to networks,
industry news, current job opportunities, professional development, forums,
international news and much more. Its website, **www.thebigidea.co.nz**,
includes a selection of recent writing on all the main creative disciplines,
collected from the press and specialist journals, as well as lots of information on
prizes, exhibitions, artists' and writers' residences, grants, festivals – and,
crucially, listings for jobs in the arts. It also has links to arts organisations, art
galleries and even individual practitioners. The Big Idea is 'committed to the
innovation of virtual community as a way of providing alternative networking
and information sharing across all the creative sectors'. While you won't necessarily find a job on the site, it will at least give you an idea of what's out there.

# Film and TV Work

Keep your ear to the ground if you're bright-eyed, bushy-tailed and eager to
work in New Zealand's burgeoning film industry. (Whether it will continue to
burgeon is anybody's guess, but the last few years have seen a run of big
productions, some indigenous, others foreign, from Peter Jackson's *Lord of the
Rings* trilogy to *Whale Rider* and *The Last Samurai*.) Whether your lifelong ambition is to be an elf extra in *The Hobbit – A Prequel*, or you are an experienced
make-up artist, art director or editor, the only way to find the jobs is to check out
what's in production and get in touch with the production companies – or hang
around film shoots looking keen until someone mistakes you for a runner and
sends you out for pizza. Listed below are some organisations, publications and
guilds that can help you to find out what's happening.

- **New Zealand Film Commission; www.nzfilm.co.nz.** The NZFC is the
  primary funding body for the development, production and distribution of
  New Zealand feature films. The commission's main focus is funding indigenous feature film production and certifying productions working under the
  official co-production treaties. It invests around NZ\$6m per year on New
  Zealand feature films and NZ\$1.5m on short films. As well as industry news,
  it can provide you with information on tax breaks and film financing in New
  Zealand, although it has often been dogged by controversy.

- **Film New Zealand; www.filmnz.com.** A primarily government-funded film locations office, which performs various industry informational and marketing services.

- **New Zealand On Air; www.nzonair.govt.nz.** Funds indigenous television production to the tune of around NZ$45m of public money.

- **New Zealand Film and Video Technicians Guild; www.nzfvtg.org.nz.** The Techos' Guild. A professional organisation representing the interests of freelance film and video crew and allied crafts in the Screen Production Industry. Information about productions currently under way, as well as useful guidelines on pay rates and standard working conditions forcrews.

- **NZCrews; www.nzcrews.tv.** An online directory of freelance New Zealand TV crews – camera, sound, directors, production and post-production.

- **Screen Directors Guild of New Zealand; www.sdgnz.co.nz.** Industry information for directors.

- **Actors' Equity; www.nduunion.org.nz/actorsequity.htm.** The entertainment sector of the national distribution union.

- **Screen Producers' and Development Association of New Zealand; www.spada.co.nz.** A membership-based organisation that represents the collective interests of independent producers on all issues that affect the business and creative aspects of independent screen production in New Zealand, SPADA is a rich source of New Zealand industry news and information. Its website spreads the word about industry news, issues and events, and puts you in touch with the screen production industry, helping you to develop professional networks.

- **New Zealand Writers' Guild; www.nzwritersguild.org.nz.** A professional association for writers in the fields of film, television, radio, theatre, video and multi-media. It is affiliated with the Writers Guilds of Great Britain, Canada and Australia.

- **Creative New Zealand; www.creativenewzealand.govt.nz.** Arts Council of New Zealand, involved in arts advocacy across all media.

- **OnFilm; www.onfilm.co.nz.** 'New Zealand's Screen Production Industry Magazine', which has monthly listings of what's in production (from pre-production to post-production). Also publishes New Zealand's most comprehensive screen production directory, *The Data Book*, available online or at bookshops, **www.databook.co.nz.**

# Starting Your Own Business

New Zealand is a 'can-do' country and a great place to start your own business. Most businesses are small, founded on the country's practical, enthusiastic ethos. It's a place of self-made men and women – after all, many of the early immigrants came here to escape the strictures of the British class system, which prevented them from getting ahead, and nothing much has changed. If you have a good idea, be it something entirely new or just a better way of doing something old, there are few obstacles to putting it into practice here – as long as you work it all out carefully and work hard at it. As a newcomer you may be particularly well placed to import innovative ideas, and you'll find plenty of people and organisations waiting to help you do it.

While most New Zealand companies remain small, partly through choice and partly as a result of the small home market, many businesses have made it to the international big-time from insignificant beginnings. The indigenous vodka maker 42 Below, merino wool sportswear designer Icebreaker, GPS manufacturers Navman and TimeZoneOne – a creative and design agency capitalizing on international time differences and exchange rates to cater for global clients – are just a few of the success stories of recent years.

# Business Types

There are for tax and legal purposes three main forms of business in New Zealand: sole traders, partnerships and companies. A **sole trader** owns all the

## Companies

A company must have a registered name, one or more shares, one or more shareholders with liability for the obligations of the company, and one or more directors. A company may have a constitution, which, in certain circumstances, can be adopted to vary the Act's rules to suit a company's individual requirements. A company is a legal entity in its own right, separate from its shareholders, and continues to exist until it is removed from the Companies Register. It may enter into contracts with its shareholders.

Not all companies are required to prepare and register financial statements. Under the Financial Reporting Act 1993, only companies that are 'reporting entities' need to prepare and register financial statements. Reporting entities are companies that issue shares, overseas companies, subsidiary companies or companies with at least one subsidiary. Companies with assets valued at NZ$450,000 or with a turnover of NZ$1 million must also file financial statements. Small companies that do not fit any of the other categories above do not need to file financial statements.

Companies that offer securities, including shares, to the public, and overseas-owned or overseas-controlled companies, must be independently audited. Unless otherwise agreed, contracts entered into by the company do not impose liability on individual members. A New Zealand company automatically has access to the Australian market under the Australia-New Zealand Closer Economic Relations (CER) Trade Agreement.

assets of the business and is solely responsible for all the business's risks, obligations and debts. On the other hand, if you want to run a business with other people in New Zealand, you can establish an ordinary or special **partnership** under the guidelines established by the Partnership Act 1908. The Companies Act 1993 provides the basic rules for establishing and operating a **company** in New Zealand. Any person, alone or with another person, may apply for registration of a company. A company must have a registered name, one or more shares, one or more shareholders with liability for the obligations of the company, and one or more directors. To register a company name and incorporate a company, go to the website **www.companies.govt.nz**, or call **t** 0508 266726 (freephone). It costs around NZ$60.

# Codes of Conduct for Business in New Zealand

## Regulation

Although business regulation in New Zealand is not very strict, businesses are required to follow some standard principles. There are three government agencies that oversee business conduct: the Commerce Commission, the Securities Commission and the Takeovers Panel.

The **Commerce Commission** is an independent organisation with the remit to promote market efficiency by fostering healthy competition, informed consumer choice and sound economic regulation. It is charged with making sure that businesses meet the provisions of regulatory acts, including the Commerce Act 1986, the Fair Trading Act 1986 and the Electricity Industry Reform Act 1988. Suspected cases of anti-competitive business practices, and unfair or misleading trade practices, can be reported to the Commerce Commission contact centre, **www.comcom.govt.nz**, **t** 0800 943600. The centre provides advice and investigates complaints.

The **Securities Commission** is an independent body established under the Securities Act 1978, which promotes efficient and cost-effective management and regulatory practices within the capital investment market. The commission also regulates the offer of securities for public subscription. It has broad powers to investigate cases of insider trading and can recommend the reform of existing securities laws and practices.

The **Takeovers Panel**, established as a body corporate under the Takeovers Act 1993, is responsible for both the operation of the Takeovers Code and promoting public awareness of issues relating to takeovers. The Takeovers Code Approval Order 2000 is intended to ensure that takeovers take place in an orderly way. It establishes standards of proper disclosure and requires that all shareholders be treated equally.

## Health and Safety

The Occupational Safety and Health Service (OSH) of the Department of Labour is responsible for setting occupational safety and health standards. The range of services provided to employers by OSH includes hazard identification and control, employee training and supervision, and emergency management. For more information visit **www.osh.govt.nz**. The Health and Safety in Employment Act 1992 aims to prevent harm to employees while they are at work. It requires employers to ensure that employees work in a safe and healthy environment.

## Employment Relations

The Employment Relations Service, run by the Department of Labour, provides information on all aspects of employer/employee responsibilities as defined by the Employment Relations Act 2000. It can supply you with full details of how to set up an employment agreement, 'good faith' relationships between employers and employees, and the legislation governing hiring and firing, retirement, holidays and other types of leave (sickness, bereavement, maternity and paternity), minimum wages, hours and overtime, and so on (*see also* 'Being Employed (Private or Public)', pp.215–20).

The ERS can also help to resolve differences of opinion between employers and employees through mediation, the Employment Relations Authority or, as a last resort, the Employment Court. For more information on anything to do with employer/employee relations, visit the website, **www.ers.govt.nz**, or call **t** 0800 800 863.

The Employment Relations Act 2000 recognises that good employment rela-tionships are built on 'good faith'. It promotes collective bargaining for pay and conditions through unions, but also protects the rights of individuals who choose not to join a union and prefer to negotiate their own employment agreement, *see* p.217.

## Resource Management

If the business you are setting up affects or uses a natural resource, you may need to apply to your local authority for a **resource consent**. You will need to provide an assessment of the impact your business activity will have on the local environment. Land use consents are dealt with by city and district councils, which are responsible for planning. Consents for the use of air, water or coastal areas are managed by regional councils, which have a broader environmental remit. Application forms are available from the local council.

# Starting a Business in New Zealand: A Step by Step Guide

Starting your own business anywhere is risky, but potentially very rewarding. For starters, you need a good business idea and heaps of commitment. Then you need to consider carefully whether it is the right choice for you. Are you prepared to work all hours? Do you have something people want to buy? Will you be able to attract customers? Are you willing to learn new skills? Can you cope without a steady income? And do you have the support of your family and friends?

First of all, you need a business idea that really works. Newcomers to New Zealand may have the edge in importing innovative ideas from overseas, but have to compete with native New Zealanders who know the market better. (Returning expats are ideally placed to exploit their combination of local knowledge and foreign ideas.) To assess how good your idea is, before putting together a full business plan draw up a basic start-up plan to see if your idea has real potential.

## Assessing Your Idea

- **Try to identify your potential customers. Ask yourself who the customers of your business might be, and how it might benefit them. How will your product or service solve your customers' problems and satisfy their needs?**

- **Consider your keys to success, by naming three or four critical factors that will be essential to the survival of your new business (for example, a restaurant will need to provide good food, value for money, service, ambience, cleanliness and consistency).**

- **Work out what makes your product or service unique. Determine your points of difference (unless you are doing something entirely new), by establishing what sets you apart from the competition (for example, a cleaning service might use only natural products, guarantee same-day service or use a team of people for each job).**

- **Do a simple market analysis, by estimating how many potential customers the business will have.**

- **Consider the ease of entry, by assessing how easy it is going to be to set up the business and how easy for competitors to follow you.**

- **Do a simple break-even analysis, by estimating how many units of sales you will need to cover your costs. Add up the costs of rent, overheads, wages, advertising and so on, then work out how much money you'll make for each unit you sell after its specific costs, and calculate how many units you need to break even.**

- **If you still feel you have a potential business, start making a business plan.**

On top of your inspired idea, you'll need a wide range of business and personal skills – such as accounting, marketing, customer service, time management and organisational skills. It may take some time for your business to become profitable, so think about the costs you will have to cover in the meantime, which might include rent, rates, phone, power and other bills, stock (and storing or freighting it), business vehicles, equipment like phones, faxes and computers, furniture like desks, chairs and filing cabinets, stationery like letterheads and business cards, wages, ACC contributions, GST and other taxes, interest on loans or hire purchases, advertising, insurance and other business services. You will be responsible for a range of administrative issues too, such as paying tax, GST, wages, PAYE and ACC, meeting health, safety and employment laws and arranging legal things like contracts, leases and agreements.

## Drawing up a Business Plan

Not only will a business plan help you to work out if your idea is viable, but you will also need it to obtain finance, grants or business and legal advice. The plan is a document that describes your business, its products or services, and how you intend to market and finance your business; it should be a living document – constantly open to revision as the business matures.

Some of the information you need to include in a business plan includes: personal details; information about the business; what the business is about and how it will operate; whether it is a sole trader, partnership or limited liability company; where the business will be located and why; regulations affecting your type of business; details of lawyers and accountants; your contingency plan; business and marketing goals; financial details.

## Financing Your Business

Once you've drawn up a business plan, you need to make a realistic assessment of how much money you need to get the business up and running. It is easy to underestimate the start-up costs of a business, which may mean that

### The New Zealand Stock Exchange

The New Zealand Stock Exchange (NZSX; **www.nzsx.co.nz**) was established in 1981 by the Sharebrokers Amendment Act, and changed its acronym from NZSE to NZSX in 2003 – to some ridicule, as the name NZSX was already being used by a pornographic website. To be listed on the NZSX a company must have a market value of NZ$5 million, must have at least 500 public shareholders, who together hold at least 25 per cent of the securities of each listed class, and must fully comply with NZSX disclosure and other continuing obligations. Once a company is listed, it must follow the rules that protect shareholders and investors, as specified in the NZSX Listing Rules.

your business takes years to make a profit. You will need a careful estimate of the 'capital' costs and 'working capital' you will need.

Now you need to raise finance for your business. Your business will either be self-financed (you have your own start-up capital), debt-financed (you borrow money to start the business) or equity-financed (a partner puts up some or all of the capital in exchange for a share in the profits). Debt-financing is typically provided by a financial institution such as a bank. Any of the major banks in New Zealand will consider business finance; take your business plan and shop around. An alternative in New Zealand is to apply to a small business investment fund such as: Just Dollar$ Trust, Nelson Enterprise Loan Trust, Poutama Trust, Prometheus, Quaker Investment Ethical Trust, Self Start, the Methodist Employment Generation Fund, the Women's Loan Fund/Angel Fund or Independent Business Foundation NZ.

## Marketing and Advertising

Once you have raised the finance for your business, you may feel that you are on the home run – but still with no guarantee of success. Now's the time to get into the nitty-gritty like choosing a location, hiring staff and setting up your accounts. At this stage you need to start advertising and marketing your business. Some of the following might be strategies you could use:

- advertise in the *Yellow Pages* of your local phone book, in the classified section of your local community newspaper (including the free papers as these are circulated widely), through leaflets posted in the mail (circulars – very popular in New Zealand) and in specialist magazines.
- design a logo for your business and display it on your business cards, fridge magnets and pens as well as staff T-shirts.
- keep regular customers informed about promotions and specials.
- provide free samples of your product or service.
- provide limited credit to regular customers.
- place a sign advertising your business outside your premises.
- sponsor an amateur sports team from a local school.
- advertise collectively with other local retailers.
- advertise on the billboard at your local supermarkets.
- build and maintain a customer database.
- advertise on radio or television.

## Paying for the Services of Others

To get your business up and running, you may need to use the services of professional advisers such as lawyers and accountants. You may well resent the

## Case Study: On a Whim, By Design

'We came here on a whim,' says Richard Cleall-Harding, who flew to New Zealand with his wife, Kelly, just before the millennium. They were headed for Wellington, but ran out of money in Napier and stopped there. 'We drove into Hawke's Bay and I saw all the apple orchards and thought, "What have I done?",' says Richard, who had previously worked as an illustrator and animator in London, and met Kelly running 'trendy bars' there. Richard was broke, still paying off his student loan, and there wasn't much work in his field in provincial New Zealand. 'There were two ad agencies in the Bay. I didn't like their stuff, and they thought I was wacky,' he says. So he 'poached' some work off the Internet for Australian magazines, and the couple moved into a seaside bach. Driven out by rats, they now live in a farmhouse, with sheep, chickens and a cat. 'In the middle of it all and out of it is our motto,' says Richard, who 'can't handle suburbia' after years in London suburbs. He's currently looking for a gun to shoot the possums.

In the last two years Richard has established a design partnership, which is starting to take off – but it's been a long haul. He has generated all his own work, sometimes in unexpected ways: he worked in an organic foods ware-house for a while, bagging rice; when the director found out he did graphics, he got him to design packaging for what is one of the country's largest organic wholesalers. Other clients – including undertakers – have come and gone. He now does some work for higher-paying Auckland companies too (his business partner has good contacts there), proving that you can work long-distance over the Internet if you know the right people.

There have been a few culture shocks along the way. 'It's all so laid back,' Richard says, adding that clients here will simply forget to turn up to meetings, in a way that would be unthinkable in England. He is also frustrated by the 'diabolical' management of small businesses, whose managers may be top-notch organic cooks, but don't know how to manage people. The small-town ethos winds him up as well: 'Everybody knows everybody here so you have to be careful what you say. People are polite, but bitchy.' As for design, Richard describes graphics in New Zealand as 'like landing back in the 1970s', with agen-cies churning out 'bad typefaces in green and purple for awful clients', and badly misses 'very good, close friends in London from art school, who are at my design level'. 'I spent seven years at art school, and now I've learnt about business too,' he says. 'But if anything went wrong I'd be out on the streets.'

fees you have to pay, but to keep your business running smoothly and profitably you may need to pay for expert advice. In particular, it is unwise to dabble in matters of the law on your own – so if your business is dealing with legal matters you should consult a lawyer, but make sure you have one who specialises in business. Talk to your lawyer regularly, as lawyers often have useful business contacts and can become part of your network.

Another professional you are almost certain to need is an accountant, with specialist financial management and tax knowledge. Your accountant can prepare your annual accounts and tax return, and can also provide you with an analysis of how your business is doing.

## Organisations that Can Help You to Start a Business

There are myriad organisations that can help you to start a business in New Zealand, by offering information, expert advice and networking opportunities.

The government **Business Development Programme** (BIZ; **www.bizinfo. govt.nz**) exists to help small and medium-sized businesses to improve their management skills. The range of services includes assessment, skills training, coaching and networking provided by a range of affiliated organisations, such as regional enterprise development agencies, consultancies, industry associations and the Open Polytechnic of New Zealand. There are 34 BIZ centres, all listed in the *Blue Pages* of the phone books.

**Industry New Zealand** is a government agency charged with helping to build a strong and vibrant economy. In addition to BIZinfo and business development programmes, it also provides access to practical advice, training and funding intended to help businesses and regions develop and grow.

**Technology New Zealand** provides a range of programmes to promote the business community's development and adoption of advanced technologies, with the help of government-funded research grants.

**Trade New Zealand** is a development agency providing expert assistance to exporters through a global network of offices and representatives. Its export consultants can provide guidance on export procedures and export markets.

The **Economic Development Association of New Zealand** (EDANZ) represents 52 Economic Development Agencies and Units run by regional, district and city councils. It provides a range of services for business migrants.

The **New Zealand Chambers of Commerce and Industry** (NZCC) are voluntary, membership-based organisations. Membership is open to all types of business and this is a particularly effective way to establish new business contacts and find out about local business conditions. Chamber services include advocacy, business education, international trade services, business advice and mentoring, and social functions for meeting and networking with new members and developing businesses. The network includes 32 chambers representing about 20,000 businesses, of which around 75 per cent are small and medium-sized businesses and more than one-third are involved in international trade. There are 52 **Small Business Enterprise Centres** in New Zealand, which specialise in helping small businesses and offer economic development programmes, business development information, business services and business support.

The **Business Migrant Liaison Unit** of the NZIS also provides essential information for migrants setting up a business in New Zealand.

## Business Tax

It is important to set up the right accounting and tax systems from the outset when you start a business. You may need to pay several sorts of tax for your business. These may include income tax, goods and services tax (GST) and tax deductions for your employees. You will need to get an IRD number for the business if it is a partnership or company, complete a tax return every year, make a number of tax payments through the year and keep your records accurately so that your accounts can be verified. Income tax for companies is currently charged at a flat rate of 33 per cent. GST is charged at 12.5 per cent to anyone purchasing goods and services. If your business turnover is more than NZ$400,000, you register for and charge GST. Below that figure GST registration is optional. If you are registered, however, you can claim back GST on expenses. There is no capital gains tax in New Zealand.

# Further Information on Starting a Business

## Government Sites

- **Business Information Zone**, t 0800 424946; **www.biz.org.nz**. A government-sponsored business development programme, run in partnership with the private sector. A wide range of information relevant to starting a business.

- **Commerce Commission**, t 0800 943600; **www.comcom.govt.nz**. Responsible for the Commerce, Fair Trading and Electricity Reform Acts. Explains how these apply to individual business operations.

- **Employment Relations Service**, t 0800 800863; **www.ers.govt.nz**. Information on all aspects of the employer/employee relationship from how to formulate an employment agreement to leave entitlements and what to do it if all turns to custard.

- **Inland Revenue Department; www.ird.govt.nz**. All about tax.

- **Ministry of Consumer Affairs; www.consumeraffairs.govt.nz.** Works with both consumers and businesses to keep the marketplace fair and informed.

- **Ministry of Agriculture and Forestry; www.maf.govt.nz**. Import and export, and biosecurity.

- **Ministry for the Environment**; **www.mfe.govt.nz**. National environmental issues, although resource consents and day-to-day environmental management are in the hands of local government.

- **New Zealand Companies Office**, t 0508 266726; **www.companies. govt.nz**. Registers all new companies. You can register your own company name and become incorporated online, or search company records.

- **Occupational Safety and Health Service; www.osh.govt.nz.** Information on health and safety in the workplace, including legal requirements.

- **Securities Commission; www.seccom.govt.nz.** Facilitates capital investment in New Zealand in accordance with the Securities Act.

- **Takeovers Panel; www.takeovers.govt.nz.** Information on the Takeovers Code.

- **New Zealand Trade and Enterprise; www.nzte.govt.nz.** Trade development agency providing expert assistance to exporters through a global network of offices and representatives. Also assists investors.

## Other Sites

- **Business NZ; www.businessnz.org.nz.** Regional business associations' policy and advocacy wing.

- **Auckland Chamber of Commerce** and **Northern Region Chambers of Commerce; www.chamber.co.nz.** Links to NZ Chambers of Commerce; local chambers of commerce may be a very good starting point for new migrants to establish business contacts.

- **Economic Development Association of New Zealand; www.edanz.org.nz.** A range of business services for business migrants.

- **Local Government New Zealand; www.lgnz.co.nz.** Links to local council websites, which you may need to contact for resource management information.

- **New Zealand Stock Exchange; www.nzsx.co.nz.**

- **UBD, t** 0800 823225; **www.ubd.co.nz.** Business directory, listing more than 150,000 businesses.

- *Yellow Pages*; **www.yellowpages.co.nz.** Telephone listings for businesses.

# Volunteering

If you have a conscience – environmental, social or animal – you'll find plenty of chances to be conscientious in New Zealand.

Whether you're more interested in conserving the kiwi, kea or kakapo, caring for children and helping the aged, or protecting the planet from the ravages of rising sea levels, there's an organisation here that can help you to help others and save the world. You can spend your evenings, weekends or the summer planting pohutakawa trees, taking troubled teenagers tramping or poisoning possums to preserve pukeko chicks.

# Environment, Conservation and Animal Welfare

The **Department of Conservation** (DOC; **www.doc.govt.nz**) manages all New Zealand's national parks and the campsites, cabins, huts and walking tracks that enable the public to access them. It is also charged with conserving the country's natural and historic heritage. In both these areas of activity DOC relies on volunteers, who may help with conservation tasks such as native bird counts, historic building restoration, habitat restoration, hut and track maintenance, weed control, whale strandings, tree planting or giving talks.

What you do will depend partly on your skills, but all DOC volunteer work requires a reasonable level of fitness ('low' fitness is classified as being able to do a three-hour tramp with a rucksack). To find out details of specific projects, check the online calendar for volunteers. As volunteering for DOC offers an opportunity to spend time in some of New Zealand's most beautiful landscapes, it is often oversubscribed, and local people come first. You can download a form from the website to register as a volunteer, or volunteer at a regional office for community-based conservation work. You may be asked to help year-round, or for a block of time.

Closely allied to the British trust, the **New Zealand Trust for Conservation Volunteers** (**www.conservationvolunteers.org.nz**) helps to maintain and improve New Zealand's ecology, including natural bush areas, parks, reserves, wildlife, waterways, walkways, urban and rural landscape. The NZTCV helps to restore New Zealand's ecosystems to their natural beauty, by participating in countrywide projects of wildlife and habitat conservation, endangered species preservation and ecology education. Some volunteering opportunities for overseas visitors include accommodation, while other short-term and ongoing conservation volunteering projects can be fitted in around the regular life of a resident. You can register online to be kept informed of projects and matched with activities in your area. The NZTCV website has good links to regional councils (responsible for environmental management) and other environmental and conservation organisations, any of which may have opportunities for volunteers.

**ECO**, a network of Environment and Conservation Organisations of Aotearoa New Zealand (**www.eco.org.nz**) is another starting point for green volunteering, with links to groups from the Biodynamic Farming and Gardening Association to Friends of the Shoreline and the Toxins Action Group. The Greenpages (**www.greenpages.org.nz**) is a comprehensive directory of greens.

**Greenpeace New Zealand** (**www.greenpeace.org/new-zealand**) is a campaigning organisation that has had a particularly high profile in New Zealand since agents of the French secret service sank its flagship, the *Rainbow Warrior*, in Auckland Harbour in 1985 as it was about to embark on a protest voyage against nuclear testing on Mururoa atoll. The organisation welcomes enthusiastic volunteers for tasks of all sorts. You can register as a volunteer online. Campaigns include lobbying for a moratorium on bottom-trawling by deep-sea commercial fishing boats and trying to put a stop to Japanese whaling in the Antarctic.

The **Society for the Prevention of Cruelty to Animals** (SPCA; **www.spca.org.nz**) always needs volunteers to help with cleaning, feeding, medicating, exercising and assisting with the adoption of the stray cats and dogs that it rescues. This volunteer work provides a good opportunity to get hands-on experience in working with animals. Another volunteer service is the Animal Outreach programme: volunteers visit the elderly, the terminally ill and those with 'ageing disorders', taking their animals with them to share with those who have no contact with the therapeutic value of companion animals.

**Willing Workers on Organic Farms** (**www.wwoof.org.nz**) is the New Zealand branch of a global network that enables people interested in organic farming, permaculture and biodynamics to travel the world, staying on 'green' farms and working a few hours a day in exchange for board and lodging – farm-stay au pairs. WWOOFers can hope to gain some knowledge of sustainability and the like in exchange for the hard labour they offer to like-minded hosts – although experiences vary widely. There are over 550 WWOOF Farms in New Zealand, spread from the far north to the deep south, and activities on each farm depend on the interests and expertise of each host, and the type of country they farm.

## Social Volunteering: Caring for People

If you are affiliated with any church or other religious organisation it is bound to be able to offer you the chance to get involved with caring for the community; if not, there are plenty of lay organisations that welcome voluntary assistance. **Volunteering New Zealand** (**www.volunteeringnz.org.nz**) is an umbrella organisation for volunteers, which runs 10 volunteer centres operating in New Zealand, matching people who wish to volunteer their time with local not-for-profit organisations that have vacancies for volunteer assistance. The **VolunteerNow** website, **www. volunteernow.org.nz**, has volunteer job listings by region and type. Volunteering organisations are especially keen to recruit experienced, skilled over-50s for all sorts of tasks.

# References

# New Zealand at a Glance

**Official name of country**: New Zealand (NZ); increasingly referred to as Aotearoa for cultural purposes

**Nationality**: New Zealander; known as Kiwis

**Capital city**: Wellington (southernmost national capital in the world)

**Administrative divisions**: Auckland, Bay of Plenty, Canterbury, Gisborne, Hawke's Bay, Marlborough, Nelson, Northland, Otago, Southland, Taranaki, Tasman, Waikato, Manawatu-Wanganui, Wellington, West Coast

**Flag**: Blue, with flag of the UK in the upper hoist-side quadrant and four red five-pointed stars edged in white centred in the outer half of the flag; the stars represent the Southern Cross constellation. Campaigners hope to replace the flag with one that better reflects the country's 21st-century identity. Designs suggested by NZ artists typically draw on the Maori koru motif, silver fern and wave patterns; while some retain the stars, all ditch the colonial association

**Type of government**: Parliamentary democracy

**Head of government**: Prime minister

**Head of state**: British monarch, represented by a Governor General

**Location**: Oceania; islands in the South Pacific Ocean, southeast of Australia

**Geographic co-ordinates**: latitude 41° 00"S, longitude 174° 00" E

**Time zone**: GMT plus 12 hours; clocks go forward one hour from early October until late March for daylight saving; New Zealand is across the International Dateline from the Western Hemisphere, and one of the first places in the world to see the sun rise each day

**Area**: 268,680 sq km (103,740 sq miles)

**Length (north to south)**: 1,300km (800 miles)

**Width (at widest point)**: 420km (260 miles)

**Geographical highlights**: North and South Islands are predominately mountainous with some large coastal plains; large inland lakes include Taupo and Wanaka; deep coastal inlets include Milford Sound and Queen Charlotte Sound; highest point is Mount Cook, 3,746 m (12,290 ft) in the Southern Alps; earthquakes are common, although usually not severe, and there is some volcanic activity

**Territories**: New Zealand territories include Antipodes, Auckland, Bounty, Chatham and Kermadec Islands and Campbell Island, as well as the North and South Islands and Stewart Island

**Dependent territories**: Cook Islands, Niue (self-governing in free association with New Zealand), Tokelau (administered by New Zealand as a non-self-governing territory)

**Coastline**: 15,134 km (9,403 miles)

**Bordering countries**: none

**Surrounding seas**: Tasman Sea (northwest) and South Pacific Ocean; the North and South Islands are separated by the Cook Strait; the South Island and Stewart Island are separated by the Foveaux Strait

**Population**: 4.25 million in 2008

**Ethnic groups**: New Zealand European (Pakeha) 67.6 per cent; Maori 14.6 per cent; New Zealander 11.1 per cent; Pacific Islander 6.9 per cent; Asian 9.2 per cent and other 11.2 per cent (not 100 per cent, as ethnicity is self-identified, meaning people can tick more than one box on census forms; the distribution of ethnic groups around the country is very uneven, with few Maori and Pacific Islanders in the South Island)

**Religions**: approx: Anglican 24 per cent, Presbyterian 18 per cent, Roman Catholic 15 per cent, Methodist 5 per cent, Baptist 2 per cent, other Protestant 3 per cent, unspecified or none 33 per cent

**Languages**: English and Maori

**Currency**: New Zealand dollar (NZ$)

**Weights and measures**: metric

**Electricity**: 230 volts; unique three-pin plug

**Internet country code**: .nz

**GDP**: purchasing power parity US$98.5 billion (fourth smallest OECD economy)

**GDP growth rate**: 4.8 per cent (seventh-fastest-growing OECD economy)

**GDP per capita**: purchasing power parity US$23,200 (88 per cent of OECD average, on a par with Spain)

**GDP by sector**: agriculture 8 per cent; industry 23 per cent; services 29 per cent

**Unemployment**: 3.5 per cent

# Further Reading and Films

## Books

### History and Travelogue

Lady Barker, *Station Life in New Zealand* (1870). One of the first accounts of life in New Zealand by an early settler.

J. C. Beaglehole, *The Discovery of New Zealand* (1961); *The Life of Captain James Cook* (1974), the standard biography of the explorer; *The Endeavour Journal of Joseph Banks 1768–1771*; *The Journals of Captain Cook on his Voyages of Discovery*.

James Belich, *Making Peoples*. Analytical history by a respected historian.

T. L. Buick, *The Treaty of Waitangi*. Early 20th-century account of the treaty.

Samuel Butler, *Erewhon*. Novel satirizing 'Victorian' New Zealand. *A First Year in Canterbury Settlement* (1863). Description of life in the high country of the South Island.

William Colenso, *The Authentic and Genuine History of the Signing of the Treaty of Waitangi* (1890). Near-contemporary account by missionary and printer.

William Fox, *The Six Colonies of New Zealand* (1851).

Michael King, *Penguin History of New Zealand* (2003). 'The best general history of New Zealand to be published in a generation', a bestseller since its author died in a road accident in 2004.

J. Mander, *The Story of a New Zealand River*.

W. H. (Bill) Oliver, *The Story of New Zealand* (1960).

W. H. (Bill) Oliver and B. R. (Bridget) Williams (eds), *The Oxford History of New Zealand*. Wide-ranging examination of NZ history (one of the most comprehensive pre-King).

Claudia Orange, *The Treaty of Waitangi* (2004). Detailed but readable account of New Zealand's 'founding' treaty, and the lasting legacy of its different significance to Pakeha and Maori (now also in an illustrated version).

William Pember Reeves, *The Long White Cloud* (1898).

Dick Scott, *Ask That Mountain: The Story of Parihaka* (1975). An attempt to rebalance accounts of early settlement and Maori relations, in connection with the Parihaka peace movement.

Keith Sinclair, *A History of New Zealand* (1961). One of the first historians to challenge historical accounts of colonial supremacy over native 'primitivism' (the best history of its generation).

Philip Temple, *A Sort of Conscience* (2002). The story of the Wakefields, who drove colonisation with their New Zealand Company.

A. S. Thomson, *The Story of New Zealand* (1859). Early history of New Zealand.

Anthony Trollope, *New Zealand* (1875). Account of his travels by the prolific author more famous for *The Barchester Chronicles*.

Dom Francisco Vaggioli, *History of New Zealand and its Inhabitants*. Damning account of British colonisation and treatment of Maori, by an Italian Catholic monk who travelled to New Zealand as a missionary in the 1870s.

## Fiction and Poetry

James K. Baxter, *Beyond the Palisade* (1944). First volume of poetry by one of New Zealand's most highly reputed – and controversial – poets.

Catherine Chidgey, *In a Fishbone Church* (1998); *Golden Deeds* (2000). Award-winning, acclaimed novels by one of New Zealand's best young writers.

Ian Cross, *God Boy* (1957). An insight into adolescence and religion.

Barry Crump, *A Good Keen Man* (1960) and 20 others. Comic popular fiction on the theme of 'going bush'.

Allen Curnow, 'Landfall in Unknown Seas'. A powerful poetic evocation of the visitor confronted by an alien but compelling land.

Alan Duff, *Once Were Warriors* (1990). A depressing tale of violence and alcoholism among dispossessed urban Maori, with a redemption theme. *What Becomes of the Broken Hearted* (1996).

Maurice Duggan, *Collected Stories* (1981), ed. C.K. Stead. Includes 'Along Rideout Road that Summer' (1961), which parodies themes of conventional NZ fiction; the Lenihan stories about an Irish immigrant family; and the Beckett-inspired monologue 'Riley's Handbook'.

Janet Frame, *To the Island* (1982), *An Angel at My Table* (1984), *The Envoy from Mirror City* (1985). Three-volume autobiographical story of growing up an unconventional and gifted writer (to become New Zealand's most distinguished) in the South Island, including a period in a mental asylum (made into the film *An Angel at My Table* by Jane Campion).

Maurice Gee, *In My Father's Den* (1972); trilogy of *Plumb* (1978), *Meg* (1981) and *Sole Survivor* (1983). Much of Gee's work is based around the then small country town of Henderson he grew up in, and confronts the mental constriction of local puritanism; critics' dislike of his 'sordidness' appears to endorse the very small-town mindset he describes.

Patricia Grace, *Mutuwhenua: The Moon Sleeps* (1978). Bittersweet coming-of-age story about a Maori girl's love for a Pakeha boy.

Keri Hulme, *The Bone People* (1984). Hard-to-define 1985 Booker-prize winner.

Witi Ihimaera, *Whale Rider* (1987). Sentimental story of a girl who wins her way to the heart of her traditional Maori grandfather by taming whales (now a film). *Tangi* (1973); *Whanau* (1974); *Bulibasha* (1994). The emotional landscape of the Maori people and their political and social reality. *Nights in the Gardens of Spain* (1996). Unusual for New Zealand exploration of gay identity.

Elizabeth Knox, *Paremata* (1989), *Pomare* (1994) and *Tawa* (1998). Trilogy of semi-autobiographical novellas based on the author's childhood and adolescence in Wellington. Novels *The Vintner's Luck* (1998), *Black Oxen* (2001), *Daylight* (2003) and *Dreamhunter* (2005) stray from New Zealand themes but have met international critical acclaim.

Jane Mander, *The Story of a New Zealand River* (1920). Novel based on the author's childhood by the Otamatea river, censured by contemporary New Zealand critics for its liberalism.

Bill Manhire (ed.), *100 NZ Poems*. An anthology of some of the best.

Katherine Mansfield, *The Garden Party and Other Stories* (1923). Keenly observed depictions of middle-class New Zealand life in the 1920s. Numerous selections of Mansfield's stories are in print.

John Mulgan, *Man Alone* (1939). Classic 'man against the elements' tale with an existential twist. Took its title from a remark in Hemingway's *To Have and Have Not*: 'a man alone ain't got no bloody fucking chance'.

Emily Perkins, *Not Her Real Name and Other Stories* (1996), *Leave Before You Go* (1998) and *The New Girl* (2001). Dismal urban tales laced with black-absurdist comedy.

Frank Sargeson, *A Man and His Wife* (1940); *That Summer, and Other Stories* (1946). Most of the more than 40 stories Sargeson wrote in the 1930s and '40s, in a social realist style that came to define the puritanical, emotionally sterile New Zealand working-class male; also *Speaking for Ourselves*, edited by Sargeson (1945). Launched the next generation of writers.

C. K. Stead, *Smith's Dream* (1971), filmed under the title *Sleeping Dogs* (1977). Novel of the Vietnam War period. *All Visitors Ashore* (1984); *The Singing Whakapapa* (1994). This 1950s protégé of Curnow and Sargeson is now best known for his reactionary attitudes.

Damien Wilkins, *The Miserables* (1993); *Little Masters* (1996). Comedy of manners. *Chemistry* (2002). A tale of bad choices. *The Fainter* (2006). Just some of the works by a writer often tagged the finest of his generation.

For more information on New Zealand authors and their works, visit **www.bookcouncil.org.nz/writers**. Follow links to the literary map for regional insights.

# Films

Barry Barclay, *Tangata Whenua – The People of the Land*. A six-part documentary about Maori people; made for TV in the 1970s, it revolutionised depictions of Maori.

Jane Campion, *An Angel at My Table*. Adaptation of Janet Frame's autobiographical novel. *The Piano*. Music and lust among early settlers. *In the Cut*. New York-set, darkly 'feminist' thriller.

Niki Caro, *Whale Rider* (*see* p.243).

Roger Donaldson, *Smash Palace*. Classic film of 'unease'. *Sleeping Dogs*.

Peter Jackson, *Heavenly Creatures*. A based-on-fact story of two teenage girls who escape into fantasy and kill one of their mothers. *Bad Taste* and *Brain Dead*. Comic splatter films. *The Lord of the Rings* trilogy.

John Laing, *Other Halves*. Urban and young Maori life.

Brad McGann, *In My Father's Den*. Bleak tale of return to small-town New Zealand, based on a novel by Maurice Gee.

Merata Mita, *Mauri, Patu!*; *Bastion Point–Day 507*; *Mana Waka*.

Geoff Murphy, *Goodbye Pork Pie*. Classic anarchic road movie of the 1970s; *Utu*, a Maori 'Western'.

Sam Pillsbury, *The Scarecrow*. A fine adaptation of the classic New Zealand novel (by Ronald Hugh Morrieson) about a crazed killer who instils fear and paranoia in a small rural community.

Gaylene Preston, *Mr Wrong*; *Ruby and Rata*; *Perfect Strangers*. Romance in which Sam Neill ends up in small parts in a freezer.

Lee Tamahori, *Once Were Warriors*. Adaptation of Alan Duff's book.

Vincent Ward, *Vigil*; *The Navigator*.

Mike Walker, *Kingpin*. Urban and young Maori life from a Pakeha point of view.

For more on literature and films, *see* **New Zealand Today**, 'Culture and Art', pp.86–92.

# Glossary

## New Zealand English Idiom

| | |
|---|---|
| *afternoon tea* | three o'clock break with home-baked cakes |
| *awesome* | good |
| *bach* (pron. 'batch') | simple seaside cottage |
| *bomb* | old banger |
| *bro'* | brother, or mate, particularly among Maori |
| *chilly bin* | portable ice box |
| *chips* | chips |
| *chippies* | crisps |
| *choice* | good |
| *crib* | South Island version of bach |
| *crook* | sick, ill |
| *cuz* | cousin, or mate; especially among Maori |
| *dag* | good bloke |
| *dairy* | corner shop |
| *domain* | grassed civic centre or picnic area |
| *dunny* | lavatory |
| *full-on* | intense |
| *Gladwrap* | clingfilm |

| | |
|---|---|
| *good as gold* | great, fine |
| *hard case* | funny guy |
| *hoe* | to eat quickly |
| *hokey pokey* | vanilla ice cream with caramel chunks |
| *hoon* | wild boy |
| *jandals* | flip flops |
| *kornies* | cornflakes |
| *L&P* | lemon and paeroa, locally made lemonade, 'world famous in New Zealand' |
| *lollies* | sweets |
| *long-drop* | compost loo |
| *Mainland* | South Island |
| *paua* | abalone, a type of shellfish with a pearly turquoise shell |
| *pavlova* | dessert with meringue, cream and fruit |
| *pie* | usually minced steak, available hot from dairies and roadside cafés |
| *pipi* | shellfish a bit like a clam |
| *Pom (whingeing)* | Englishman |
| *rattle your dags* | hurry up |
| *rough as guts* | unpolished (of a person) |
| *scull* | to chug (beer) |
| *skiting* | bragging |
| *smoko* | break, rest from work |
| *stubby* | small bottle of beer |
| *sweet as* | great, cool |
| *tea* | often refers to full afternoon meal |
| *tiki tour* | scenic tour |
| *togs* | swimming costume |
| *ute* | pick-up truck ('utility vehicle') |
| *wopwops* | the back of beyond |

## Select Glossary of Commonly Used Maori Terms

| | |
|---|---|
| *ao* | cloud |
| *Aotearoa* | 'land of the long white cloud', Maori name for New Zealand |
| *atua* | gods, spirits |
| *awa* | river, valley |
| *e noho ra* | goodbye (from the person going to the one staying) |

| | |
|---|---|
| *haere mai* | welcome |
| *haere ra* | goodbye (from the person staying to the one going) |
| *haka* | war dance and song (most often seen today at rugby matches) |
| *hangi* | traditional Maori style of cooking food in an earth oven where the heat is provided by hot stones. |
| *hapu* | regional community (subtribe of an iwi) |
| *hau* | wind |
| *Hawaiki* | mythical ancient homeland of Maori people |
| *hoa* | friend |
| *hongi* | Maori welcome expressed by touching noses |
| *hui* | (tribal) meeting |
| *ika* | fish |
| *iti* | small |
| *iwi* | tribe, people, nation |
| *ka pai* | thank you |
| *kai* | food |
| *kainga* | village |
| *kapa haka* | war dance done for display |
| *karakia* | chants, prayer |
| *karanga* | chant of welcome |
| *kare* | ripening |
| *kaumatua* | elder, or respected member of tribe |
| *kauri* | huge forest tree growing in northern New Zealand; few left after most were felled by early European settlers for timber |
| *kea* | rare, inquisitive alpine parrot |
| *kia ora* | hello, good health |
| *kina* | sea urchins |
| *kiwi* | flightless, nocturnal indigenous bird; symbol of New Zealand, although nearly extinct |
| *korero* | stories |
| *koru* | spiral, used in Maori carving, inspired by the unfurling fern frond; signifies awakening and joy |
| *kumara* | sweet potato |
| *mana* | prestige, power |
| *manga* | river, stream |
| *manuka* | shrubby plant also known as tea tree, source of honey and oils with anti-bacterial qualities |

| | |
|---|---|
| *manga* | stream, tributary |
| *manu* | bird |
| *Maori* | originally meant ordinary or usual, used by indigenous New Zealanders, as opposed to Pakeha (stranger or different); now commonly used to differentiate original settlers from later European colonists |
| *Maoritanga* | Maori culture |
| *marae* | meeting place, sacred ground |
| *maunga* | mountain |
| *mere* | flat greenstone war club, highly prized weapon |
| *moana* | sea, lake |
| *moko* | facial tattoo |
| *motu* | island |
| *namu* | sandfly |
| *nga* | the (plural) |
| *ngai, ngati* | tribe, people or clan |
| *nui* | big |
| *one* | beach, sand, mud |
| *ora* | healthy, safe, alive |
| *pa* | fortified hilltop village |
| *Pakeha* | European person or foreigner |
| *pakihi* | swampland |
| *papa* | flat, broad slab |
| *po* | night |
| *pohutakawa* | large spreading coastal tree with red flowers in early summer, known as the New Zealand Christmas tree |
| *ponga* | tree fern |
| *pounamu* | greenstone or jade, precious stone found in the South Island and used in jewellery and weapons |
| *powhiri* | formal ceremony of welcome |
| *puke* | hill |
| *puku* | tummy |
| *puna* | spring |
| *rangi* | the sky, heavens |
| *roa* | long |
| *roto* | lake |
| *rua* | two |
| *tane* | man |
| *tangata* | people |

| | |
|---|---|
| *tangata whenua* | 'people of the land', indigenous Maori |
| *tangi* | funeral |
| *taniwha* | demon, spirit |
| *taonga* | treasures, cultural artefacts such as carvings or woven cloaks passed down through generations |
| *tapu* | holy, sacrosanct, taboo |
| *te* | the (singular) |
| *Te Ika a Maui* | the fish of Maui, the North Island |
| *tena koe* | hello (to one person) |
| *tena koutou* | hello (to several) |
| *te reo Maori* | the Maori language |
| *Te Wai Pounamu* | the water of greenstone, the South Island |
| *tiki* | small, very stylised carved figure of a human in wood, stone or greenstone |
| *toi toi* | tall clumps of native grass |
| *tukutuku* | Maori wall panels in marae |
| *wai* | water |
| *waiata* | songs |
| *waka* | canoe, such as those that the first Polynesian settlers arrived on; waka taua are elaborately carved war canoes. |
| *wero* | challenge |
| *whakapapa* | ancestry |
| *whanau* | extended family |
| *whanga* | bay, inlet |
| *whare* | house (*whare runanga*, meeting house; *whare puni*, family sleeping house) |
| *whakairo* | carved house |
| *whenua* | land, country |

# National Holidays

## Festivals and Annual Events

| | |
|---|---|
| **Late Jan** | Auckland Anniversary Regatta. One of the world's largest one-day regattas, on Waitemata Harbour. |
| **6 Feb** | Waitangi Day. Waitangi National Trust celebrates signing of the Treaty of Waitangi. Usually some political egg-throwing. |

| | |
|---|---|
| **Second Sat in Feb** | Marlborough Wine Festival. Wine, food and entertainment in Marlborough vineyards. |
| **Mid-Feb** | Art Deco Weekend, Napier. Fun celebration of the city's Art Deco style. |
| **Feb–Mar** | New Zealand International Arts Festival. The most prestigious event in the country's cultural calendar, featuring world-class performances in Wellington. |
| **Late Feb** | Tainui Waka Kapa Haka Festival. Festival of Maori performing arts and culture in Waikato. |
| **Late Feb** | Dunedin Fashion Week. |
| **First week Mar** | Golden Shears. National shearing competition in Masterton, Wairarapa. |
| **Mid-Mar** | Wildfoods Festival. Possum stew galore in Hokitika. |
| | World of Music and Dance (WOMAD). The world franchise comes to Taranaki. |
| | Wairarapa Wines Harvest Festival. Inaugurates the grape harvest. |
| **End Mar** | Round the Bays Run. Huge fun run around Auckland's bays, with 60,000 participants. |
| **Late Mar** | Ngaruawahia Regatta. Maori canoes (waka) compete on the Waikato River in Ngaruawahia, the home town of the Maori Queen. |
| **Mid-April** | Bluff Oyster and Seafood Festival. Seafood and wine to welcome the start of the new oyster season. |
| **Mid-April** | Classic Southern Traverse. Multisport adventure race across the South Island. |
| **Second week April** | Royal Easter Show. Livestock competitions and the largest equestrian show in the country, in Auckland. Most regions host their own 'A&P' (Agricultural and Pastoral) shows at some point in the year. |
| **Easter weekend** | Warbirds Over Wanaka. Vintage and veteran warplanes vie to crash into the lake. |
| **Easter weekend** | Montana National Jazz Festival. Tauranga, Bay of Plenty. |
| **Mid-June** | National Agricultural Fieldays. One of the world's largest agricultural events, showcasing New Zealand produce and technology, in Hamilton. |
| **21 June** | Matariki (around the Winter Solstice). Events around the country celebrate the beginning of the Maori |

new year, marked by the appearance of the Pleiades at the new moon, with fireworks and bonfires.

**Third week July**  Queenstown Winter Festival. Highlight of the Queenstown winter sports calendar, with night skiing and fireworks.

**Last week July**  Christchurch Arts Festival. Mid-winter festival of music, dance, theatre, film and visual arts.

**Mid-Aug**  Bay of Islands Jazz and Blues Festival. Popular jazz festival in Northland.

**Late Aug**  Gay Ski Week. Queenstown.

**Second week in Sept**  Hastings Blossom Festival. Spring is ushered in to this fruit-growing region with parades and concerts.

**Late Sept**  World of Wearable Art Awards, Wellington. Costume as art, or art as costume.

**Mid-Oct**  Nelson Arts Festival. Theatre, dance and music.

**Mid-Nov**  Royal New Zealand Show. Christchurch. Agricultural and Pastoral show to beat all others.

**Mid-Nov**  Toast Martinborough. Wairarapa wines and food.

**Last week Nov**  Ellerslie Flower Show. The largest flower show in the Southern Hemisphere, with all the atmosphere of Chelsea at the Auckland Regional Botanical Gardens.

Major sporting events, especially rugby and cricket, take place throughout the year. Keep an eye on the sports pages of newspapers for event dates.

# Official Public Holidays

**1 January** New Year's Day
**2 January** day after New Year's Day
**6 February** Waitangi Day
**March/April** Good Friday and Easter Monday
**25 April** ANZAC Day
**6 June** Queen's Birthday
**late October** Labour Day
**25 December** Christmas Day
**26 December** Boxing Day

All holidays are celebrated on the nearest Monday (except Good Friday, Waitangi Day and ANZAC Day).

In addition, each region has its own anniversary holiday.

# Regional Climate

New Zealand has a temperate climate, with rainfall spread evenly throughout the year, but very changeable weather and diverse microclimates around the country. Summer and autumn (Dec–May) tend to be the most settled periods.

## Temperature Ranges in the Main Centres

|  | winter | summer |
|---|---|---|
| **Auckland** | 8–15°C (48–59°F) | 14–23°C (57–74°F) |
| **Christchurch** | 2–11°C (33–52°F) | 10–22°C (50–73°F) |
| **Dunedin** | 4–12°C (39–53°F) | 9–19°C (48–66°F) |
| **Queenstown** | 1–10°C (33–50°F) | 19–22°C (66–73°F) |
| **Wellington** | 6–13°C (43–55°F) | 12–21°C (53–70°F) |

# Regional Calling Codes

For a full list of **regional calling codes**, consult any New Zealand telephone book (delivered annually to your home, or available free from post offices).

Note that while local calls are free, not all areas with the same code count as local (e.g. calls from Napier (06) to New Plymouth (06) will be toll calls). These are the codes for the main administrative capitals:

| | |
|---|---|
| Auckland and region | 09 |
| Christchurch and South Island | 03 |
| Dunedin | 03 |
| Gisborne and East Cape | 06 |
| Hamilton and central North Island | 07 |
| Hastings and Hawke's Bay region | 06 |
| Napier | 06 |
| Nelson | 03 |
| New Plymouth | 06 |
| Oamaru | 03 |
| Palmerston North | 06 |
| Queenstown | 03 |
| Rotorua | 07 |
| Taupo | 07 |
| Tauranga and Bay of Plenty | 07 |
| Wanganui | 06 |
| Wellington and region | 04 |
| Whangarei and Northland | 09 |

# Postal Codes

All addresses in New Zealand have recently been given new post codes. A directory of these is available from post offices or online at **www.nzpost.co.nz**.

# Embassies and Consulates

## British High Commission
**Head of Mission**: His Excellency Mr George Fergusson, High Commissioner
44 Hill Street, Wellington
**Postal address**: PO Box 1812, Wellington
**t** (04) 924 2888; consular **t** (04) 924 2889; press **t** (04) 924 2857; economic/commercial **t** (04) 924 2868; defence **t** (04) 924 2875
political **f** (04) 924 2831; passports **f** (04 924 2810; immigration **f** (04) 924 2822; management **f** (04) 924 2809; other sections **f** (04) 473 4982
**Office hours**: Mon–Fri 8.45–5

## British Consulate-General, Auckland
Level 17, 151 Queen Street, Auckland
**Postal address**: Private Bag 92 014, Auckland
**t** (09) 303 2973
**f** (09) 303 1836

## British Consulate, Christchurch
First Floor, Harley Chambers, 137 Cambridge Terrace, Christchurch
**Postal address**: Box 802, Christchurch
**t** (03) 374 3367
**f** (03) 374 3368

## Canadian High Commission
**Head of Mission**: Her Excellency Ms Penny Reedie, High Commissioner
61 Molesworth Level 11, 125 The Terrace, Wellington
**Postal address**: PO Box 8047, Wellington
**t** (04) 473 9577
**f** (04) 471 2082; political **f** (04) 495 4119
**Office hours**: Mon–Fri 8.30–12.30 and 1.30–4.30

## Canadian Consulate, Auckland
9th Floor, 48 Emily Place, Auckland
**Postal address**: PO Box 6186, Wellesley Street PO, Auckland
**t** (09) 309 3690
**f** (09) 307 3111
**Office hours**: Mon–Fri 8.30–12.30 and 1.30–4.30

## Embassy of the United States of America

**Head of Mission**: His Excellency Mr William Paul McCormick, Ambassador
29 Fitzherbert Terrace, Wellington
**Postal address**: PO Box 1190, Wellington
**t** (04) 462 6000
**f** (04) 472 3537
http://newzealand.usembassy.gov
**Office hours**: Mon–Fri 8.15–5

## Consulate-General of the United States of America

Level 3, Citibank Center, 23 Custom Street East,
cnr Commerce Street, Auckland
**Postal address**: Private Bag 92022, Auckland
**t** (09) 303 2724
**f** (09) 366 0870
**Office hours**: Mon–Fri 8–12 and 2–3.30

# Immigration

## Immigration New Zealand (Te Ratonga Manene)

www.immigration.govt.nz
Everything you ever wanted to know about how to get a visa or permit, residency or citizenship of New Zealand. The well-designed website demon- strates how keen New Zealand is to attract skilled people or investment. Guides you through the immigration process.

## Immigration Consultants

It is possible to use immigration consultants to help with getting visas, permits and residency. Their value is to help you identify what New Zealand will see as your greatest assets, and make your application accordingly. Business applicants may find them invaluable in deciphering the small print, but do ask pertinent questions to ascertain that they add value to the information provided by Immigration New Zealand before you employ one.

- **Immigration Unit**, UK **t** 0845 260 6030, from abroad **t** + 44 (0)1784 497 690; **info@immigrationunit.com, www.immigrationunit.com.**
- **New Zealand Association for Migration and Investment (NZAMI); www.nzami.co.nz.**
- **Malcolm Pacific; www.malcolmpacific.com.**
- **Opportunities New Zealand; www.expo-newzealand.com.** Regular shows in the UK where you can meet employers and recruitment consultants.

Many legal firms do immigration consultancy too. *See* also p.129.

# New Zealand Government Websites

If you need to contact a New Zealand government department for any reason, the phone book conveniently lists all government phone numbers in Blue Pages at the front of the phone book. Departments are listed alphabetically, and there is also an index to help you identify the department you need. The **government** website **http://newzealand.govt.nz** has links to all departments and to parliament. If you know what you're looking for, here are some useful web addresses.

## Accident Compensation Corporation (ACC)
**t** 0800 101 996
**www.acc.co.nz**
The government organisation that administers claims for accident-related injuries and compensation.

## Ministry of Agriculture and Forestry
**www.maf.govt.nz**
Oversees the agricultural, horticultural and forestry industries, and promotes their interests. Useful reference point for biosecurity.
**www.maf.govt.nz/quarantine**
Information on plant and animal imports.

## Alcohol Advisory Council of New Zealand
**www.alcohol.org.nz**
Policy and advice relating to alcohol use and abuse.

## Archives New Zealand
**www.archives.govt.nz**
In case you decide to delve into New Zealand's past.

## BIZ Business Information Services
**www.biz.org.nz**
**t** 0800 424 946
A very useful website for setting up and running a business.

## Department of Building and Housing
**t** 0800 242 243
**www.dbh.govt.nz**
Regulates the building industry and oversees tenancy agreements.

## Career Services
**t** 0800 222 733
**www.kiwicareers.govt.nz**
Careers advice.

## Child Youth and Family
**t** 0508 326 549
**www.cyf.govt.nz**
Social services, tackling family and child abuse.

## Ministry of Civil Defence and Emergency Management
**www.civildefence.govt.nz**
Information and advice on how to prepare for earthquakes, tsunamis and other potential emergencies. (A short emergency checklist is printed at the front of every phone book too, and all school-age children will be drilled in emergency procedures.)

## Commerce Commission
**www.comcom.govt.nz**
Charged with preventing misleading trading practices, anti-competitive behaviour and mergers, and promoting fair trading. Offices in the three main cities.

## Ministry of Consumer Affairs
**www.consumeraffairs.govt.nz**
Government body that oversees consumer practices.

## New Zealand Customs Service
**t** 0800 428 786, from overseas **t** + 64 (0)9 300 5399
**www.customs.govt.nz**
All you need to know about what you can and can't bring into the country, and customs duties that may apply.

## Earthquake Commission
**t** 0800 652 333
**www.eqc.govt.nz**
Government insurance for earthquakes and other disasters. When you take out a commercial insurance policy, a levy is paid to the EQC to cover eventual damage caused by natural havoc.

## Ministry of Economic Development
**www.med.govt.nz**
Works to ensure New Zealand is one of the best places in the world to do business.

## Fish and Game New Zealand
**www.fishandgame.org.nz**
Information on fresh-water fishing and game-hunting, including hunting permits and trout-fishing licences.

## Ministry of Foreign Affairs and Trade
**www.mfat.govt.nz**
Overseas relations.

## Ministry of Health
**www.moh.govt.nz**
Everything to do with the management and funding of health services, public health, training and maternity services.

## Human Rights Commission
**t** 0800 4496 877
**www.hrc.govt.nz**
A semi-independent agency charged with investigating and resolving complaints about discrimination and human rights, many of which are enshrined in New Zealand law.

## Inland Revenue Department
**t** 0800 227 774 (personal)
**t** 0800 377 774 (business)
**www.ird.govt.nz**
The tax office. All tax enquiries are handled centrally. Forms and calculators are available online.

## Department of Internal Affairs
**www.dia.govt.nz**
**t** 0800 225 050 for passports
**t** 0800 225 252 for births, deaths and marriages
**t** 0800 225 151 for citizenship
**www.bdm.govt.nz**
Processes citizenship applications, birth, death, marriage and civil union (gay marriage) certificates and New Zealand passports.

## Ministry of Justice
**www.justice.govt.nz**
Legal system, courts and criminal records.

## Department of Labour
**www.dol.govt.nz**
The labour market, immigration, employment, holiday, parental and sick leave.
**www.worksite.govt.nz**
More employee-friendly version of the DoL website.
**www.osh.dol.govt.nz**

## Land Transport Safety Authority
**t** 0800 822 422 (driver licensing)
**www.ltsa.govt.nz**
Rules the roads. Info on transport regulation and driver safety campaigns on New Zealand roads. Alternatively, for New Zealand licences (obligatory after 12 months in the country, and enforceable with a fine of NZ$400 and a driving ban), contact the **New Zealand Automobile Association**, **t** 0800 500 444, **www.nzaa.co.nz**. The AA also offers insurance and breakdown services.

## Leaky Buildings (Weathertight Homes Resolution Services)
**t** 0800 116 926
**www.weathertightness.govt.nz**
Call this number if you end up in a shoddily built house, or need guidance on how to avoid doing so.

## Maritime Safety Authority of New Zealand
**www.msa.govt.nz**
Co-ordinates rescues at sea.

## Mental Health Commission
**www.mhc.govt.nz**
Looks after the mental health of the nation.

## National Library of New Zealand Te Puna Matauranga O Aotearoa
**www.natlib.govt.nz**
The place to research New Zealand history and find good books.

## NZ On Air
**www.nzonair.govt.nz**
Promotes broadcasting.

## New Zealand Qualifications Authority
**www.nzqa.govt.nz**
Sets standards for and assesses professional qualifications and the school curriculum. The people to call if you are a teacher or medical professional and need to check the validity of your credentials.

## New Zealand Trade and Enterprise
**www.nzte.govt.nz**
Promotes entrepreneurship.

## Retirement Commission
**www.retirement.org.nz**
Sort out your pension here.
**www.sorted.org.nz**
And your finances here.

### Security Intelligence Service
**www.nzsis.govt.nz**
The New Zealand secret services.

### Serious Fraud Office
**www.sfo.govt.nz**
Investigates, deals with and aims to prevent fraud.

### Ministry of Social Development
**wwww.msd.govt.nz**
Promotes social development through education and welfare. Umbrella organisation for Work and Income, Child, Youth and Family and so on.

### Statistics New Zealand
**t** 0508 525 525
**www.stats.govt.nz**
A goldmine of information about who New Zealanders are and what they get up to.

### TeachNZ
**t** 0800 832 246
**www.teachnz.govt.nz**
Teacher recruitment and training.

### Tenancy Services
**t** 0800 836 262
**www.tenancy.govt.nz**
Mediates in disputes between landlords and tenants, and helps to set up watertight contracts to avoid these disputes.

### Work and Income (WINZ)
**t** 0800 559 009
**www.workandincome.govt.nz**
The welfare agency, responsible for the dole, childcare subsidies and war pensions.

# Local Government

### Local Government New Zealand
**www.lgnz.co.nz**
Information on New Zealand's local government system, with links to the 85 local and regional councils.

## Northland

Northland Regional Council, t 0800 002 004; **www.nrc.govt.nz.**

Far North District Council, t 0800 920 029; **www.fndc.govt.nz.**

Kaipara District Council, t (09) 439 7059; **www.kaipara.govt.nz.**

Whangarei District Council, t (09) 430 4200; **www.wdc.govt.nz.**

## Auckland

Auckland Regional Council, t (09) 366 2070; **www.arc.govt.nz.**

Auckland City Council, t (09) 379 2020; **www.aucklandcity.govt.nz.**

Franklin District Council, t (09) 237 1300; **www.franklindistrict.govt.nz.**

Manukau City Council, t (09) 263 7100; **www.manukau.govt.nz.**

North Shore City Council, t (09) 486 8600; **www.northshorecity.govt.nz.**

Papakura District Council, t (09) 299 8870; **www.pdc.govt.nz.**

Rodney District Council, t (09) 426 5169; **www.rodney.govt.nz.**

Waitakere City Council, t (09) 839 0400; **www.waitakere.govt.nz.**

## Waikato

Environment Waikato, t (07) 856 7184; **www.ew.govt.nz.**

Hamilton City Council, t (07) 838 6699; **www.hcc.govt.nz.**

Hauraki District Council, t (07) 862 8609; **www.hauraki-dc.govt.nz.**

Matamata-Piako District Council, t (07) 884 0060; **www.mpdc.govt.nz.**

Otorohanga District Council, t (07) 873 8199; **www.otodc.govt.dc.**

South Waikato District Council, t (07) 886 1710; **www.swktdc.govt.nz.**

Thames-Coromandel District Council, t (07) 868 6025; **www.tcdc.govt.nz.**

Waikato District Council, t (07) 824 8633; **www.waikatodistrict.govt.nz.**

Waipa District Council, t (07) 872 0030; **www.waipadc.govt.nz.**

Waitomo District Council, t (07) 878 8801; **www.waitomo.govt.nz.**

## Bay of Plenty

Bay of Plenty Regional Council, t 0800 ENV BOP (0800 368 267); **www.envbop. govt.nz.**

Kawerau District Council, t (07) 323 8779; **www.kaweraudc.govt.nz.**

Opotiki District Council, t (07) 315 6167; **www.odc.govt.nz.**

Rotorua District Council, t (07) 348 4199; **www.rdc.govt.nz.**

Taupo District Council, t (07) 376 0899; **www.taupodc.govt.nz.**

Tauranga City Council, t (07) 577 7000 or t (07) 577 7285 (VIC); **www. tauranga.govt.nz.**

Western Bay of Plenty District Council, t (07) 571 8008; **www.wbop.govt.nz.**

Whakatane District Council, t (07) 306 0500; **www.whakatane.com.**

## Gisborne

Gisborne District Council, t (06) 867 2049; **www.gdc.govt.nz.**

## Hawke's Bay

Hawke's Bay Regional Council, t (06) 835 9200; **www.hbrc.govt.nz.**

Central Hawke's Bay District Council, t (06) 857 8060; **www.chbdc.govt.nz.**

Hastings District Council, t (06) 878 0500; **www.hastingsdc.govt.nz.**

Napier City Council, t (06) 835 7579; **www.napier.govt.nz.**

Wairoa District Council, t (06) 838 7309; **www.wairoadc.govt.nz.**

## Taranaki

Taranaki Regional Council, t (06) 765 7127; **www.trc.govt.nz.**

New Plymouth District Council, t (06) 759 6060; **www.npdc.govt.nz.**

South Taranaki District Council, t (06) 278 8010; **www.stdc.govt.nz.**

Stratford District Council, t (06) 765 6099; **www.stratford.govt.nz.**

## Chatham Islands

Chatham Islands Council, t (03) 305 0033; **www.cic.govt.nz.**

## Manawatu

'Horizons' (Manawatu-Wanganui) Regional Council, t (06) 952 2800; **www.horizons.govt.nz.**

Horowhenua District Council, t (06) 949 4949; **www.horowhenua.govt.nz.**

Manawatu District Council, t (06) 323 0000; **www.mdc.govt.nz.**

Palmerston North City Council, t (06) 356 8199; **www.pncc.govt.nz.**

Rangitikei District Council, t (06) 327 8174; **www.rangdc.govt.nz.**

Ruapehu District Council, t (07) 895 8188; **www.ruapehudc.govt.nz.**

Tararua District Council, t (06) 374 4080; **www.tararua.com.**

Wanganui District Council, t (06) 349 0001; **www.wanganui.govt.nz.**

## Wellington

Wellington Regional Council, t (04) 384 5708; **www.gw.govt.nz.**

Carterton District Council, t (06) 379 6626; **www.cartertondc.govt.nz.**

Hutt City Council, t (04) 570 6666; **www.huttcity.info.**

Kapiti Coast District Council, t (04) 904 5700; **www.kapiticoastdc.govt.nz.**

Masterton District Council, t (06) 378 9666; **www.mstn.govt.nz.**

Porirua City Council, t (04) 237 5089; **www.pcc.govt.nz.**

South Wairarapa District Council, t (06) 306 9611; **www.swdc.govt.nz.**

Upper Hutt City Council, t (04) 527 2169; **www.upperhuttcity.com.**

Wellington City Council, t (04) 499 4444; **www.wellington.govt.nz.**

## Marlborough

Marlborough District Council, t (03) 578 5249; **www.marlborough.govt.nz.**

## Nelson

Nelson City Council, t (03) 546 0200; **www.ncc.govt.nz.**

Tasman District Council, t (03) 544 8176; **www.tdc.govt.nz.**

## Westland

West Coast Regional Council, t (03) 768 0466; **www.wcrc.govt.nz.**

Buller District Council, t (03) 789 7239; **www.bullerdc.govt.nz.**

Grey District Council, t (03) 768 1700; **www.greydc.govt.nz.**

Westland District Council, t (03) 755 8321; **www.westlanddc.govt.nz.**

## Canterbury

Environment Canterbury, t (03) 365 3828; **www.ecan.govt.nz.**

Ashburton District Council, t (03) 308 5139; **www.ashburtondc.govt.nz.**

Christchurch City Council, t (03) 371 1999; **www.ccc.govt.nz.**

Hurunui District Council, t (03) 314 8816; **www.hurunui.govt.nz.**

Kaikoura District Council, t (03) 319 5026; **www.kaikoura.govt.nz.**

Mackenzie District Council, t (03) 685 8514; **www.mackenzie.govt.nz.**

Selwyn District Council, t (03) 324 8080; **www.selwyn.govt.nz.**

Timaru District Council, t (03) 684 8199; **www.timaru.govt.nz.**

Waimakariri District Council, t (03) 313 6136; **www.waimakariri.govt.nz.**

Waimate District Council, t (03) 689 8079; **www.waimatedc.govt.nz.**

## Otago

Otago Regional Council, t (03) 474 0827; **www.orc.govt.nz.**

Central Otago District Council, t (03) 448 6979; **www.codc.govt.nz.**

Clutha District Council, t (03) 418 1350; **www.cluthadc.govt.nz.**

Dunedin City Council, t (03) 477 4000; **www.cityofdunedin.com.**

Queenstown-Lakes District Council, t (03) 443 8197; **www.qldc.govt.nz.**

Waitaki District Council, t (03) 434 8060; **www.waitaki.govt.nz.**

## Southland

Environment Southland, t (03) 211 5115; **www.envirosouth.govt.nz.**

Gore District Council, t (03) 208 9080; **www.goredc.govt.nz.**

Invercargill City Council, t (03) 211 1777; **www.invercargill.org.nz.**

Southland District Council, t (03) 218 7259; **www.southlanddc.govt.nz.**

# General Advice, Help and Support

The best starting point for all sorts of advice and information, such as the law, translation services, social welfare, health, education, housing, budgeting, employment rights, consumer rights and personal and family issues, is the **Citizens Advice Bureau** (CAB). If nothing else, it will be able to point you in the direction of the most relevant body to help you. All its services are confidential. There is one in every town (see the *White Pages*), or you can visit the website, **www.cab.org.nz**, or call **t** 0800 367 222.

There are also a number of church- and charity-run community support services, which may vary from area to area. These include **Child & Family**, a branch of Presbyterian Support (**www.ps.org.nz**), **Age Concern**, the **Deaf Association of New Zealand**, **DOVE** (combating domestic violence), **Heart Foundation**, the **Rape and Sexual Abuse Centre**, **Salvation Army**, and various organisations offering support to specific sectors of the community (e.g. Maori). They are listed in the *Yellow Pages* under 'Community Services', where you may also find local **Community Law Centres**.

The **Consumers' Institute of New Zealand**, **www.consumer.org.nz**, can investigate complaints about misleading advertising and unfair trading practices on your behalf, and offers consumer advice (at a modest price).

# Emergency Services

Dial **t** 111 for fire, ambulance and police.

For your local police station, look under P in the *Blue Pages* at the front of the telephone book.

For general police information, including crime statistics and police recruitment, visit the **New Zealand Police** website, **www.police.govt.nz**.

In the event that you become a victim of crime, **Victim Support**, **t** 0800 842 846, **www.victim support.org.nz**, provides counselling support services.

You may be able to get involved in a community-based crime prevention programme (no vigilantes, please) through **www.neighbourhoodsupport.co.nz**.

# Government Housing Regulatory Bodies

## Department of Building and Housing

The Department of Building and Housing oversees all legislation relating to the building, renovation and conversion, and letting of properties. Its website, **www.dbh.govt.nz**, provides information about building regulations and controls, the laws governing tenancy and where to seek redress if problems arise with a building project or rental.

Tenancy Agreement forms, Property Inspection Report forms, Bond Lodgement forms, Bond Refund forms, Bond Transfer forms and useful information such as a New Tenant's Checklist and sample standard letters for resolving differences between landlords and tenants (10 Working Day Notices to Remedy a Breach) can all be downloaded from **www.dbh.govt.nz/housing/tenancy/ Forms**. The forms can also be purchased at stationery shops such as Whitcoulls and Warehouse Stationery. The website also lists current rental market values by region and type of housing. **Tenancy Services** can be contacted by phone on **t** 0800 83 62 62 or from outside New Zealand on **t** + 64 (0)4 238 4695.

### Housing New Zealand Corporation

The Housing New Zealand Corporation provides subsidised rental accommodation to those on low incomes, known in New Zealand as state housing. Visit the website, **www.hnzc.co.nz**, for more information, or call **t** 0800 739717.

### Land-online

**www.landonline.govt.nz**. An online database of land title and survey information (user pay service).

### Consumer Rights for House Buyers And Builders

The **Consumer Build** website, **www.consumerbuild.org.nz**, a combined initiative by the Department of Building and Housing and the Consumers' Institute, has masses of useful information on how to protect your interests when buying, building or renovating a house. Information ranges from how to do your research when buying a house or section, to how to find architects, builders and other tradespeople, and the legal issues around building.

# Professional Bodies Related to the Buying and Selling of Property

### Quotable Value New Zealand

For current house sale prices, visit the website of Quotable Value New Zealand (the ratings valuation body), **www.qv.co.nz**. This is not a free service, but can provide you (for a small fee) with price trends and recent sale values in a specific area, a demographic profile of the area and a full market valuation of any property you are interested in.

### Real Estate

Real Estate New Zealand, **t** 0800 732 536; **www.realestate.co.nz**, publishes up-to-date price surveys on national, regional, city and neighbourhood levels. It can also provide individual reports on rates, sales history, property history and comparative valuations for a modest fee. Also publishes comprehensive national and regional property listings.

The Real Estate Institute of New Zealand, **www.reinz.co.nz**, is the professional body governing real estate agents. It, too, publishes information on property trends.

# Lawyers

It is impossible to list lawyers, as there are so many and they are locally based. However the New Zealand legal system is very similar to the British one, with barristers and solicitors, each dealing in certain areas of the law (e.g. family, property, criminal). The best way to find a lawyer, should you need one, is to ask around for personal recommendations, trust your instincts on personal meetings, and ask for the fees and services to be clearly laid out before you sign up with a lawyer. The **Citizens Advice Bureau** may also be able to help.

**Public Trust** is a government-backed organisation with a long history that exists to help ordinary people put their financial and legal affairs in order without paying exorbitant lawyers' fees. It has offices in main towns and can help with drawing up trust documents, house buying and so forth. Public Trust, **t** 0800 371 471; **www.publictrust.co.nz**.

The **Law Commission, www.lawcom.govt.nz**, is the governing body for the legal profession. **Crown Law, www.crownlaw.govt.nz**, is the New Zealand equivalent of the Crown Prosecution Service.

The **Ministry of Justice, www.justice.govt.nz**, has a good outline of the New Zealand legal system on its website, while the **Department for Courts, www. courts.govt.nz**, has comprehensive information on the structure of New Zealand's courts and tribunals, and **www.courts.govt.nz/family** takes you straight to the Family Court of New Zealand, which deals with custody and family issues (and may be relevant to mixed New Zealand/foreign marriages).

The **Human Rights Commission, www.hrc.govt.nz**, is an independent agency responsible for investigating and resolving complaints about broader human rights issues such as discrimination, as they are enshrined in New Zealand law.

The **Legal Services Agency, www.lsa.govt.nz**, is a government-funded agency providing legal aid.

The **Office of the Ombudsmen, t** 0800 802 602, **www.ombudsmen.govt.nz**, reviews requests for official information and adjudicates disputes with local and central government agencies.

Locally, you may find **Community Law Services** that offer cheap or free legal advice. Look in the *Yellow Pages* under Community Services.

# New Zealand-based Removal Companies

There are many more than it is possible to list. For companies based in the UK, *see* pp.115–16.

- Allied Pickfords, t 0800 255 433; **www.alliedpickfords.co.nz**.
- AXXA, t (09) 6255 800; **www.axxatrailerhire.co.nz**.
- Backload Moving Company, t 0800 321 000; **www.backloadmoving.co.nz**.
- Budget Moving and Baggage Express International, t (09) 275 0452; **www. budgetmoving.co.nz**.
- Conroy Removals Limited;**www.removals.co.nz**. Offices round the country.
- Crown Relocations, t 0800 227 696; **www.crownrelo.com**.
- Dolphin Movers, from New Zealand t +44 (0)20 8804 7700, **removals@dolphinmovers.com**, **www.dolphinmovers.com**.
- Handy; **www.handy.co.nz**.
- Mr Shifter, t 0800 355 0077; **www.mrshifter.co.nz**.
- NZ Van Lines; **www.nzvanlines.co.nz**. Lots of branches.
- TSL; **www.www.tslnz.com**.

# Insurance Companies

Most companies cover all categories (home, car, contents, boat, bike, etc.), and some also do medical and life insurance. Many offer discounts if you take out more than one policy with them.

The main health insurer is **Southern Cross**, t 0800 800 181; **www.southern cross.co.nz**. A look at the *Yellow Pages* will identify local branches of insurance companies, as well as brokers and consultants operating in your area, who may help you to find the best deal. Listed below are those companies that have a website and/or an 0800 number. Most banks offer insurance too.

- AA Insurance, t 0800 500 221; **www.aainsurance.co.nz**.
- AMI Insurance, t 0800 100 200; **www.ami.co.nz**. Helpful and reliable.
- AMP, t 0800 808 267; **www.amp.co.nz**.
- AXA New Zealand, t 0800 106 652; **www.axa.co.nz**.
- Crown Insurance, t 0800 246 787; **www.crowninsurance.co.nz**.
- FinTel, t 0800 801 801; **www.fintel.co.nz**.
- FMG, t 0800 366 466; **www.fmg.co.nz**. Caters specially for the rural sector.
- InsuranceLine, t 0800 697 654; **www.insuranceline.co.nz**. Life and death (funeral) insurance.
- Lumley General Insurance (NZ) Limited, t 0800 801 210; **www.lumley.co.nz**.

- **NZI, t** 0800 800 800; **www.nzi.co.nz.**
- **SIS** (over-50s only), **t** 0800 801 701; **www.greypower.co.nz.**
- **Sovereign, t** 0800 500 103; **www.sovereign.co.nz.**
- **State, t** 0800 802 424; **www.state.co.nz.**
- **Tower, t** 0800 808 808; **www.tower.co.nz.**
- **Vero** (Star Alliance rebranded), **t** 0800 800 786; **www.vero.co.nz.**

# Banks

- **ANZ;** www.anz.com.
- **ASB;** www.asb.co.nz.
- **Bank of New Zealand (BNZ);** www.bnz.co.nz.
- **Kiwibank;** www.kiwibank.co.nz. The only New Zealand-owned one; operates from post offices.
- **National Australian Bank, t** + 61 3 8641 9083, www.nab.com.au.
- **National Bank;** www.nationalbank.co.nz.
- **TSB;** www.tsb.co.nz.
- **Westpac;** www.westpactrust.co.nz.

# News Sites

The Internet has obviously made it easier to keep track of international news and events. You can also follow New Zealand news online:

- The Wellington-based *Dominion Post* and other Fairfax-owned newspapers; **www.stuff.co.nz.**
- The Auckland-based *New Zealand Herald* and its stablemates; **www.nzherald.co.nz.**

# Index

Page references to maps are in *italics*.